Intermediate French

Edited by
Shaina Malkin and Cindy Hazelton

LIVING LANGUAGE®

Content in this program has been modified and enhanced from Starting Out in French and Complete Course French: The Basics, both published in 2008.

Living Language and colophon are registered trademarks of Random House, Inc.

Published in the United States by Living Language, an imprint of Random House, Inc.

www.livinglanguage.com

Editor: Shaina Malkin
Production Editor: Carolyn Roth
Production Manager: Tom Marshall
Interior Design: Sophie Chin
Illustrations: Sophie Chin

First Edition

ISBN: 978-0-307-97154-8

This book is available at special discounts for bulk purchases for sales promotions or premiums. Special editions, including personalized covers, excerpts of existing books, and corporate imprints, can be created in large quantities for special needs. For more information, write to Special Markets/ Premium Sales, 1745 Broadway, MD 3-1, New York, New York 10019 or e-mail specialmarkets@ randomhouse.com.

PRINTED IN THE UNITED STATES OF AMERICA

10 9 8 7

Acknowledgments

Thanks to the Living Language team: Amanda D'Acierno, Christopher Warnasch, Suzanne McQuade, Shaina Malkin, Laura Riggio, Erin Quirk, Amanda Muñoz, Fabrizio LaRocca, Siobhan O'Hare, Sophie Chin, Sue Daulton, Alison Skrabek, Carolyn Roth, Ciara Robinson, and Tom Marshall.

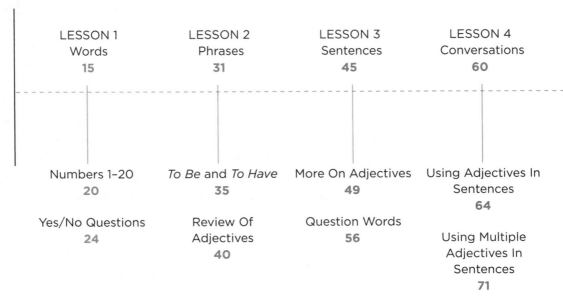
C O U R S E

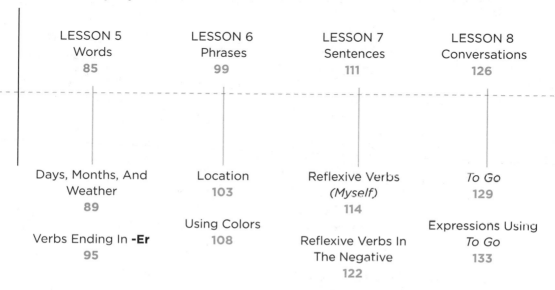
OUTLINE

COURSE

OUTLINE

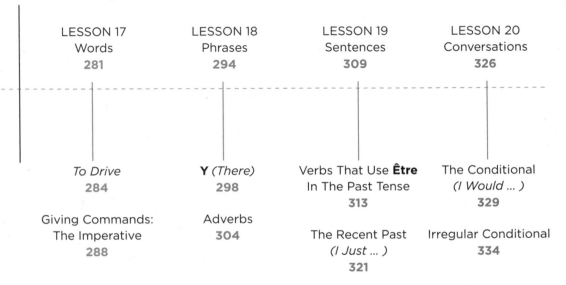

How to Use This Course

Bienvenue ! Welcome to *Living Language Intermediate French*!

Before we begin, let's take a quick look at what you'll see in this course.

CONTENT

Intermediate French is a continuation of *Essential French*. It will review, expand on, and add to the foundation that you received in *Essential French*. In other words, this course contains:

1. an in-depth review of important vocabulary and grammar from *Essential French*;
2. an expanded and more advanced look at some key vocabulary and grammar from *Essential French*;
3. an introduction to idiomatic language and more challenging French grammar.

UNITS

There are five units in this course. Each unit has four lessons arranged in a "building block" structure: the first lesson will present essential *words*, the second will introduce longer *phrases*, the third will teach *sentences*, and the fourth will show how everything works together in everyday *conversations*.

At the beginning of each unit is an introduction highlighting what you'll learn in that unit. At the end of each unit you'll find the Unit Essentials, which reviews the key information from that unit, and a self-graded Unit Quiz, which tests what you've learned.

LESSONS

There are four lessons per unit for a total of 20 lessons in the course. Each lesson has the following components:

- **Introduction** outlining what you will cover in the lesson.

- **Word Builder 1** (first lesson of the unit) presenting key words and phrases.

- **Phrase Builder 1** (second lesson of the unit) introducing longer phrases and expressions.

- **Sentence Builder 1** (third lesson of the unit) teaching sentences.

- **Conversation 1** (fourth lesson of the unit) for a natural dialogue that brings together important vocabulary and grammar from the unit.

- **Take It Further** providing extra information about the new vocabulary you just saw, expanding on certain grammar points, or introducing additional words and phrases.

- **Word / Phrase / Sentence / Conversation Practice 1** practicing what you learned in Word Builder 1, Phrase Builder 1, Sentence Builder 1, or Conversation 1.

- **Word Recall** reviewing important vocabulary and grammar from any of the previous lessons in *Intermediate* or *Essential French*.

- **Grammar Builder 1** guiding you through important French grammar that you need to know.

- **Work Out 1** for a comprehensive practice of what you saw in Grammar Builder 1.

- **Word Builder 2 / Phrase Builder 2 / Sentence Builder 2 / Conversation 2** for more key words, phrases, or sentences, or a second dialogue.

- **Take It Further** for expansion on what you've seen so far and additional vocabulary.

- **Word / Phrase / Sentence / Conversation Practice 2** practicing what you learned in Word Builder 2, Phrase Builder 2, Sentence Builder 2, or Conversation 2.

- **Word Recall** reviewing important vocabulary and grammar from any of the previous lessons in *Intermediate* or *Essential French*.

- **Grammar Builder 2** for more information on French grammar.

- **Work Out 2** for a comprehensive practice of what you saw in Grammar Builder 2.

- **Drive It Home** ingraining an important point of French grammar for the long term.

- **Tip** or **Culture Note** for a helpful language tip or useful cultural information related to the lesson or unit.

- **How Did You Do?** outlining what you learned in the lesson.

UNIT ESSENTIALS

You will see the **Unit Essentials** at the end of every unit. This section summarizes and reviews the key information from the unit, but with missing vocabulary information for you to fill in. In other words, each Unit Essentials works as both a study guide and a blank "cheat sheet." Once you complete it, you'll have your very own reference for the most essential vocabulary and grammar from the unit.

UNIT QUIZ

After each Unit Essentials, you'll see a **Unit Quiz**. The quizzes are self-graded so it's easy for you to test your progress and see if you should go back and review.

PROGRESS BAR

You will see a **Progress Bar** on each page that has course material. It indicates your current position within the unit and lets you know how much progress you're making. Each line in the bar represents a Grammar Builder section.

AUDIO

Look for the symbol ▶ to help guide you through the audio as you're reading the book. It will tell you which track to listen to for each section that has audio. When you see the symbol, select the indicated track and start listening! If you don't see the symbol, then there isn't any audio for that section. You'll also see ⏸, which will tell you where that track ends.

The audio can be used on its own—in other words, without the book—when you're on the go. Whether in your car or at the gym, you can listen to the audio on its own to brush up on your pronunciation or review what you've learned in the book.

PHONETICS

Phonetics will occasionally be used in this course (in other words, [boh(n)-zhoor] in addition to bonjour), usually in order to highlight a point about French pronunciation. Remember that phonetics are not exact—they're just a general approximation of sounds—and so you should rely most on the audio, *not* the phonetics, to further your pronunciation skills.

For a guide to our phonetics system, see the Pronunciation Guide at the end of the course.

PRONUNCIATION GUIDE, GRAMMAR SUMMARY, GLOSSARY

At the back of this book you will find a **Pronunciation Guide**, **Grammar Summary**, and **Glossary**. The Pronunciation Guide provides information on French pronunciation and the phonetics system used in this course. The Grammar Summary contains a brief overview of key French grammar from *Essential* and *Intermediate French*. The Glossary (French–English and English–

French) includes all of the essential words from *Essential* and *Intermediate French*, as well as additional vocabulary.

FREE ONLINE TOOLS

Go to ***www.livinglanguage.com/languagelab*** to access your free online tools. The tools are organized around the units in this course, with audiovisual flashcards, and interactive games and quizzes. These tools will help you to review and practice the vocabulary and grammar that you've seen in the units, as well as provide some bonus words and phrases related to the unit's topic.

Unit 1:
Greetings and Introductions

Welcome to *Intermediate French*! In this course, we're going to review, expand on, and add to the foundation that you received in *Essential French*.

There are five units in *Intermediate French*, and four lessons in each unit. Within a unit, you will gradually build from words in the first lesson, then to phrases, sentences, and finally conversations in the last lesson.

It might help to think of the first few units of this course as a bridge, strengthening and expanding on what you learned in *Essential French* so that you can move forward with ease in the later units.

On y va !

By the end of this unit, you should be able to:

☐ Address and answer people politely and appropriately

☐ Easily recite numbers 1–20

☐ Ask and respond to *how are you?* or *what's up?*

☐ Ask any type of yes/no question

☐ Say *I'm hungry, I'm thirsty, I need*, and *I feel like*

☐ Know when to use *to have* or *to be*

☐ Express opinions and make exclamations

☐ Use words like *funny* and *strange*

☐ Talk about nationalities, origins, and languages

☐ Use words like *Parisian, serious, proud,* and *equal*

☐ Say where you're from

☐ Name different countries

☐ Ask *of what, how much, how many, at what time, why,* and *when*

☐ Talk about beauty, age, size, and whether something is good

☐ Talk about holidays and birthdays

☐ Use more than one word to describe something

Remember to look for the symbol ⊳ to help guide you through the audio as you're reading the book. It will tell you which track to listen to for each section that has audio. When you see the symbol, select the indicated track and start listening! If you don't see the symbol, then there isn't any audio for that section. You'll also see ⏸, which will tell you where that track ends. Finally, keep in mind that the audio can also be used on its own when you're on the go!

Lesson 1: Words

By the end of this lesson, you will be able to:

☐ Address and answer people politely and appropriately

☐ Easily recite numbers 1–20

☐ Ask and respond to *how are you?* or *what's up?*

☐ Ask any type of yes/no question

Word Builder 1

To get started, let's review some essentials, such as *yes, no,* and *there is/there are,* and crucial polite expressions like *please* and *thank you.* You'll see both new and familiar vocabulary.

▶ 1A Lesson 1 Word Builder 1 (CD 4, Track 1)

yes	oui
no	non
there is, there are	voilà
here is, here are	voici
me	moi
you (infml.)	toi
also	aussi
okay, all right	d'accord
all right (understood)	entendu
please	s'il vous plaît*
thank you	merci
you're welcome (it's nothing)	de rien
you're welcome	il n'y a pas de quoi
you're welcome (fml.)	je vous en prie
pardon (me) (excuse me)	pardon
excuse me	excusez-moi

Ⅱ * Remember that the informal form is s'il te plaît.

Note that the following abbreviations will be used in this course: (*m.*) = masculine, (*f.*) = feminine, (*sg.*) = singular, (*pl.*) = plural, (*fml.*) = formal/polite, (*infml.*) = informal/familiar, (*lit.,*) = literally. If a word has two grammatical genders, (*m./f.*) or (*f./m.*) is used.

Take It Further

In these sections, we'll expand on what you've seen so far.

We might break down new phrases, look more closely at specific words, introduce related vocabulary and grammar, or expand on some of the grammar points. You'll get a better sense of the phrases and dialogues in the unit, and how they are constructed. You'll also get a basic introduction to vocabulary and grammar that will be covered more in detail later on the course, or in *Advanced French*.

For now, we'll look at some vocabulary related to what you just saw in Word Builder 1.

Let's review forms of address, since those are of course very important if you want to be polite and address people correctly.

sir	monsieur
ma'am, madam	madame
miss	mademoiselle

Their abbreviations are:

Mr.	M.
Mrs., Ms.	Mme
Miss	Mlle

Note that you do not put a period after **Mme** and **Mlle**, even though you do put one after **M.**

For more than one person, use:

gentlemen	messieurs
ladies	mesdames
misses	mesdemoiselles

Mesdames et messieurs...
Ladies and gentlemen ...

You might also hear the abbreviated version messieurs et dames (*ladies and gentlemen*).

✎ Word Practice 1

Translate the following sentences into French.

1. *Excuse me, sir.* _____

2. *Thank you, miss.* _____

3. *You're welcome (fml.), madam.* _____

4. *Ladies and gentlemen, here is ...* _____

5. *Okay, Mrs. Smith.* _____

ANSWER KEY:
1. Excusez-moi/Pardon, monsieur. 2. Merci, mademoiselle. 3. Je vous en prie, madame. 4. Mesdames et messieurs, voici... 5. D'accord, Mme Smith.

✎ Word Recall

These exercises will review important vocabulary and grammar from any of the previous lessons in the program, from the first lesson of *Essential French* up to your current point in *Intermediate French*. The exercises will reinforce what you've learned so far and help you retain the information for the long term.

Choose the correct French word to fill in the blank, based on the English translation provided. You will see a full translation of each sentence in the Answer Key.

1. M. Dupont est un _____ (man).
   a. fille
   b. garçon
   c. femme
   d. homme
   e. mari

2. Suzanne est mon _____ (friend) préférée.
   a. mari
   b. amie
   c. garçon
   d. homme
   e. ami

3. Mme Beaulieu est une _____ (woman).
   a. amie
   b. homme
   c. fille
   d. ami
   e. femme

4. Le _____ (boy) s'appelle Jean-Pierre.
   a. garçon
   b. femme
   c. homme
   d. mari
   e. français

5. J'apprends le _____ (French).
   a. fille
   b. français
   c. garçon
   d. ami
   e. mari

ANSWER KEY:
1. d (*Mr. Dupont is a man.*); 2. b (*Suzanne is my favorite friend.*); 3. e (*Mrs./Ms. Beaulieu is a woman.*); 4. a (*The boy's name is Jean-Pierre./The boy is called Jean-Pierre.*); 5. b (*I'm learning French.*)

Grammar Builder 1
NUMBERS 1–20

▶ 1B Lesson 1 Grammar Builder 1 (CD 4, Track 2)

Please note that in *Intermediate* and *Advanced French*, only example sentences, tables, and charts are recorded.

As you know, numbers are very important for many different situations, including shopping, telling time, talking about age, and so on. You were first introduced to numbers in *Essential French*, but let's review some of them here.

Here are numbers 1–20 in French:

un/une *(m./f.)*	one	onze	eleven
deux	two	douze	twelve
trois	three	treize	thirteen
quatre	four	quatorze	fourteen
cinq	five	quinze	fifteen
six	six	seize	sixteen
sept	seven	dix-sept	seventeen
huit	eight	dix-huit	eighteen
neuf	nine	dix-neuf	nineteen
dix	ten	vingt	twenty

Remember that **un/une** can mean both *one* and *a/an*. In other words, **une table** can mean *a table* or *one table*.

⏸

✎ Work Out 1

Write out the following numbers in French.

1. *sixteen* _____

2. *six* _____

3. *three* _____

4. *eighteen* _____

5. *twenty* _____

ANSWER KEY:
1. **seize**; 2. **six**; 3. **trois**; 4. **dix-huit**; 5. **vingt**

Word Builder 2

Now let's go over basic greetings, introductions, and good-byes, which are also very important to remember.

Don't forget that, in writing, French usually adds a space before the punctuation marks **! ? :** and **;**. As a result, you will see **Bonjour !** and not **Bonjour!**

▶ 1C Lesson 1 Word Builder 2 (CD 4, Track 3)

Good day!/Hello!	**Bonjour !**
Hello!/Hi!/Bye!	**Salut !**
Welcome!	**Bienvenue !**
Come in! (lit., Enter!)	**Entrez !***
How's everything? (How's it going?)	**(Comment) ça va ?**
Everything is well. (It's going well.)	**Ça va bien.**

* **Entrez !** is used when speaking formally or to a group of people. The informal, singular form is **Entre !**

Everything is really well. (It's going really well.)	**Ça va très bien.**
It's not going well. (It's going badly.)	**Ça va mal.**
How are you? (fml.)	**Comment allez-vous ?**
How are you? (infml.)	**Comment vas-tu ?**
Very well.	**Très bien.**
Pleased to meet you. (Nice to meet you.)	**Enchanté/Enchantée (de faire votre connaissance).**
I'm delighted to make your acquaintance.	**Je suis ravi/ravie de faire votre connaissance.**
Good-bye!	**Au revoir !**
See you soon!	**À bientôt !**
See you later!	**À tout à l'heure !/À plus tard !**
Good evening!	**Bonsoir !**
Good night!	**Bonne nuit !**

Take It Further

Here is an informal greeting that you could use in casual conversation:

What's up?/What's new?	**Quoi de neuf ?**

And you could respond:

Nothing new.	**Rien de neuf.**
Not a lot.	**Pas grand-chose.**
Nothing much.	**Rien de particulier.**

Finally, here are two more ways to say *see you later*:

See you later!	À plus !
See you later!	À la prochaine !

À plus is an informal version of À plus tard ! It's pronounced [ah plews].

✎ Word Practice 2

Fill in the blanks in the sentences below based on the English translations provided.

1. **Quoi de neuf ?** _____ . *(What's up? Not a lot.)*

2. **Au revoir !** _____ ! *(Good-bye! See you soon!)*

3. **Bonjour, monsieur.** _____ .

   (Hello, sir. I'm delighted to make your acquaintance.)

4. _____ ?

   Très bien, merci. *(How are you [fml.]? Very well, thank you.)*

5. **Bonjour, madame.** _____ , _____

   _____ . *(Hello, madam. Come in, please [fml].)*

ANSWER KEY:

1. **Pas grand-chose;** 2. **À bientôt;** 3. **Je suis ravi/ravie de faire votre connaissance;** 4. **Comment allez-vous;** 5. **Entrez, s'il vous plaît**

✎ Word Recall

You reviewed numbers 1–20 in Grammar Builder 1. How well do you remember numbers above twenty? Complete the following equations with the correct number written out in French.

1. **dix + dix =** _____

2. **trente-six – neuf =** _____

3. **quarante-huit + deux =** _____

4. **soixante + onze =** _____

5. **cent – quinze =** _____

ANSWER KEY:
1. **vingt** (*ten + ten = twenty*); 2. **vingt-sept** (*thirty-six – nine = twenty-seven*); 3. **cinquante** (*forty-eight + two = fifty*); 4. **soixante et onze** (*sixty + eleven = seventy-one*); 5. **quatre-vingt-cinq** (*one hundred – fifteen = eighty-five*)

Grammar Builder 2
YES/NO QUESTIONS

▶ 1D Lesson 1 Grammar Builder 2 (CD 4, Track 4)

Keep in mind that in Intermediate and Advanced French, only example sentences, tables, and charts are recorded.

Remember yes/no questions from *Essential French*? Let's review and expand on what you learned.

There are three ways to form yes/no questions in French.

1. When talking, simply raise your intonation at the end of the sentence. When writing, place a question mark at the end of the sentence: **Je chante bien** (*I sing well*) becomes **Je chante bien ?** (*I sing well?/Do I sing well?*).

2. Place **est-ce que** at the beginning of a sentence to turn it into a question. Note that **est-ce que** becomes **est-ce qu'** before a word that begins with a vowel or silent **h**.

Je chante bien.
I sing well.

Est-ce que je chante bien ?
Do I sing well?

3. Switch the verb and the subject. This method is often called "inversion."

In other words, place the verb before the subject with a hyphen connecting them. Perhaps the most classic example of this type of yes/no question is:

Parlez-vous français ?
Do you speak French?

In this case, the verb **parlez** comes before the subject pronoun **vous** to form the question.

Remember that if the verb ends with a vowel, and the subject pronoun is **il**, **elle**, or **on**, then **-t-** needs to be inserted in between the verb and the pronoun: **Parle-t-elle français ?** (*Does she speak French?*)

It's also important to mention that there is actually a "sub-category" of this third type of yes/no question.

If the subject of the sentence is a noun (*Luc is French, my parents eat dinner, Paris has museums*) rather than a subject pronoun (*he is French, they eat dinner, it has museums*), then you need to use the following format to create an "inversion" question:

subject + verb + hyphen + subject pronoun

For example, you can't say **Est-Luc français ?** That would be incorrect. Instead, you would have to say:

Luc est-il français ?
Is Luc French? (lit., Luc is he French?)

As you can see, the subject **Luc** comes first, followed by the verb **est** (*is*), then a hyphen, and then the subject pronoun **il** (*he*). You should use the subject pronoun that would normally replace the noun, such as *Luc (he), Marie (she), my parents (they), Paris (it)*, etc.

Here's another example: **Ta fille est-elle grande ?** (*Is your daughter tall?* or literally, *Your daughter is she tall?*)

For this type of question, you still need to insert a -t- in between the verb and the subject pronoun if the verb ends with a vowel and the pronoun is **il, elle,** or **on**:

Marie parle-t-elle anglais ?
Does Marie speak English? (lit., Marie speaks she English?)

Anglais, as you can probably guess, means *English* (both the language and the nationality).

To summarize, here are examples of the three ways to form yes/no questions in French.

Tu aimes Paris ?	Est-ce que tu aimes Paris ?	Aimes-tu Paris ?	*Do you like Paris?*
Luc aime Marie ?	Est-ce que Luc aime Marie ?	Luc aime-t-il Marie ?	*Does Luc like Marie?*
Nous jouons ?	Est-ce que nous jouons ?	Jouons-nous ?	*Are we playing?*
Vous travaillez ?	Est-ce que vous travaillez ?	Travaillez-vous ?	*Do you work?*
Elles dansent ?	Est-ce qu'elles dansent ?	Dansent-elles ?	*Are they dancing?*
Il donne le livre à son ami ?	Est-ce qu'il donne le livre à son ami ?	Donne-t-il le livre à son ami ?	*Is he giving the book to his friend?*
Elle décide ?	Est-ce qu'elle décide ?	Décide-t-elle ?	*Is she deciding?*

Ⅱ

✎ Work Out 2

Change the following sentences into questions using est-ce que.

1. **Christine danse.** *(Christine is dancing.)*

   _____

2. **Tu aimes la maison blanche.** *(You like the white house.)*

   _____

3. **Tes parents dînent à la maison.** *(Your parents are having dinner at home.)*

   _____

4. **Vous parlez anglais.** *(You speak English.)*

_____

5. **Elles aiment les films français.** *(They like French films.)*

_____

ANSWER KEY:
1. **Est-ce que Christine danse ?** *(Is Christine dancing?)* 2. **Est-ce que tu aimes la maison blanche ?** *(Do you like the white house?)* 3. **Est-ce que tes parents dînent à la maison ?** *(Are your parents having dinner at home?)* 4. **Est-ce que vous parlez anglais ?** *(Do you speak English?)* 5. **Est-ce qu'elles aiment les films français ?** *(Do they like French films?)*

✎ Drive It Home

Now let's do one more practice.

This exercise is designed to instill key information about French structure. Although it may seem repetitive, it is **very** important that you read through each question carefully, write out each response, and then read the whole question out loud. It will help you to retain the information beyond just this lesson and course.

Change the following French sentences into questions using the inversion method.

1. **Vous aimez danser.** *(You like to dance.)*

_____

2. **Il aime danser.** *(He likes to dance.)*

_____

3. **Ils aiment danser.** *(They like to dance.)*

_____

4. **Marc aime danser.** (*Marc likes to dance.*)

5. **Nous aimons danser.** (*We like to dance.*)

6. **Hélène aime danser.** (*Hélène likes to dance.*)

ANSWER KEY:

1. **Aimez-vous danser ?** (*Do you like to dance?*) 2. **Aime-t-il danser ?** (*Does he like to dance?*) 3. **Aiment-ils danser ?** (*Do they like to dance?*) 4. **Marc aime-t-il danser ?** (*Does Marc like to dance?*) 5. **Aimons-nous danser ?** (*Do we like to dance?*) 6. **Hélène aime-t-elle danser ?** (*Does Hélène like to dance?*)

Tip

Here's a quick tip to help you pronounce numbers.

A **liaison**, or *linking* of words, is used in between a number that ends in **s** (like **trois**) and a word that starts with a vowel, such as **enfants** (*children*), or a word that starts with a silent **h**, such as **heures** (*hours, o'clock*) and **hommes** (*men*).

For example, look at the following two pronunciations (note the phonetics):

| *three girls* | **trois filles** | trwah feey |
| *three children* | **trois enfants** | trwah zah(n)-fah(n) |

In the first example, the **s** in **trois** is silent. However, in the second example, the **s** in **trois** is pronounced like a *z* and "linked" to the word **enfants** so that the phrase is pronounced [trwah zah(n)-fah(n)].

The same thing happens with the numbers **deux**, **six**, and **dix**. The letter **x** is pronounced like a *z* when it is followed by a word beginning with a vowel or silent **h**. The letter **x** is also pronounced like a *z* in the number **dix-neuf** [deez-nuhf] (*nineteen*).

In the number *nine*, **neuf**, the *f* sound changes to a *v* sound in front of a word beginning with a vowel or silent **h**. For instance:

| *nine o'clock, nine hours* | **neuf heures** | nuh-vuhr |

Finally, note that when the numbers **cinq**, **six**, **huit**, and **dix** are followed by a word beginning with a consonant, the final letter of the number is silent.

five minutes	**cinq minutes**	sa(n) mee-newt
six girls	**six filles**	see feey
ten boys	**dix garçons**	dee gahr-soh(n)

However, **cinq** does not always follow this rule.

How Did You Do?

Let's see how you did! By now, you should be able to:

☐ Address and answer people politely and appropriately
(Still unsure? Jump back to page 17)

☐ Easily recite numbers 1–20
(Still unsure? Jump back to page 20)

☐ Ask and respond to *how are you?* or *what's up?*
(Still unsure? Jump back to page 21)

☐ Ask any type of yes/no question
(Still unsure? Jump back to page 24)

Lesson 2: Phrases

By the end of this lesson, you will be able to:

☐ Say *I'm hungry, I'm thirsty, I need,* and *I feel like*

☐ Know when to use *to have* or *to be*

☐ Express opinions and make exclamations

☐ Use words like *funny* and *strange*

Phrase Builder 1

Let's look at some helpful expressions that use avoir (*to have*). As you can see below, avoir is used in many fixed expressions where English normally uses *to be*. Many of these phrases should already be familiar to you, but they're important to review.

▶ 2A Lesson 2 Phrase Builder 1 (CD 4, Track 5)

to be hungry (lit., to have hunger)	avoir faim
I'm hungry.	J'ai faim.
to be thirsty (lit., to have thirst)	avoir soif
She's thirsty.	Elle a soif.
to be cold (lit., to have cold)	avoir froid
to be hot, to be warm (lit., to have heat)	avoir chaud
to be afraid (lit., to have fear)	avoir peur
to be right (lit., to have reason)	avoir raison
to be sleepy (lit., to have sleep)	avoir sommeil
to be wrong (lit., to have wrong)	avoir tort

to take place, to be held (lit., to have place)	avoir lieu
to be ashamed (lit., to have shame)	avoir honte
to feel like (lit., to have desire for)	avoir envie de
to need (lit., to have need of)	avoir besoin de
to have brown/blond/red/black hair	avoir les cheveux bruns/blonds/ roux/noirs*
to have blue/brown/green eyes	avoir les yeux bleus/bruns/verts
My father has blue eyes.	Mon père a les yeux bleus.
My brother is twenty years old. (lit., My brother has twenty years.)	Mon frère a vingt ans.

* Remember that French uses articles like le/la/les (*the*) or un/une/des (*a, an*) a lot more than English does. As a result, French articles won't always translate into English. Also note that roux (*red*) is mainly used to describe hair. Otherwise, the word rouge is used to mean *red*.

Take It Further

Let's take a closer look at irregular plurals in French.

As you probably guessed, yeux means *eyes*. The singular, however, is actually un œil (*an eye*). Most French nouns simply add an -s in the plural, but unfortunately, yeux is just an irregular plural that you have to learn separately.

You already know about some other irregular plurals. For example, you know that many words that end in -eau and -eu, and some words that end in -ou, add -x in the plural in French. For example: le château (*the castle*) and les châteaux (*the castles*). One exception is pneu (*tire*), which is pneus in the plural.

It is also important to note that many nouns ending in **-al** and **-ail** change to **-aux** in the plural. For example: **le journal** (*the newspaper*) and **les journaux** (*the newspapers*).

Finally, if a noun ends in **-s**, **-x**, or **-z**, there is no change in the plural. For example: **le fils** (*the son*) and **les fils** (*the sons*). The masculine noun **l'os** (*the bone*) behaves the same way (**les os**) although it is actually pronounced [ohs] in the singular and [oh] in the plural. Just to keep things interesting!

 # Phrase Practice 1

Match the following French phrases to their correct English translations.

1. **avoir soif**	a. *to be hungry*
2. **avoir raison**	b. *to be afraid*
3. **avoir faim**	c. *to be right*
4. **avoir froid**	d. *to be cold*
5. **avoir peur**	e. *to be thirsty*

ANSWER KEY:
1. e; 2. c; 3. a; 4. d; 5. b

✎ Word Recall

Fill in the following family tree with the correct French word for each member of the family. Make sure to include **le** or **la** (or **l'**) before each French word.

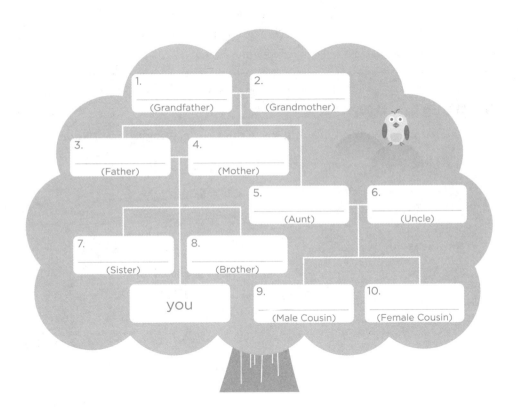

1. _____ (Grandfather)
2. _____ (Grandmother)
3. _____ (Father)
4. _____ (Mother)
5. _____ (Aunt)
6. _____ (Uncle)
7. _____ (Sister)
8. _____ (Brother)
you
9. _____ (Male Cousin)
10. _____ (Female Cousin)

ANSWER KEY:
1. le grand-père (*the grandfather*); 2. la grand-mère (*the grandmother*); 3. le père (*the father*); 4. la mère (*the mother*); 5. la tante (*the aunt*); 6. l'oncle (*the uncle*); 7. la sœur (*the sister*); 8. le frère (*the brother*); 9. le cousin (*the male cousin*); 10. la cousine (*the female cousin*)

Grammar Builder 1
TO BE AND *TO HAVE*

▶ 2B Lesson 2 Grammar Builder 1 (CD 4, Track 6) Again, remember that in *Intermediate* and *Advanced French*, only example sentences, tables, and charts are recorded.

In Phrase Builder 1, you saw a lot of expressions using the irregular verb avoir (*to have*). Let's review its full conjugation:

AVOIR *(TO HAVE)*	
j'ai	*I have*
tu as	*you have (infml.)*
il a	*he has*
elle a	*she has*
nous avons	*we have*
vous avez	*you have (pl./fml.)*
ils ont	*they have (m.)*
elles ont	*they have (f.)*

Let's also review the full conjugation of another important irregular verb: être (*to be*).

ÊTRE *(TO BE)*	
je suis	*I am*
tu es	*you are (infml.)*
il est	*he is*
elle est	*she is*
nous sommes	*we are*
vous êtes	*you are (pl./fml.)*
ils sont	*they are (m.)*
elles sont	*they are (f.)*

Avoir and **être** are the two most important verbs in French, and you will be using them *a lot* in upcoming units. Make sure to memorize their conjugations.

Finally, remember that the verb avoir (and not être) is used to talk about age:

J'ai vingt ans.
I'm twenty years old. (lit., I have twenty years.)

A good related phrase to know is:

Quel âge as-tu ?
How old are you? (lit., What age do you have?)

(II)

✎ Work Out 1

Fill in the blanks with the correct avoir expression from the word bank below. Don't forget to conjugate avoir.

avoir besoin de	avoir envie de
avoir tort	avoir honte

1. Elle _____. *(She is ashamed.)*

2. Il _____. *(My brother is wrong.)*

3. Ils _____ danser. *(My grandparents feel like dancing.)*

4. Tu _____. *(You are wrong.)*

5. J' _____ _____ mes amis. *(I need my friends.)*

ANSWER KEY:
1. a honte; 2. a tort; 3. ont envie de; 4. as tort; 5. ai besoin de

Phrase Builder 2

The phrase **c'est** (*it is*) is often used with various adjectives to express opinions. Keep in mind that **c'est** can mean *this is* or *that is*, in addition to *it is*, so the following expressions can also be translated as *That's good*, *That's true*, *This is amusing*, etc.

▶ 2C Lesson 2 Phrase Builder 2 (CD 4, Track 7)

It's good.	C'est bon.
It's true.	C'est vrai.
It's amusing.	C'est amusant.
It's delicious.	C'est délicieux.
It's interesting.	C'est intéressant.
It's cool.	C'est cool.
It's super. (It's great.)	C'est super.
It's great.	C'est extra.

Take It Further

Note that you can also use **c'est vrai** as a question (**C'est vrai ?**) to mean *Is that true?* or *Really?*

Here are some more expressions of opinion, as well as some common exclamations:

It's good! (cannot be used to refer to food)	C'est bien !
It's great!	C'est formidable !
What? (surprise, question)	Quoi ?
Really?	Vraiment ?

Absolutely!	**Absolument !**
Say!/Hey! (surprise)	**Tiens !**
Man!/You don't say!/Say! (lit., Say so!)	**Dis donc !**
Wow!/No way!	**Oh là là !**
My god!	**Mon dieu !**
I don't believe it!/Oh man!/It's not possible! (disappointment, anger)	**Ce n'est pas possible !**
No luck!	**Pas de chance !**
Good luck!	**Bonne chance !**
Of course!	**Bien sûr !**

And here are a few other good words to know to make your sentences sound more natural:

Oh well … /Well …	**Eh bien…** or **Ben…** *(infml.)*
Oh really … /Oh okay …	**Ah bon…**
Then … /So … /Well …	**Alors…**
Well … (lit., So there …)	**Alors là…**
Therefore … /So… /Then …	**Donc…**
Then … /Next …	**Ensuite…**
Then …	**Puis…**
because …	**parce que…**
but …	**mais…**
maybe …, possibly …	**peut-être…**
probably …	**probablement…**
… isn't it?/… right?/… isn't that so?	**… n'est-ce pas ?**

Note that **ben** is pronounced like **bien** but without the **i**, so ba[n].

✎ Phrase Practice 2

Match the following English phrases to their correct French translations.

1. *It's good.*	a. **C'est amusant.**
2. *It's great.*	b. **C'est vrai.**
3. *It's true.*	c. **C'est bon.**
4. *It's delicious.*	d. **C'est extra.**
5. *It's amusing.*	e. **C'est délicieux.**

Answer Key:
1. c; 2. d; 3. b; 4. e; 5. a

✎ Word Recall

Let's practice verbs. Can you translate the following French verbs? (Some may have more than one translation; you only need to provide one.)

1. habiter _____

2. parler _____

3. étudier _____

4. arriver _____

5. travailler _____

ANSWER KEY:
1. *to live;* 2. *to speak, to talk;* 3. *to study;* 4. *to arrive, to get somewhere, to reach;* 5. *to work*

Grammar Builder 2
REVIEW OF ADJECTIVES

▶ 2D Lesson 2 Grammar Builder 2 (CD 4, Track 8)

You just learned how to express opinions with adjectives (**c'est bon**, **c'est intéressant**, etc.) in French. Before we learn more about adjectives, let's review the basics.

As you know, adjectives in French agree with the noun they're describing in gender (masculine or feminine) and in number (singular or plural). So:

Luc est intelligent.
Luc is intelligent.

But:

Martine est intelligente.
Martine is intelligent.

And:

Luc et Joseph sont intelligents.
Luc and Joseph are intelligent.

Typically, feminine adjectives are marked by the feminine ending -**e** and plural adjectives are marked by the plural ending -**s**. If the noun is feminine *and* plural, you would therefore add -**es**.

Here are some more examples:

MASCULINE SINGULAR	FEMININE SINGULAR	MASCULINE PLURAL	FEMININE PLURAL	
important	importante	importants	importantes	*important*
grand	grande	grands	grandes	*big, tall*
petit	petite	petits	petites	*small (little, short)*
bleu	bleue	bleus	bleues	*blue*
brun*	brune	bruns	brunes	*brown*

* Note that the word brun is usually used to describe hair. It is also used sometimes used to describe eyes. Otherwise, *brown* is usually marron. Marron does not change form, no matter the gender or number of the noun.

However, if the masculine singular form of an adjective already ends in a silent -e, the feminine singular form is the same as the masculine singular form. For example, rouge (*red*) and sincère (*sincere*) do not change form in the feminine singular.

Here are other adjectives like sincère and rouge. Some of them should be familiar to you.

MASCULINE/FEMININE SINGULAR	MASCULINE/FEMININE PLURAL	
agréable	agréables	*pleasant*
aimable	aimables	*kind, nice*
autre	autres	*other*
brave	braves	*brave*
difficile	difficiles	*difficult*
drôle	drôles	*funny*
énorme	énormes	*enormous*
étrange	étranges	*strange*
facile	faciles	*easy*
large	larges	*wide*

MASCULINE/FEMININE SINGULAR	MASCULINE/FEMININE PLURAL	
magnifique	magnifiques	*magnificent*
mince	minces	*thin*
rapide	rapides	*quick*
sympathique	sympathiques	*friendly, nice*
jaune	jaunes	*yellow*
rose	roses	*pink*

✎ Work Out 2

Choose the correct form of the adjective.

1. Elle est (américain, américaine).

2. L'homme est (intelligent, intelligente).

3. Le garçon et la fille sont (sincères, sincère).

4. La femme est (grand, grande).

5. Elles sont (drôle, drôles).

ANSWER KEY:
1. américaine (*She is American.*); 2. intelligent (*The man is intelligent.*); 3. sincères (*The boy and the girl are sincere.*); 4. grande (*The woman is big/tall.*); 5. drôles (*They [f.] are funny.*)

✎ Drive It Home

Remember, this exercise may seem repetitive, but it's designed that way to help you remember an important point of grammar for the long term. Read through and respond to each question carefully, and then read it out loud.

A. Fill in each blank with the correct form of the verb avoir (*to have*):

1. Nous _____ une maison blanche. (*We have a white house.*)

2. J' _____ une maison blanche. (*I have a white house.*)

3. Tu _____ une maison blanche. (*You have a white house.*)

4. Vous _____ une maison blanche. (*You have a white house.*)

5. Elles _____ une maison blanche. (*They have a white house.*)

B. Now fill in each blank with the correct form of the verb être (*to be*):

1. Je _____ intelligent. (*I am intelligent.*)

2. Elle _____ intelligente. (*She is intelligent.*)

3. _____ -vous intelligent ? (*Are you intelligent? [fml.]*)

4. Ils _____ intelligents. (*They are intelligent.*)

5. Tu _____ intelligent. (*You are intelligent.*)

ANSWER KEY:
A. 1. avons; 2. ai; 3. as; 4. avez; 5. ont
B. 1. suis; 2. est; 3. Êtes; 4. sont; 5. es

 # Tip

Let's go back to yes/no questions for a second.

In order to respond positively to a yes/no question, you know that you can use oui
to mean *yes*.

Parlez-vous français ?
Do you speak French?

Oui, je parle français.
Yes, I speak French.

Oui is the general word for *yes*. However, there are actually some cases where you *cannot* use **oui**. In fact, there are two different words for *yes*: **oui** and **si**.

When responding to yes/no questions, use **oui** to answer a positive question like **Parlez-vous français ?** but **si** to answer a negative question like **Vous ne parlez pas français ?**

Vous ne parlez pas français ?
You don't speak French?

Si, je parle français.
Yes, I speak French.

(Remember that **ne** and **pas** are used around the verb to form a negative sentence. We'll review this more in detail later on in the course.)

Si can also be used in this way to contradict a negative sentence:

Elle ne chante pas bien.
She doesn't sing well.

Si !
Yes (she does)!

So, to summarize, use **si** to mean *yes* when you want to contradict a negative statement. But note that **si** is *only* used to mean *yes* when responding to a negative question or sentence. Otherwise, it usually means *if* or *so*.

How Did You Do?

Let's see how you did! By now, you should be able to:

☐ Say *I'm hungry, I'm thirsty, I need*, and *I feel like*
(Still unsure? Jump back to page 31)

☐ Know when to use *to have* or *to be*
(Still unsure? Jump back to page 35)

☐ Express opinions and make exclamations
(Still unsure? Jump back to page 37)

☐ Use words like *funny* and *strange*
(Still unsure? Jump back to page 40)

Lesson 3: Sentences

By the end of this lesson, you will be able to:

☐ Talk about nationalities, origins, and languages

☐ Use words like *Parisian, serious, proud*, and *equal*

☐ Say where you're from

☐ Name different countries

☐ Ask *of what, how much, how many, at what time, why*, and *when*

Sentence Builder 1

▶ 3A Lesson 3 Sentence Builder 1 (CD 4, Track 9)

I am Italian/Canadian/Irish. (m.)	**Je suis italien/canadien/irlandais.**
The man is French.	**L'homme est français.**
The woman is French.	**La femme est française.**
The man and the woman are French.	**L'homme et la femme sont français.**
Here is a French woman.	**Voici une femme française.**
Here is an American woman.	**Voici une femme américaine.**
I am of American origin.	**Je suis d'origine américaine.**
Pierre is of Irish origin.	**Pierre est d'origine irlandaise.**
Jean-Luc is of Canadian origin.	**Jean-Luc est d'origine canadienne.**

Take It Further

You've seen the following adjectives of nationality:

American	**américain/américaine**
Canadian	**canadien/canadienne**
French	**français/française**
Italian	**italien/italienne**
English	**anglais/anglaise**
Irish	**irlandais/irlandaise**

Here are a few more:

Scottish	**écossais/écossaise**
Spanish	**espagnol/espagnole**
Portuguese	**portugais/portugaise**
Belgian	**belge**

Swiss	suisse
German	allemand/allemande
Greek	grec/grecque
Russian	russe
Indian	indien/indienne
Chinese	chinois/chinoise
Japanese	japonais/japonaise
Australian	australien/australienne
Brazilian	brésilien/brésilienne
Algerian	algérien/algérienne
Moroccan	marocain/marocaine
Mexican	mexicain/mexicaine

And here are some other useful words related to nationality:

origin	l'origine (f.)
nationality	la nationalité

The word **origine** is often used in the phrase **d'origine** + nationality adjective, which means *of … origin*. Keep in mind that **origine** is a feminine noun, so the nationality adjective needs to be in its feminine form. For example: **Jean-Luc est d'origine canadienne.** (*Jean-Luc is of Canadian origin.*)

Note that, in general, the names for **les langues** (*f.*) (*languages*) are the same as the masculine form of the nationality. For example:

French language	le français
English language	l'anglais (m.)
Spanish language	l'espagnol (m.)
Chinese language	le chinois (m.)

If you want to say something is *in* the language, use **en: en français** (*in French*), **en anglais** (*in English*), etc.

Finally, you can also use adjectives of nationality as nouns. As nouns, they are capitalized.

an Irish man	**un homme irlandais**
an Irishman	**un Irlandais**

✎ Sentence Practice 1

Complete the table below with the correct sentences based on the example provided. For example, if you saw *Italian* and **Elle**, you would write **Elle est italienne.** (*She is Italian.*)

Make sure to use the correct form of the nationality adjective and the verb **être** (*to be*).

	FRENCH	AMERICAN	CANADIAN	IRISH
Il	1. Il est français.	4.	7.	10.
Elle	2.	5.	8.	11.
Elles	3.	6.	9.	12.

ANSWER KEY:
1. Il est français. 2. Elle est française. 3. Elles sont françaises. 4. Il est américain. 5. Elle est américaine. 6. Elles sont américaines. 7. Il est canadien. 8. Elle est canadienne. 9. Elles sont canadiennes. 10. Il est irlandais. 11. Elle est irlandaise. 12. Elles sont irlandaises.

Word Recall

Now let's take a look at words that help you to connect sentences and make them sound more natural.

Match the French words on the left to the correct English translations on the right. You saw all of these words in *Essential French*.

1. pour	a. *together*
2. ensemble	b. *for*
3. avec	c. *after, afterwards*
4. toujours	d. *before*
5. sans	e. *always*
6. après	f. *with*
7. avant	g. *without*

Answer Key:
1. b; 2. a; 3. f; 4. e; 5. g; 6. c; 7. d

Grammar Builder 1
MORE ON ADJECTIVES

▶ 3B Lesson 3 Grammar Builder 1 (CD 4, Track 10) Remember that in *Intermediate* and *Advanced French*, only example sentences, tables, and charts are recorded.

Okay, so you know that regular adjectives add an -e to form the feminine and an -s to form the plural. You also know that if the masculine singular form already ends in a silent -e, the feminine form is the same as the masculine form.

It's also good to know that if the masculine singular form ends in -s or -x, the masculine plural is the same as the masculine singular.

Il est français.
He is French.

Ils sont français.
They are French.

It's important to remember that some adjectives, like canadien/canadienne, double the final consonant and then add an -e to form the feminine. For example:

MASCULINE SINGULAR	FEMININE SINGULAR	MASCULINE PLURAL	FEMININE PLURAL	
ancien	ancienne	anciens	anciennes	*old*
bon	bonne	bons	bonnes	*good*
gentil	gentille	gentils	gentilles	*nice, kind*
parisien	parisienne	parisien	parisiennes	*Parisian*

There are also irregular adjectives. You're already familiar with the following adjectives, which are completely irregular and don't follow a pattern:

MASCULINE SINGULAR	FEMININE SINGULAR	MASCULINE PLURAL	FEMININE PLURAL	MASCULINE SINGULAR BEFORE A VOWEL OR SILENT H	
beau	belle	beaux	belles	bel	*beautiful*
vieux*	vieille	vieux	vieilles	vieil	*old*
nouveau	nouvelle	nouveaux	nouvelles	nouvel	*new*

*What's the difference between vieux and ancien? Well, in general, ancien means *old* in the sense of *former* (as in, an *old colleague* or a *former colleague*), *ancient* (as in, *ancient culture*), and *antique/ vintage*. Vieux, on the other hand, means *elderly*, *old* in terms of age, and *outdated*.

Another irregular adjective that doesn't follow a pattern is blanc (*white*), which becomes blanche in the feminine.

However, there are some irregular adjectives that do follow a pattern, such as sportif and sportive (*athletic*), heureux and heureuse (*happy*), and cher and chère (*dear, expensive*).

Here is the pattern:

MASCULINE SINGULAR	FEMININE SINGULAR	MASCULINE PLURAL	FEMININE PLURAL
-x	-se	-x	-ses
-f	-ve	-fs	-ves
-er	-ère	-ers	-ères
-et	-ète/-ette	-ets	-ètes/-ettes

So for example:

MASCULINE SINGULAR	FEMININE SINGULAR	MASCULINE PLURAL	FEMININE PLURAL	
sérieux	sérieuse	sérieux	sérieuses	*serious*
actif	active	actifs	actives	*active*
fier	fière	fiers	fières	*proud*
inquiet	inquiète	inquiets	inquiètes	*worried (anxious)*
violet	violette	violets	violettes	*violet (purple)*

Finally, most masculine adjectives that end in -al in the masculine singular, change that ending to -aux in the masculine plural.

MASCULINE SINGULAR	FEMININE SINGULAR	MASCULINE PLURAL	FEMININE PLURAL	
égal	égale	égaux	égales	*equal*
général	générale	généraux	générales	*general*

MASCULINE SINGULAR	FEMININE SINGULAR	MASCULINE PLURAL	FEMININE PLURAL	
principal	principale	principaux	principales	*principal (main)*
national	nationale	nationaux	nationales	*national*

✎ Work Out 1

Choose the correct form of the adjective.

1. **Elles sont (actifs, actives).**

2. **Elle est (fier, fière).**

3. **Ils sont (sérieux, sérieuses).**

4. **C'est un (vieux, vieil) homme.**

5. **Voilà une femme (parisien, parisienne).**

ANSWER KEY:
1. actives (*They are active.*); 2. fière (*She is proud.*); 3. sérieux (*They are serious.*); 4. vieil (*He is an old man.*); 5. parisienne (*Here/There is a Parisian woman.*)

Sentence Builder 2

▶ 3C Lesson 3 Sentence Builder 2 (CD 4, Track 11)

in France	en France
from Paris	de Paris
from the United States	des États-Unis
to the United States (in the United States)	aux États-Unis
Where do you live? (fml.)	Où habitez-vous ?

Where do you live? (infml.)	Où habites-tu ?
I live in the United States.	J'habite aux États-Unis.
I'm from the United States.	Je suis des États-Unis.
What's your nationality? (fml.)	De quelle nationalité êtes-vous ?
What's your nationality? (infml.)	De quelle nationalité es-tu ?

Take It Further

Now that we've looked at nationalities and languages, let's look at the names of
les pays (m.) (countries). Just like any other French noun, each country's name
has a gender.

You already know:

| France | la France |
| the United States | les États-Unis (m. pl.) |

Here are the other country names for the nationalities you saw earlier in the
lesson:

Canada	le Canada
Italy	l'Italie (f.)
England	l'Angleterre (f.)
Ireland	l'Irlande (f.)
Scotland	l'Écosse (f.)
Spain	l'Espagne (f.)
Portugal	le Portugal
Belgium	la Belgique
Switzerland	la Suisse
Germany	l'Allemagne (f.)

Greece	la Grèce
Russia	la Russie
India	l'Inde (f.)
China	la Chine
Japan	le Japon
Australia	l'Australie (f.)
Brazil	le Brésil
Algeria	l'Algérie (f.)
Morocco	le Maroc
Mexico	le Mexique

In French, *in* or *to* is usually en with feminine countries, au with masculine ones, and aux with plural ones. For countries that are singular and start with a vowel or silent h, it's usually en.

Tu es en France. Tu vas en France.
You're in France. You're going to France.

Nous sommes au Brésil. Nous allons au Brésil.
We're in Brazil. We're going to Brazil.

Je suis aux États-Unis. Je vais aux États-Unis.
I'm in the United States. I'm going to the United States.

To say *from*, use de la with feminine countries, du with masculine ones, des with plural ones, and d' with countries that are singular and begin with a vowel or silent h.

Tu viens de la France ?
You come from France?

Intermediate French

Nous venons du Maroc.
We come from Morocco.

Elles sont des États-Unis.
They're from the United States.

With cities, use à for *in* and *to*, and de for *from*.

Je suis à New York. Je suis de New York.
I'm in New York. I'm from New York.

Elle va à Paris. Elle vient de Paris.
She's going to Paris. She comes from Paris.

Finally, the *European Union* is l'Union *(f.)* européenne. If you're *European,* you're européen/européenne.

✎ Sentence Practice 2

Fill in the blanks with the correct word from the word bank below:

en	aux	de	des

1. **Nous sommes** _____ États-Unis. *(We're from the United States.)*

2. **Je suis** _____ France. *(I'm in France.)*

3. **Vous habitez** _____ États-Unis. *(You live in the United States.)*

4. **Elle habite** _____ France ? *(She lives in France?)*

5. **Tu es** _____ Paris. *(You're from Paris.)*

   ANSWER KEY:

   1. des; 2. en; 3. aux; 4. en; 5. de

✎ Word Recall

Do you remember which French words combine to form **aux** and **des**? Let's review. Complete the following equations with the correct words in French.

1. **au** = _____ + _____

2. **aux** = _____ + _____

3. **du** = _____ + _____

4. **des** = _____ + _____

ANSWER KEY:
1. à + le; 2. à + les; 3. de + le; 4. de + les

Grammar Builder 2
QUESTION WORDS

▶ 3D Lesson 3 Grammar Builder 2 (CD 4, Track 12)

First, let's review the question words and phrases that you already know:

où	*where*
comment	*how*
qui	*who*
quel/quelle *(m./f.)*, quels/quelles *(m. pl./f. pl.)*	*what, which*
qu'est-ce que	*what*

Some other commonly used question words are:

de quel + noun	*what/of what* + noun
combien (de)	*how much, how many*
à quelle heure	*at what time*

| pourquoi | *why* |
| quand | *when* |

Note that the **quel** in **de quel** needs to agree with the noun in gender and number using the forms of **quel** shown in the first table above.

Here are some examples:

De quelle nationalité es-tu ?
What's your nationality? (lit., Of what nationality are you?)

De quelle origine es-tu ?
What's your origin? (lit., Of what origin are you?)

Il y a combien de personnes dans ta famille ?
How many people are there in your family?
(lit., There are how many people in your family?)

Combien de frères as-tu ?
How many brothers do you have?

À quelle heure arrive-t-elle ?
At what time is she arriving?

Pourquoi aimez-vous le français ?
Why do you like French?

Quand partez-vous en vacances ?
When are you leaving on vacation?

✎ Work Out 2

Supply the missing word in French.

1. **Il y a** _____ (*how many*) **de personnes dans ta famille ?**

2. _____ (*Which*) **homme est ton père ?**

3. _____ (*Which*) **fille est ta sœur ?**

4. **Tu as** _____ (*how many*) **d'enfants ?**

5. _____ (*Where*) **est Martine ?**

6. _____ (*Of what/What*) **origine est Marc ?**

7. _____ (*Why*) **étudiez-vous ?**

8. _____ (*Where*) **se trouve la Tour Eiffel ?**

ANSWER KEY:
1. **combien** (*How many people are there in your family?/There are how many people in your family?*);
2. **Quel** (*Which man is your father?*); 3. **Quelle** (*Which girl is your sister?*); 4. **combien** (*How many children do you have?/You have how many children?*); 5. **Où** (*Where is Martine?*); 6. **De quelle** (*What's Marc's origin?/Of what origin is Marc?*); 7. **Pourquoi** (*Why are you studying?*); 8. **Où** (*Where is the Eiffel Tower?*)

✎ Drive It Home

Rewrite the following sentences by putting the adjectives in the feminine. Don't forget to read each sentence out loud once you're done.

1. **Je suis sérieux.** (*I am serious.*) _____

2. **Je suis fier.** (*I am proud.*) _____

3. **Je suis actif.** (*I am active.*) _____

4. **Je suis inquiet.** (*I am worried.*) _____

5. **Je suis sportif.** (*I am athletic.*) _____

6. **Je suis heureux.** (*I am happy.*) _____

ANSWER KEY:
1. Je suis sérieuse. 2. Je suis fière. 3. Je suis active. 4. Je suis inquiète. 5. Je suis sportive. 6. Je suis heureuse.

🌐 Culture Note

Although metropolitan France is smaller than the state of Texas, it has a population of more than sixty million people, almost three times that of Texas. Metropolitan France is made up of twenty-two **régions** (*f.*) (*regions*). Here are their names in French: **Alsace, Aquitaine, Auvergne, Basse-Normandie, Bourgogne, Bretagne, Centre, Champagne-Ardenne, Corse, Franche-Comté, Haute-Normandie, Île-de-France, Languedoc-Roussillon, Limousin, Lorraine, Midi-Pyrénées, Nord-Pas-de-Calais, Pays de la Loire, Picardie, Poitou-Charentes, Provence-Alpes-Côte d'Azur**, and **Rhône-Alpes**.

The scenery, weather, and way of life vary greatly from region to region. In **Rhône-Alpes** to the east, the mountains of the Alps are covered with snow all year round and are a popular skiing destination. **Basse-Normandie** (*Lower Normandy*), in the north, has a flat coastline with long sandy beaches. **Bretagne** (*Brittany*), located in the northwest, has a rocky coastline with many inlets. **Provence-Alpes-Côte d'Azur** lies to the south and includes the famous Mediterranean coastline known as the **Côte d'Azur** or French Riviera. And **Île-de-France** contains the city of Paris.

France also has **départements d'outre-mer** (*overseas departments*): **Guyane** (*French Guiana*) in northern South America, **Guadeloupe** and **Martinique** in the Caribbean, and **Réunion** in the Indian Ocean.

How Did You Do?

Let's see how you did! By now, you should be able to:

☐ Talk about nationalities, origins, and languages
(Still unsure? Jump back to page 46)

☐ Use words like *Parisian*, *serious*, *proud*, and *equal*
(Still unsure? Jump back to page 49)

☐ Say where you're from
(Still unsure? Jump back to page 52)

☐ Name different countries
(Still unsure? Jump back to page 53)

☐ Ask *of what*, *how much*, *how many*, *at what time*, *why*, and *when*
(Still unsure? Jump back to page 56)

Lesson 4: Conversations

By the end of this lesson, you will be able to:

☐ Talk about beauty, age, size, and whether something is good

☐ Talk about holidays and birthdays

☐ Use more than one word to describe something

Conversation 1

Fabienne and her cousin Martine are at a café. Luc, Fabienne's friend, arrives just as Martine excuses herself from the table.

▶ 4A Lesson 4 Conversation 1 (CD 4, Track 13)

Luc :	Salut, Fabienne ! Comment vas-tu, chère amie ?
Fabienne :	Ah ! Bonjour Luc. Ça va très bien, et toi ?
Luc :	Pas mal, merci. La fille blonde, c'est une amie ?
Fabienne :	C'est ma cousine Martine.
Luc :	Elle est française ?
Fabienne :	Non, elle est américaine.
Luc :	Elle est mariée ?
Fabinne :	Non, Martine est célibataire.
Luc :	C'est bien. Elle habite ici ?
Fabienne :	Non, elle est des États-Unis.
Luc :	Eh bien ! Pas de chance !

Luc:	*Hi, Fabienne! How are you, dear friend?*
Fabienne:	*Ah! Hello, Luc. Everything's going really well, and you?*
Luc:	*Not bad, thank you. The blonde girl, it's a friend?*
Fabienne:	*It's my cousin Martine.*
Luc:	*She's French?*
Fabienne:	*No, she's American.*
Luc:	*She's married?*
Fabienne:	*No, Martine is single.*
Luc:	*That's good. She lives here?*
Fabienne:	*No, she's from the United States.*
Luc:	*Oh well! No luck!*

Take It Further

Let's look at some words that have to do with people:

single	célibataire
married	marié/mariée
to be engaged (to)	être fiancé/fiancée (à)
girlfriend	la petite amie, la copine

boyfriend	le petit ami, le copain
someone	quelqu'un
person	la personne
people	les gens (m.)
human being	l'être (m.) humain
individual	l'individu (m.)
adult, grown-up	l'adulte (m./f.)
adolescent, teenager	l'adolescent/l'adolescente
baby	le bébé
newborn	le nouveau-né
youngest child	le cadet/la cadette
oldest child	l'aîné/l'aînée
elderly person	la personne âgée

And some helpful related phrases:

It's a crowd.	C'est une foule.
There are a lot of people.	Il y a beaucoup de monde.

Le monde means *world*, but it can also be used to mean *people*. For example, tout le monde is an expression meaning *everybody* or *everyone*. It literally means *all of the world* or *all of the people*. This expression is frequently used in French conversation.

Bonjour tout le monde !
Hello, everyone!

Tout le monde est ici.
Everybody is here.

✎ Conversation Practice 1

Unscramble the following sentences from Conversation 1.

1. est / Martine / cousine / ma / C' / .

   _____

2. va / toi / très / Ça / bien / et / ? / ,

   _____

3. elle / États-Unis / des / est / Non / . / ,

   _____

4. est / célibataire / Martine / Non / . / ,

   _____

5. vas / amie / Comment / tu / chère / ? / , / -

   _____

ANSWER KEY:
1. C'est ma cousine Martine. 2. Ça va très bien, et toi ? 3. Non, elle est des États-Unis. 4. Non, Martine est célibataire. 5. Comment vas-tu, chère amie ?

✎ Word Recall

Let's practice replacing nouns with pronouns. Rewrite the following sentences using subject pronouns (je, tu, il, elle, etc.)

For example, if you saw **Sophie est américaine.** (*Sophie is American.*), you would write **Elle est américaine.** (*She is American.*)

1. **Marc a peur.** (*Marc is afraid.*) _____

2. **Mes parents sont sportifs.** (*My parents are athletic.*) _____

   _____

3. **Hélène et Sophie sont parisiennes.** (*Hélène and Sophie are Parisian.*) _____

   _____

4. **Marc et Sophie ont raison.** (*Marc and Sophie are right.*) _____

   _____

5. **Les tables sont grandes.** (*The tables are big.*) _____

   ANSWER KEY:
   1. **Il a peur.** (*He is afraid.*) 2. **Ils sont sportifs.** (*They are athletic.*) 3. **Elles sont parisiennes.** (*They are Parisian.*) 4. **Ils ont raison.** (*They are right.*) 5. **Elles sont grandes.** (*They are big.*)

Grammar Builder 1
USING ADJECTIVES IN SENTENCES

▶ 4B Lesson 4 Grammar Builder 1 (CD 4, Track 14)

You know that, in French, most adjectives come *after* the noun.

une femme intelligente
an intelligent woman

However, you also know that there are some adjectives that come *before* the noun:

un beau garçon
a handsome boy

les petits enfants
the little children

Let's look at those types of adjectives more in detail. It can be helpful to think of adjectives that come before the noun as "BAGS adjectives," or Beauty-Age-Goodness-Size adjectives.

BEAUTY	
beau/bel/belle	*beautiful, handsome*
joli/jolie	*pretty*

AGE	
jeune	*young*
vieux/vieil/vieille	*old*
nouveau/nouvel/nouvelle	*new*
ancien/ancienne	*old, former*

GOODNESS	
bon/bonne	*good*
mauvais/mauvaise	*bad*

SIZE	
petit/petite	*small, little*
grand/grande	*big, tall*
long/longue	*long*
mince	*thin*

Here are some example sentences:

Marc est un beau garçon.
Marc is a handsome boy.

Christine est une belle fille.
Christine is a beautiful girl.

Nous avons un long voyage.
We have a long trip.

C'est une longue histoire.
It's a long story.

(Note that **le voyage** means *trip*, *voyage*, or *travel*, and **l'histoire** is a feminine noun meaning *story* or *history*.)

It's important to mention that **vieux** and **ancien** can actually come before *or* after the noun. You'll learn more in Unit 4.

✎ Work Out 1

Translate the adjective in parentheses, and then place it in the correct position in the sentence.

1. **C'est un jardin.** (*small*) _____

2. **Tu as une maison.** (*beautiful*) _____

3. **C'est un homme.** (*French*) _____

4. **Ils ont une cuisine.** (*new*) _____

5. **C'est une histoire.** (*serious*) _____

ANSWER KEY:
1. **C'est un petit jardin.** (*It/This/That is a small garden.*) 2. **Tu as une belle maison.** (*You have a beautiful house/home.*) 3. **C'est un homme français.** (*It/This/That is a French man.*) 4. **Ils ont une nouvelle cuisine.** (*They have a new kitchen.*) 5. **C'est une histoire sérieuse.** (*It/This/That is a serious story.*)

🗨 Conversation 2

Julia and her friend Jean are discussing their families and **Noël** (*Christmas*).

▶ 4C Lesson 4 Conversation 2 (CD 4, Track 15)

Julia :	Eh bien, qu'est-ce que tu fais pour la fête de Noël ?
Jean :	Tout le monde est à la maison pour la fête.
Julia :	C'est extra ! Tes enfants sont mariés, n'est-ce pas ? Ils sont là ?
Jean :	Oui. Mes enfants sont là avec leurs femmes et leurs maris, et nous avons des parents de Paris. C'est bon d'avoir la famille ensemble.
Julia :	Bien sûr, et vous avez une grande famille.
Jean :	Et toi, qu'est-ce que tu fais pour la fête ?
Julia :	Le dîner* a lieu à la maison. Mon fils, Robert, qui est étudiant à l'université, est à la maison aussi avec mon mari et moi, et ses grands-parents.
Jean :	Tu as une photo de Robert ?
Julia :	Oui, voilà une photo de Robert avec ses cousins et ses cousines.
Jean :	Il a les cheveux blonds comme toi, Julia.
Julia :	Et il a les yeux bleus comme son père.

Julia:	*Well, what are you doing for the Christmas holiday?*
Jean:	*Everyone is at home for the holiday.*
Julia:	*That's great! Your children are married, right? Are they there?*
Jean:	*Yes. My children are there with their wives and their husbands, and we have some relatives from Paris. It's good to have the family together.*
Julia:	*Of course, and you have a big family.*
Jean:	*And you, what are you doing for the holiday?*
Julia:	*The dinner is taking place at home. My son, Robert, who is a student at the university, is also at home with my husband and me, and his grandparents.*

Jean:	*Do you have a photo of Robert?*
Julia:	*Yes, here is a photo of Robert with his male and female cousins.*
Jean:	*He has blond hair like you, Julia.*
Julia:	*And he has blue eyes like his father.*

* Note that dîner can be used as a verb to mean *to dine* or *to have dinner*, and **also** as a masculine noun meaning *dinner*.

Take It Further

Remember that comme means *like, as,* or *how.*

Also, comme can mean *for* or *as* in phrases like:

comme dessert...	*as (a) dessert ... , for (a) dessert ...*
comme boisson...	*as (a) drink ... , for (a) drink ...*

For example:

Comme dessert, je mange...
For dessert, I'm eating ... /As a dessert, I'm eating ...

Also notice that qui (*who*) can be used in both questions and sentences:

Qui est là ?
Who is there?

Mon fils, Robert, qui est étudiant à l'université...
My son, Robert, who is a student at the university ...

You'll learn more about how to use qui in sentences in *Advanced French.*

In Conversation 2, you also saw some words related to the holidays:

| holiday, festival, party | les vacances, la fête |
| Christmas | Noël (*m.*) |

Here is some other holiday-related vocabulary:

Christmas Eve	le réveillon de Noël, la veille de Noël
Hanukkah	Hanoukka (*f.*), Hanoucca (*f.*)
Ramadan	Ramadan (*m.*)
national holiday	la fête nationale
Bastille Day, July 14th (France's national holiday)	le 14 (Quatorze) Juillet, la fête nationale de la France
New Year's Eve	la Saint-Sylvestre, le réveillon (du jour de l'An)
New Year's Day	le jour de l'An
New Year	le Nouvel An
birthday, anniversary	l'anniversaire (*m.*)

And some phrases:

Happy New Year!	Bonne Année !
Happy Holidays!	Bonnes/Joyeuses Fêtes !
Merry Christmas!	Joyeux Noël !
Happy birthday/anniversary!	Joyeux/Bon anniversaire !

✎ Conversation Practice 2

Re-read Conversation 2. Then choose the best word or phrase to complete each sentence.

1. Pour la fête de Noël, la famille de Jean est...

   a. ... au cinéma.

   b. ... à la maison.

   c. ... au restaurant.

2. Les enfants de Jean sont...

   a. ... célibataires.

   b. ... étudiants.

   c. ... mariés.

3. La famille de Jean est...

   a. ... petite.

   b. ... grande.

   c. ... triste

4. Le fils de Julia est...

   a. ... médecin.

   b. ... professeur.

   c. ... étudiant.

5. Robert a les cheveux blonds comme...

   a. ... ses cousins.

   b. ... sa mère.

   c. ... son père.

ANSWER KEY:

1. b (*For the Christmas holiday, Jean's family is at home.*); 2. c (*Jean's children are married.*); 3. b (*Jean's family is big.*); 4. c (*Julia's son is a student.*); 5. b (*Robert has blond hair like his mother.*)

✎ Word Recall

Let's practice possessives. Fill in the blanks with the correct possessives by translating the English words in parentheses.

1. J'ai trois sœurs. Voici _____ (*my*) sœurs.

2. Tu as une voiture. Voici _____ (*your, infml.*) voiture.

3. Ils ont un vélo. Tu as _____ *(their)* vélo.

4. Hélène est l'amie de Sophie. Elle est _____ *(her)* amie.

ANSWER KEY:
1. mes (*I have three sisters. Here are my sisters.*); 2. ta (*You have a car. Here is your car.*); 3. leur (*They have a bike. You have their bike.*); 4. son (*Hélène is Sophie's friend. She is her friend.*)

Grammar Builder 2
USING MULTIPLE ADJECTIVES IN SENTENCES

▶ 4D Lesson 4 Grammar Builder 2 (CD 4, Track 16)

You've seen examples of nouns modified by one adjective. Here are examples of nouns modified by more than one adjective.

un nouveau garçon intelligent
a new, intelligent boy

une vieille dame charmante
a charming old lady

une jeune fille sincère
a sincere young girl

les bons amis sincères
the sincere good friends

You just learned the new word la dame (*lady*). Of course, you've actually seen the word dame before, in the name of the Paris cathedral Notre-Dame, which literally means *Our Lady*.

Ⅱ

✎ Work Out 2

Choose the correct translation of each English sentence.

1. *This is an intelligent old lady.*
   a. C'est une vieille dame intelligente.
   b. C'est une intelligente vieille dame.
   c. C'est une dame vieille intelligente.

2. *It's a good, amusing day.*
   a. C'est un amusant jour bon.
   b. C'est un bon jour amusant.
   c. C'est un bon amusant jour.

3. *He is watching a new French film.*
   a. Il regarde un nouveau film français.
   b. Il regarde un français film nouveau.
   c. Il regarde un nouveau français film.

ANSWER KEY:
1. a; 2. b; 3. a

✎ Drive It Home

Translate the following sentences into French based on the sentence C'est un livre. (*This is a book.*)

1. *This is a big book.* _____

2. *This is a beautiful book.* _____

3. *This is a new book.* _____

4. *This is a bad book.* _____

5. *This is a good book.* _____

6. *This is a long book.* _____

ANSWER KEY:
1. C'est un grand livre. 2. C'est un beau livre. 3. C'est un nouveau livre. 4. C'est un mauvais livre.
5. C'est un bon livre. 6. C'est un long livre.

Culture Note

The average worker in France has five to six weeks of vacation time. Most people use a large part of their vacation in the summer, particularly in August. In fact, the last Saturday in July (and sometimes also the first Saturday in August) is often known as "Black Saturday" in France due to the large number of people traveling on that day. Traffic on France's highways is notoriously terrible at that time.

Summer vacation is referred to as les grandes (*f.*) vacances (*lit., the big vacation*). The time off from school in the winter is called les vacances (*f.*) d'hiver (*lit., winter vacation*).

How Did You Do?

Let's see how you did! By now, you should be able to:

☐ Talk naturally about beauty, age, size, and whether something is good
(Still unsure? Jump back to page 64)

☐ Talk about holidays and birthdays
(Still unsure? Jump back to page 67)

☐ Use more than one word to describe something
(Still unsure? Jump back to page 71)

Unit 1 Essentials

You're almost at the end of the first unit of *Intermediate French*! Félicitations !

You will see Unit Essentials at the end of every unit. They are divided into two sections: Vocabulary Essentials and Grammar Essentials. The Vocabulary Essentials section is a blank "cheat sheet" for you to fill in and test yourself on the vocabulary you learned in the past four lessons. Once you've completed it, you will be able to use it along with the Grammar Essentials as your very own reference guide for all of the key material from each Unit.

And don't forget to go to *www.livinglanguage.com/languagelab* to access your free online tools for this lesson: audiovisual flashcards, interactive games and quizzes.

Vocabulary Essentials

Note that if a word has more than one translation, or different masculine and feminine forms, make sure to write them all down.

BASICS

yes		okay	
no		please	
there is, there are		thank you	
here is, here are		you're welcome	
me		excuse me	
also			

[Pg. 16] (If you're stuck, visit this page to review!)

GREETINGS

Good day!/Hello!	
Hello!/Hi!/Bye!	
How's everything?/How's it going?	
Everything is well./I'm fine.	
Everything's well./It's going well.	
Everything's really well./It's going really well.	
It's not going well./It's going badly.	
How are you? (fml.)	
How are you? (infml.)	
Very well.	
Pleased to meet you./Nice to meet you.	
Good-bye!	
See you soon!	
See you later!	
Good evening!	
Good night!	

[Pg. 21]

EXPRESSIONS USING AVOIR

How old are you?	
I am ... years old.	
I'm hungry.	
I'm thirsty.	
I'm hot.	

I'm cold.	
I need ...	

[Pg. 31]

EXCLAMATIONS AND EXPRESSIONS OF OPINION

It's good.	
It's true.	
It's delicious.	
It's great.	

[Pg. 37]

NATIONALITY

I am of ... origin.	
French	
American	
in France	
from Paris	
from the United States	
in/to the United States	
Where do you live? (fml.)	
Where do you live? (infml.)	
I live ...	
What's your nationality? (fml.)	
What's your nationality? (infml.)	

[Pgs. 46 & 52]

NUMBERS 1-20

one		eleven	
two		twelve	
three		thirteen	
four		fourteen	
five		fifteen	
six		sixteen	
seven		seventeen	
eight		eighteen	
nine		nineteen	
ten		twenty	

[Pg. 20]

QUESTION WORDS AND PHRASES

where		of what, what	
how		how much, how many	
who		at what time	
which, what		why	
what		when	

[Pg. 56]

Grammar Essentials
YES/NO QUESTIONS

The three ways to form yes/no questions in French are:

1. When talking, simply raise your intonation at the end of the sentence. When writing, place a question mark at the end of the sentence:

2. Place est-ce que at the beginning of a sentence to turn it into a question. Note that est-ce que becomes est-ce qu' before a word that begins with a vowel or silent h.

3. Inversion, or switching the verb and the subject. In other words, place the verb before the subject with a hyphen connecting them.

Remember that if the verb ends with a vowel, and the subject pronoun is il, elle, or on, then -t- needs to be inserted in between the verb and the pronoun. It's also important to mention that there is actually a "sub-category" of this third type of yes/no question.

If the subject of the sentence is a noun rather than a subject pronoun, then you need to use the following format to create an "inversion" question:

subject + verb + hyphen + subject pronoun

ADJECTIVES

1. Most French adjectives come after the noun.
2. BAGS (Beauty-Age-Goodness-Size) adjectives come before the noun.

Regular adjectives

MASCULINE SINGULAR	FEMININE SINGULAR	MASCULINE PLURAL	FEMININE PLURAL	
important	importante	importants	importantes	*important*
grand	grande	grands	grandes	*big, tall*

Intermediate French

Adjectives where masculine singular form ends in a silent -e

MASCULINE SINGULAR	FEMININE SINGULAR	MASCULINE PLURAL	FEMININE PLURAL	
difficile	difficile	difficiles	difficiles	*difficult*
étrange	étrange	étranges	étranges	*strange*

Adjectives where masculine singular form ends in -s or -x

MASCULINE SINGULAR	FEMININE SINGULAR	MASCULINE PLURAL	FEMININE PLURAL	
français	française	français	françaises	*French*

Adjectives that double the final consonant and add e to form the feminine

MASCULINE SINGULAR	FEMININE SINGULAR	MASCULINE PLURAL	FEMININE PLURAL	
bon	bonne	bons	bonnes	*good*

Irregular adjectives with no pattern

MASCULINE SINGULAR	FEMININE SINGULAR	MASCULINE PLURAL	FEMININE PLURAL	MASCULINE SINGULAR BEFORE A VOWEL OR SILENT H	
beau	belle	beaux	belles	bel	*beautiful*
vieux	vieille	vieux	vieilles	vieil	*old*
nouveau	nouvelle	nouveaux	nouvelles	nouvel	*new*

Irregular adjectives with a pattern:

MASCULINE SINGULAR	FEMININE SINGULAR	MASCULINE PLURAL	FEMININE PLURAL
-x	-se	-x	-ses
-f	-ve	-fs	-ves
-er	-ère	-ers	-ères
-et	-ète/-ette	-ets	-ètes/-ettes

VERBS

AVOIR (*TO HAVE*)			
I have	j'ai	*we have*	nous avons
you have (infml.)	tu as	*you have (pl./fml.)*	vous avez
he has	il a	*they have (m.)*	ils ont
she has	elle a	*they have (f.)*	elles ont

ÊTRE (*TO BE*)			
I am	je suis	*we are*	nous sommes
you are (infml.)	tu es	*you are (pl./fml.)*	vous êtes
he is	il est	*they are (m.)*	ils sont
she is	elle est	*they are (f.)*	elles sont

Unit 1 Quiz

Now let's see how you've done so far.

In this section you'll find a short quiz testing what you learned in Unit 1. After you've answered all of the questions, score yourself to see how you did! If you find that you need to go back and review, please do so before continuing on to Unit 2.

There will be a quiz at the end of every unit.

A. Translate the following greetings.

1. *How's it going?*_____

2. *Pleased to meet you.*_____

3. *Good-bye!*_____

4. *Hi!*_____

5. *See you soon!*_____

B. Give each person's nationality. Pay attention to gender and number!

1. **Marie habite aux États-Unis. Elle est**_____.

2. **Elles habitent au Canada. Elles sont**_____.

3. **3.Hélène habite en France. Elle est**_____.

4. **Pierre habite aux États-Unis. Il est**_____.

5. **Ils habitent à Paris. Ils sont**_____.

C. Insert the correct form of avoir or être.

1. Elle _____ trente ans. (*She is thirty years old.*)

2. Ma tante _____ heureuse. (*My aunt is happy.*)

3. Est-ce que vous _____ faim ? (*Are you hungry?*)

4. Nous _____ froid. (*We are cold.*)

5. Ils_____ très sérieux. (*They are very serious.*)

D. Match the question words on the left to the correct English translations on the right.

1. quand	a. *who*
2. où	b. *what*
3. qui	c. *where*
4. pourquoi	d. *when*
5. qu'est-ce que	e. *why*

ANSWER KEY:

A. 1. (Comment) ça va ? 2. Enchanté/Enchantée (de faire votre connaissance). 3. Au revoir ! 4. Salut ! 5. À bientôt !

B. 1. américaine; 2. canadiennes; 3. française; 4. américain; 5. français (parisiens)

C. 1. a; 2. est; 3. avez; 4. avons; 5. sont

D. 1. d; 2. c; 3. a; 4. e; 5. b

How Did You Do?

Give yourself a point for every correct answer, then use the following key to determine whether or not you're ready to move on:

0–7 points: It's probably best to go back and study the lessons again to make sure you understood everything completely. Take your time; it's not a race! Make sure you spend time reviewing the vocabulary and reading through each grammar note carefully.

8–16 points: If the questions you missed were in Section A or B, you may want to review the vocabulary again; if you missed answers mostly in Section C or D, check the Unit 1 Essentials to make sure you have your conjugations and other grammar basics down.

17–20 points: Feel free to move on to the next unit! You're doing a great job.

 Points

Unit 2:
Everyday Life

Congratulations on completing Unit 1!

In this next unit, you will learn more vocabulary, expressions, and verbs for everyday life. You'll also learn how to talk about location.

By the end of this unit, you should be able to:

☐ Talk about days and months

☐ Discuss the weather

☐ Give a date

☐ Say what you're doing in the present

☐ Name objects and rooms around the house

☐ Talk about *under, behind, next to,* and other locations

☐ Discuss the color of something

☐ Say whether something is *boring, bad,* or *perfect*

☐ Say *I get dressed* and *I hurry*

☐ Say *I don't get dressed* and *I don't hurry*

☐ Talk about *going*

☐ Talk about *how everything's going*

Don't forget to look for the symbol ▷ to help guide you through the audio as you're reading the book. It will tell you which track to listen to for each section that has audio. If you don't see the symbol, then there isn't any audio for that section. You'll also see ⅠⅠ, which will tell you where that track ends.

Lesson 5: Words

By the end of this lesson, you will be able to:

☐ Talk about days and months

☐ Discuss the weather

☐ Give a date

☐ Say what you're doing in the present

Word Builder 1

Here is a quick review of the days of the week, the months of the year, and weather expressions. Remember that days and months are not capitalized in French.

Note that, from now on, the vocabulary in this course will include an article like le, la, or les where appropriate to indicate gender and number, but the article will usually not be translated. For example, les jours will be translated as *days* not *the days*. If the article is les or l', additional gender information will be provided.

▷ 5A Lesson 5 Word Builder 1 (CD 4, Track 17)

days of the week	les jours (*m.*) de la semaine
Monday	lundi

Tuesday	**mardi**
Wednesday	**mercredi**
Thursday	**jeudi**
Friday	**vendredi**
Saturday	**samedi**
Sunday	**dimanche**
months of the year	**les mois (m.) de l'année**
January	**janvier**
February	**février**
March	**mars**
April	**avril**
May	**mai**
June	**juin**
July	**juillet**
August	**août**
September	**septembre**
October	**octobre**
November	**novembre**
December	**décembre**
It's beautiful (outside).	**Il fait beau.**
It's hot.	**Il fait chaud.**
It's cold.	**Il fait froid.**
It's sunny.	**Il fait soleil./Il fait du soleil./ Il y a du soleil.**
It's windy.	**Il fait du vent./Il y a du vent.**
It's raining. (It rains.)	**Il pleut.**
It's snowing. (It snows.)	**Il neige.**

Take It Further

Here are some words related to days and months. You should already be familiar with some of them.

day	le jour
week	la semaine
weekend	le week-end
month	le mois
year	l'année (*f.*), l'an (*m.*)
yesterday	hier
today	aujourd'hui
tomorrow	demain
morning	le matin
afternoon	l'après-midi (*m./f.*)
evening, night	le soir
night	la nuit

Similar to the phrase le week-end, which can mean *the weekend* but also *over the weekend* and *on the weekend*, the phrase le soir can mean *the evening* and also *in the evening*. The same goes for le matin, l'après-midi, and la nuit. For example: Tu n'es pas gentil le matin. (*You are not nice (m.) in the morning.*) Also remember that soir is used to mean both *evening* and *night*. So, for example, ce soir can mean *this evening* or *tonight*.

And here are some words related to activities and everyday life that you will see later on in this unit:

class, grade	la classe
meeting, appointment, date	le rendez-vous
concert	le concert

When Americans hear the expression rendez-vous, they often think of a secret getaway or dinner date. In French, however, the term rendez-vous can refer to any kind of appointment, such as a doctor's appointment, a business meeting, or a lunch date with a friend.

✎ Word Practice 1

Identify the following weather conditions by filling in the correct sentence in French.

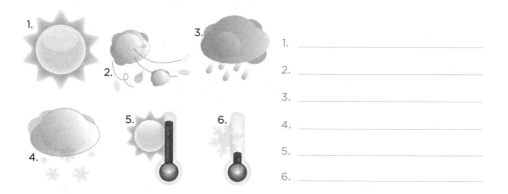

1. _____
2. _____
3. _____
4. _____
5. _____
6. _____

ANSWER KEY:
1. Il fait soleil./Il fait du soleil./Il y a du soleil. (*It's sunny.*) 2. Il fait du vent./Il y a du vent.
(*It's windy.*) 3. Il pleut. (*It's raining.*) 4. Il neige. (*It's snowing.*) 5. Il fait chaud. (*It's hot.*) 6. Il fait froid.
(*It's cold.*)

✎ Word Recall

Match the statements on the left with the best match on the right.

1. J'ai faim.	a. Je vais au stade.
2. Je suis médecin.	b. Je vais au restaurant.
3. Je suis footballeur.	c. Je vais à la librairie.
4. J'ai besoin de livres.	d. Je sors en boîte.
5. J'aime danser.	e. Je vais à l'hôpital.

ANSWER KEY:

1. b (*I'm hungry. I go to the restaurant.*) 2. e (*I'm a doctor. I go to the hospital.*) 3. a (*I'm a soccer player. I go to the stadium.*) 4. c (*I need books. I go to the bookstore.*) 5. d (*I like to dance. I go out clubbing/to clubs.*)

Grammar Builder 1
DAYS, MONTHS, AND WEATHER

▶ 5B Lesson 5 Grammar Builder 1 (CD 4, Track 18)

Remember that to say something happens *on* a particular day in French, just say the name of the day. You don't need a word like *on*, as you usually do in English.

Samedi, il y a un concert.
On Saturday, there is a concert. (lit., Saturday, there is a concert.)

J'ai un rendez-vous mardi.
I have an appointment on Tuesday. (lit., I have an appointment Tuesday.)

However, if you want to say that something takes place repeatedly or habitually, add le (never la) before the day of the week.

Le lundi, j'ai ma classe de français.
On Mondays, I have my French class.

Le dimanche, je suis à la maison.
On Sundays, I am at home.

As you know, you can also use tous (*every, all*) + les + a day of the week in the plural to talk about something that happens *every* week. For example, tous les samedis means *every Saturday*.

When giving une date (*a date*) in French, always say: le + number (+ month).

La date de la fête nationale française est le quatorze juillet.
The date of the French national holiday is (on) the fourteenth of July.

La fête de Noël est le vingt-cinq décembre.
Christmas (lit., The holiday of Christmas) is on the twenty-fifth of December.

Mon anniversaire est le vingt et un mai.
My birthday is on the twenty-first of May.

And finally, here are some weather expressions that include the months of the year. Notice that they all use en (*in, to, into*), and all but three of them use the il form of the verb faire (*to do, to make*): il fait (*lit., it does, it makes*).

Il fait beau en mai.
It's beautiful (outside) in May.

Il fait frais en mars.
It's cool in March.

Il fait chaud en juillet.
It's hot in July.

Il fait froid en janvier.
It's cold in January.

Il fait du vent en mars.
It's windy in March.

Il fait (du) soleil en juin.
It's sunny in June.

Il pleut en avril.
It rains in April.

Il neige en décembre.
It snows in December.

Il y a une tempête de neige en janvier.
There is a snow storm (blizzard) in January.

Il gèle en février.
It's freezing in February. (It freezes in February.)

✎ Work Out 1

Decide whether le is needed in the following sentences. If it isn't, leave the space blank. Make sure to pay careful attention to the English translations.

1. Marie a une classe _____ lundi et _____jeudi.

   (*Marie has a class on Mondays and Thursdays.*)

2. _____ samedi, nous avons une fête. (*On Saturday, we have a party.*)

3. Mes collègues ont un rendez-vous _____ mardi. (*My colleagues have a meeting on Tuesday.*)

4. _____ mercredi, je visite le Louvre. (*On Wednesday, I am visiting the Louvre.*)

5. Julie est heureuse _____ dimanche. (*Julie is happy on Sundays.*)

   ANSWER KEY:
   1. le, le; 2. blank; 3. blank; 4. blank; 5. le

Word Builder 2

Here are some useful -er verbs.

▶ 5C Lesson 5 Word Builder 2 (CD 4, Track 19)

to accompany	accompagner
to help	aider
to sing	chanter
to decide	décider
to dine (to have dinner)	dîner
to give	donner
to wash	laver

to walk	marcher
to leave	quitter
to ski	skier
to work	travailler
to visit (a place)	visiter
to speak (to talk)	parler
to dance	danser
to play	jouer
to like, to love	aimer
to prepare	préparer
to watch, to look at	regarder
to listen (to)	écouter

Take It Further

From *Essential French* up to this point, you have seen three ways to say *to leave*:

1. **partir (de)**

2. **quitter**

3. **sortir (de)**

Partir is probably the most general way to say that you're leaving. It also means *to go away* somewhere or *to depart*. You can use it to say that you're going away for the weekend, or leaving the house, the party, the building, the office, etc.

Like **partir**, **quitter** can also mean *to depart*. Depending on context, sometimes **quitter** and **partir** are interchangeable. However, **quitter** can have more of a permanent sense to it; it can mean *to quit* as well. Therefore, you can also use quitter when you leave a job, a person, a city, etc.

Finally, sortir primarily means *to go out* or *to come out*. It carries more of a sense of *to exit*, hence the related word la sortie (*exit*). It can even mean *to be released* or *to get out*. You can use it to talk about going out to a club or getting out of bed, or to say that you're coming out of a house, room, building, or area (as in, *How do I get out of this airport terminal?*). You can also use sortir + avec (*with*) to mean *to go out with (someone)* or *to date (someone)*.

Word Practice 2

Match the French verbs to their correct English translations.

1. dîner	a. *to play*
2. laver	b. *to watch*
3. regarder	c. *to help*
4. aider	d. *to have dinner*
5. marcher	e. *to wash*
6. jouer	f. *to walk*

ANSWER KEY:
1. d; 2. e; 3. b; 4. c; 5. f; 6. a

✎ Word Recall

Remember how to talk about *this* and *that*? Change the following phrases to say *this bus, this man, these flowers,* etc.

1. le bus *(the bus)* _____

2. l'homme *(the man)* _____

3. la carte *(the menu)* _____

4. l'amie *(the female friend)* _____

5. les fleurs *(the flowers)* _____

ANSWER KEY:

1. ce bus; 2. cet homme; 3. cette carte; 4. cette amie [remember that you only use cet with ***masculine*** nouns beginning with a vowel or silent h]; 5. ces fleurs

Grammar Builder 2
VERBS ENDING IN -ER

▶ 5D Lesson 5 Grammar Builder 2 (CD 4, Track 20)

Let's review French verbs. There are three types of regular verbs in French:

1. Verbs ending in -er (such as **parler**, *to speak*)

2. Verbs ending in -re (such as **vendre**, *to sell*)

3. Verbs ending in -ir (such as **finir**, *to finish*)

As you can see, the types are based on the final letters in the verb's ***infinitive*** form. The infinitive form is the most basic form of the verb. It's equivalent to the *to* form in English (*to speak, to sell,* etc.).

Verbs Ending in **-ER**

Most verbs end in -er. Let's review how they're conjugated: just drop the -er from the infinitive and add the following endings.

PRONOUN	ENDING	PRONOUN	ENDING
je	-e	nous	-ons
tu	-es	vous	-ez
il	-e	ils	-ent
elle	-e	elles	-ent

Here are some examples using parler (*to speak*):

Joelle parle italien avec moi.
Joelle speaks Italian with me.

Le professeur parle devant la classe.
The professor is speaking in front of the class.

Oui, je parle français.
Yes, I speak French.

Note that this conjugation is the "present tense" of -er verbs. The present tense in French can be translated into English as, for example, *speak, speaks, am speaking, is speaking, are speaking*, etc. In other words, you're talking about things that are currently taking place. You'll learn how to talk about the past and the future later on in *Intermediate French*.

Also remember that only *regular* verbs conjugate this way. Some verbs that end in -er may be irregular and conjugate differently, such as aller (*to go*).

✎ Work Out 2

Fill in the blanks with the correct present tense form of the verb in parentheses.

1. Jean _____ (regarder) un film. (*Jean is watching a movie.*)

2. Ils _____ (danser) ensemble. (*They are dancing together.*)

3. Je _____ (préparer) le dîner pour ma famille.

   (*I prepare dinner for my family.*)

4. Vous _____ (jouer) au football. (*You play soccer.*)

5. Nous _____ (regarder) la télévision. (*We are watching television.*)

ANSWER KEY:
1. regarde; 2. dansent; 3. prépare; 4. jouez; 5. regardons

✎ Drive It Home

Rewrite the following phrases in the **nous** form of the verb.

1. j'aide _____

2. elles lavent _____

3. il marche _____

4. je quitte _____

5. tu aimes _____

6. tu écoutes _____

7. elle danse _____

8. ils travaillent _____

ANSWER KEY:
1. nous aidons; 2. nous lavons; 3. nous marchons; 4. nous quittons; 5. nous aimons; 6. nous écoutons; 7. nous dansons; 8. nous travaillons

Tip

As you know, there are many words in French that look very similar to their English translations. They may be pronounced differently in the two languages, but they are usually spelled similarly and have the same meaning.

Here is a list of some of those words. Look at how many French words you already know!

blond	la blouse
certain	la boutique
cruel	la nation
différent	la photo
élégant	la phrase
excellent	la question
horrible	la table
le boulevard	l'accident (*m.*)
le bureau	l'âge (*m.*)
le chef	l'animal (*m.*)
le client	l'automobile (*f.*)
le fruit	l'avenue (*f.*)
le guide	l'éléphant (*m.*)
le menu	l'hôtel (*m.*)
le zoo	l'océan (*m.*)
orange, l'orange (*f.*)	la télévision
la rose	le T-shirt

However, just remember that there are also "false" similar words, like la librairie (*bookstore*) and le collège (*secondary school, junior high school, middle school*). Other examples include sale (*dirty*), which doesn't refer to discounts, and blessé/ blessée, which may look similar to *blessed*, but actually means *wounded*.

How Did You Do?

Let's see how you did! By now, you should be able to:

☐ Talk about days and months
   (Still unsure? Jump back to page 85)

☐ Discuss the weather
   (Still unsure? Jump back to page 85)

☐ Give a date
   (Still unsure? Jump back to page 89)

☐ Say what you're doing in the present
   (Still unsure? Jump back to page 95)

Lesson 6: Phrases

By the end of this lesson, you will be able to:

☐ Name objects and rooms around the house

☐ Talk about *under, behind, next to,* and other locations

☐ Discuss the color of something

Phrase Builder 1

Here are some words for common rooms and objects in a house. Notice that some of the vocabulary involves location as well. We'll discuss those location words in Grammar Builder 1.

▶ 6A Lesson 6 Phrase Builder 1 (CD 4, Track 21)

at the house, at home	à la maison
room	la pièce (la salle)
kitchen	la cuisine
in the dining room	dans la salle à manger
bedroom	la chambre (à coucher)
bathroom	la salle de bains
restroom (toilet)	les toilettes (f.)
parlor, living room	le salon
garden	le jardin
under the bed	sous le lit
chair	la chaise
on the table	sur la table
behind the sofa	derrière le canapé
lamp	la lampe
(a piece of) furniture*	le meuble

* If you want to talk about furniture in general, rather than one piece of furniture, use les meubles.

Take It Further

You may have noticed two words with similar meanings in the list above: les toilettes (*restroom, toilet*) and la salle de bains (*bathroom*). We looked at the difference between these two rooms briefly in the Review Dialogues in *Essential French*, but let's go into a little more detail here.

In France, la salle de bains is a room set aside for the sole purpose of bathing and washing up. In a salle de bains, you would generally find the following items:

sink	le lavabo
bathtub	la baignoire
shower	la douche
bidet	le bidet

You will generally **not** find a toilet in the **salle de bains**. Instead, the toilet is in a separate room called **les toilettes** or **les W.C.** [lay vay-say] (from the English term *water closet*).

The word **toilettes** is also used to refer to the actual *toilet* (even when referring to a single *toilet*, you always use the plural form) and to the *restroom* at a restaurant or other public place.

Finally, here are some more words related to the home:

rug	le tapis
carpet	la moquette
floor (of a room)	le sol
floor (as in, second floor, third floor, etc.)	l'étage (*m.*)
wall	le mur
ceiling	le plafond
door	la porte
window	la fenêtre

✎ Phrase Practice 1

Fill in the floor plan below with the correct French word for each room.

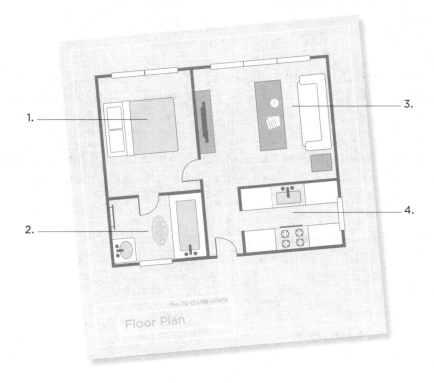

1. _____

2. _____

3. _____

4. _____

ANSWER KEY:

1. la chambre (à coucher) (*bedroom*); 2. la salle de bains (*bathroom*); 3. le salon (*living room*);
4. la cuisine (*kitchen*)

Reflexive Verbs (*Myself*) To Go

Reflexive Verbs in
the Negative

Expressions
Using *To Go*

✎ Word Recall

Choose the correct translation of the following French words.

1. **un ordinateur**

   a. *a car*

   b. *a microwave*

   c. *a computer*

   d. *a cellar*

2. **un micro-ondes**

   a. *a computer*

   b. *a clock*

   c. *a microwave*

   d. *a refrigerator*

3. **une bibliothèque**

   a. *a library*

   b. *a bakery*

   c. *a store*

   d. *a drugstore*

4. **une télé**

   a. *a computer*

   b. *a TV*

   c. *a mirror*

   d. *a clock*

ANSWER KEY:
1. c; 2. c; 3. a; 4. b

Grammar Builder 1
LOCATION

▶ 6B Lesson 6 Grammar Builder 1 (CD 4, Track 22)

Here are some basic prepositions and prepositional phrases dealing with location.

à	*to, at, in*
dans	*in (into)*
sur	*on*
sous	*under*
derrière	*behind*
devant	*in front of*

UNIT 2 Lesson 6: Phrases   103

à côté de	next to
en face de	facing, across from

If you want to say *in*, when do you use à and when do you use **dans**? Well, you know that you use à to mean *in* when you want to say someone or something is *in* a city or other similar location. You use **dans** when you want to say someone or something is *inside* or *within* something, like a room, a swimming pool, or a car.

For example, you would say:

à Paris
in Paris

dans la salle de bains
in the bathroom

Now let's look at some examples of those prepositions and prepositional phrases in sentences:

Je suis dans la baignoire.
I'm in the bathtub.

Le journal est sur la table.
The newspaper is on the table.

Le chien est sous la table.
The dog is under the table.

La lampe est derrière le canapé.
The lamp is behind the sofa.

La table est devant le canapé.
The table is in front of the sofa.

La chaise est en face du lit.
The chair is across from the bed.

La table est à côté du lit.
The table is next to the bed.

✎ Work Out 1

Choose the correct preposition from the word bank below to complete the
following sentences.

dans	devant	à	derrière

1. **Le jardin est** _____ **la maison.** (*The garden is behind the house.*)

2. **Mon frère est** _____ **la cuisine.** (*My brother is in the kitchen.*)

3. **Ma sœur est** _____ **New York.** (*My sister is in New York.*)

4. **Sophie est** _____ **le garage.** (*Sophie is in front of the garage.*)

ANSWER KEY:
1. **derrière**; 2. **dans**; 3. **à**; 4. **devant**

Phrase Builder 2

You've already seen a good amount of colors, both in *Essential French* and here in
Intermediate French. Let's take a look at a more complete list of common colors.

▶ 6C Lesson 6 Phrase Builder 2 (CD 4, Track 23)

blue	bleu/bleue
black	noir/noire
green	vert/verte
brown	brun/brune, marron*
orange	orange
red	rouge
beige, tan	beige
yellow	jaune
pink	rose
white	blanc/blanche
violet (purple)	violet/violette

* Remember that brun/brune is typically used for hair and sometimes for eyes as well. Otherwise, *brown* is usually marron. Also remember that marron does not change form, no matter the gender or number.

Take It Further

You've learned vocabulary for talking about the home in this unit, so now might be a good time to review how to say *first, second, third,* and so on in French, just in case you want to talk about the different étages *(m.) (floors)* of a house or building. (See the Culture Note in this lesson for more information about floors in France.)

Remember that these kinds of numbers are known as "ordinal numbers."

ORDINAL NUMBERS	
first	premier/première
second	deuxième, second/seconde
third	troisième
fourth	quatrième

ORDINAL NUMBERS	
fifth	cinquième
sixth	sixième
seventh	septième
eighth	huitième
ninth	neuvième
tenth	dixième
eleventh	onzième
fifteenth	quinzième
twentieth	vingtième

Note that there are two ways to say *second* in French: deuxième and second/seconde. The two terms are mostly interchangeable, although second/seconde tends to be used when there are *only* two of something, while deuxième sometimes implies that there is at least a third item.

Phrase Practice 2
Give the feminine form of each color, and then translate it into English.

1. blanc _____

2. violet _____

3. rouge _____

4. vert _____

5. noir _____

6. bleu _____

ANSWER KEY:
1. blanche (*white*); 2. violette (*violet, purple*); 3. rouge (*red*); 4. verte (*green*); 5. noire (*black*); 6. bleue (*blue*)

✎ Word Recall

Unscramble the following greetings and introductions and then translate them into English.

1. vous / je / présente _____

2. appelle / m' / je _____

3. ci / comme / comme / ça / , _____

4. va / très / ça / bien _____

ANSWER KEY:
1. je vous présente (*let me introduce*); 2. je m'appelle (*my name is/I am called*); 3. comme ci, comme ça (*so-so*); 4. ça va très bien (*everything is really well/it's going really well*)

Grammar Builder 2
USING COLORS

▶ 6D Lesson 6 Grammar Builder 2 (CD 4, Track 24)

Like other French adjectives, color adjectives must agree with the noun in gender (masculine or feminine) and number (singular or plural). Again like most adjectives, color adjectives are placed after the noun.

Here are some examples:

le canapé vert
the green sofa

la maison verte
the green house

les canapés verts
the green sofas

les maisons vertes
the green houses

le mur blanc
the white wall

la maison blanche
the white house

le tapis violet
the violet rug

la table violette
the violet table

✎ Work Out 2

Choose the correct sentence.

1. **C'est un long canapé vert. / C'est vert canapé long.**

2. **Voici le blanc mur grand. / Voici le grand mur blanc.**

3. **C'est un nouveau meuble marron. / C'est un marron meuble nouveau.**

4. **Vous avez une jolie chaise blanche. / Vous avez une blanche chaise jolie.**

ANSWER KEY:
1. **C'est un long canapé vert.** (*It's a long green couch.*) 2. **Voici le grand mur blanc.** (*Here is the big white wall.*) 3. **C'est un nouveau meuble marron.** (*It's a new piece of brown furniture./It's new brown furniture.*) 4. **Vous avez une jolie chaise blanche.** (*You have a pretty white chair.*)

✎ Drive It Home

Fill in the blanks with the appropriate preposition.

1. Le vélo est _____ (*in*) la maison.

2. Le vélo est _____ (*behind*) la maison.

3. Le vélo est _____ (*next to*) la maison.

4. Le vélo est _____ (*across from*) la maison.

5. Le vélo est _____ (*in front of*) la maison.

ANSWER KEY:

1. **dans** (*The bike is in the house.*); 2. **derrière** (*The bike is behind the house.*); 3. **à côté de** (*The bike is next to the house.*); 4. **en face de** (*The bike is across from the house.*); 5. **devant** (*The bike is in front of the house.*)

🌐 Culture Note

It is important to note that the numbering of floors in France differs from the numbering of floors in the United States. The floor on which a building is entered, sometimes called *the first floor* in the United States, is considered *the ground floor* in France and is referred to as **le rez-de-chaussée.** The floor above **le rez-de-chaussée** is called **le premier étage** (*the first floor* in France, but *the second floor* in the U.S.); the floor above that is **le deuxième étage** (*the second floor* in France, but *the third floor* in the U.S.); the next floor is **le troisième étage** (*the third floor* in France, but *the fourth floor* in the U.S.), and so on.

How Did You Do?

Let's see how you did! By now, you should be able to:

☐ Name objects and rooms around the house
(Still unsure? Jump back to page 99)

☐ Talk about *under, behind, next to,* and other locations
(Still unsure? Jump back to page 103)

☐ Discuss the color of something
(Still unsure? Jump back to page 105)

Lesson 7: Sentences

By the end of this lesson, you will be able to:

☐ Say whether something is *boring, bad,* or *perfect*

☐ Say *I get dressed* and *I hurry*

☐ Say *I don't get dressed* and *I don't hurry*

Sentence Builder 1

Remember that ça can mean *that, this,* or *it*. As a result, c'est, which is literally a combination of ça and est (*is*), can mean *that is, this is,* or *it is*. Only one version will be provided below, but the others are possible as well.

▶ 7A Lesson 7 Sentence Builder 1 (CD 4, Track 25)

I (really) like ...	J'aime bien...
I like that./I love that.	J'aime ça.
I'm having a good time. (I'm having fun.)	Je m'amuse.

It's perfect.	C'est parfait.
It's bad. / That's bad.	C'est mauvais.
It's strange.	C'est bizarre. (C'est étrange.)
It's boring.	C'est ennuyeux.

Take It Further

You've seen **bien** used to mean *well* or *good* in phrases like **Ça va bien** (*It's going well*) and **C'est bien !** (*It's good!*).

However, **bien** is also used in French to mean *very, really,* or *definitely*. In addition, it can just be added to a sentence for emphasis, somewhat similar to the word *even* or the *do* in *I do like that.*

Here are some examples:

I really like that./I do like that.	J'aime bien ça.
I really want ... /I do want ...	Je veux bien...
I would really like ...	Je voudrais bien...
I do have ...	J'ai bien...
Thank you very much.	Merci bien.
I do understand./Completely understood./Of course.	Bien entendu.
or even, or else, either, or	ou bien
and even more, and much more	et bien plus
quite the opposite, quite the contrary	bien au contraire

Bien is also used in certain set expressions. You've already seen some examples, such as:

Oh well … /Well …	Eh bien…
Of course! (lit., Very certain/sure!)	Bien sûr !

✎ Sentence Practice 1

Fill in the blanks in the conversations below.

1. **Aimez-vous le cinéma ? Oui,** _____

   les films. (*Do you like movies? Yes, I really like movies.*)

2. **Aimez-vous le livre ? Non,** _____ .

   (*Do you like the book? No, it's boring.*)

3. **Aimez-vous ce meuble ? Non,** _____ .

   (*Do you like that piece of furniture? No, it's strange.*)

4. **Aimez-vous le concert ? Non,** _____ .

   (*Do you like the concert? No, it's bad.*)

5. **Aimez-vous le jardin ? Oui,** _____ .

   (*Do you like the garden? Yes, it's perfect.*)

   ANSWER KEY:
   1. j'aime bien; 2. c'est ennuyeux; 3. c'est bizarre/c'est étrange; 4. c'est mauvais; 5. c'est parfait

✎ Word Recall

Match the French adjectives on the left to the correct English translations on the right.

1. facile	a. *difficult*
2. mince	b. *easy*
3. sympathique	c. *worried*
4. difficile	d. *nice*
5. inquiet	e. *thin*

ANSWER KEY:
1. b; 2. e; 3. d; 4. a; 5. c

Grammar Builder 1
REFLEXIVE VERBS (*MYSELF*)

▶ 7B Lesson 7 Grammar Builder 1 (CD 4, Track 26)

In Sentence Builder 1, you saw the phrase Je m'amuse (*I'm having a good time, I'm having fun*). This is an example of a reflexive verb; in this case, s'amuser (*to have a good time, to enjoy oneself, to have fun*).

Reflexive verbs are verbs that usually point the action or feeling back to the person or *oneself*. In other words, *I wash myself* or *he hurt himself* or *they enjoyed themselves*.

Let's review this important type of verb, which you were first introduced to in *Essential French*. Here are the reflexive pronouns:

REFLEXIVE PRONOUNS			
me (m')	*myself*	**nous**	*ourselves*
te (t')	*yourself (infml.)*	**vous**	*yourselves (or yourself, fml.)*
se (s')	*himself, herself, itself*	**se**	*themselves*

Keep in mind that the pronouns aren't always translated as *myself, yourself,* etc. in English. Those are literal translations.

Now let's look at the pronouns in use.

First, let's look at a regular **-er** verb that's not reflexive: **laver** (*to wash*).

LAVER (*TO WASH*) - **PRESENT**			
je lave	*I wash*	**nous lavons**	*we wash*
tu laves	*you wash (infml.)*	**vous lavez**	*you wash (pl./fml.)*
il lave	*he washes (or it washes, m.)*	**ils lavent**	*they wash (m.)*
elle lave	*she washes (or it washes, f.)*	**elles lavent**	*they wash (f.)*

Now let's look at the reflexive form of **laver**: **se laver** (*to wash oneself, to wash up*). Note that the infinitive form of a reflexive verb is always preceded by **se** (or **s'**).

SE LAVER *(TO WASH ONESELF, TO WASH UP)* - **PRESENT**			
je me lave	*I wash myself*	nous nous lavons	*we wash ourselves*
tu te laves	*you wash yourself (infml.)*	vous vous lavez	*you wash yourselves* (or *you wash yourself, fml.*)
il se lave	*he washes himself* (or *it washes itself, m.*)	ils se lavent	*they wash themselves (m.)*
elle se lave	*she washes herself* (or *it washes itself, f.*)	elles se lavent	*they wash themselves (f.)*

Almost any verb in French can be made reflexive by adding the pronouns (and se/s' before the infinitive), as with laver and se laver. However, doing so can change the meaning more significantly than just *to wash* and *to wash up*. For example, appeler means *to call*, as in *I'll call you tomorrow*, but remember that s'appeler means *to be called*, as in *I am called Sophie*. Another example is tromper, which means *to deceive*, while se tromper means *to be mistaken*.

Note that there are some verbs that **only** have a reflexive form. For instance, se souvenir means *to remember*, but the non-reflexive verb souvenir does not exist.

Here is a list of common reflexive verbs. The only verb here that doesn't have a non-reflexive form is se souvenir. To compare the reflexive and non-reflexive forms of the verbs below, see the Tip at the end of this lesson.

REFLEXIVE VERBS	
s'amuser	*to have a good time, to enjoy oneself (to have fun)*
s'appeler	*to be called (to call oneself)*
se blesser	*to hurt oneself*
se brosser	*to brush oneself (hair, teeth, etc.)*
se coucher	*to go to bed, to lie down (to lie oneself down)*
se demander	*to wonder, to ask oneself*
se dépêcher	*to hurry*
s'ennuyer	*to get bored (to be bored)*
s'habiller	*to dress oneself, to get dressed*
se lever	*to get up, to rise (to get oneself up)*
se promener	*to take a walk*
se reposer	*to rest (oneself) (to relax)*
se réveiller	*to wake up (to wake oneself up)*
se souvenir	*to remember*
se tromper	*to be mistaken, to make a mistake*
se trouver	*to be situated (to find oneself somewhere)*

As you can see, not all French reflexive verbs correspond to English reflexive verbs. For example, se souvenir just means *to remember*, not *to remember oneself* or something similar.

Here are some examples of reflexive verbs used in sentences:

Je me couche quand j'ai sommeil.
I go to bed when I'm sleepy.

Nous nous habillons pour la soirée.
We get dressed for the party.

Les garçons se dépêchent.
The boys hurry.

Il s'appelle Paul.
His name is Paul. (He is called Paul.)

Don't forget that s'appeler conjugates irregularly. It doubles the l in every form except **nous** and **vous**. Let's review:

S'APPELER *(TO BE CALLED)* - **PRESENT**			
je m'appelle	*I am called*	**nous nous appelons**	*we are called*
tu t'appelles	*you are called (infml.)*	**vous vous appelez**	*you are called (pl./fml.)*
il s'appelle	*he/it is called*	**ils s'appellent**	*they are called (m.)*
elle s'appelle	*she/it is called*	**elles s'appellent**	*they are called (f.)*

The non-reflexive form appeler conjugates in the same way, but, of course, without the reflexive pronouns.

Ⅱ

🖊 Work Out 1

Fill in the blanks with the correct form of the reflexive verb in parentheses.

1. Madame Dumas _____ (s'habiller) pour la soirée.

2. Les enfants _____ (se coucher).

3. Comment _____ (s'appeler)-ils ?

4. Vous _____ (s'amuser) avec vos amis.

5. En vacances, je _____ (se reposer).

ANSWER KEY:
1. s'habille (*Madame Dumas gets dressed for the party.*); 2. se couchent (*The children go to bed/lie down.*); 3. s'appellent (*What are they called?/What are their names?*); 4. vous amusez (*You have fun/a good time with your friends.*); 5. me repose (*I rest/relax on vacation.*)

Sentence Builder 2

You know that to form the negative (*not*) in French, two words are used: ne, placed before the verb, and pas, placed *immediately* after the verb. Remember that ne becomes n' when the verb begins with a vowel or silent h.

▶ 7C Lesson 7 Sentence Builder 2 (CD 4, Track 27)

I walk.	**Je marche.**
I do not walk.	**Je ne marche pas.**
You watch.	**Tu regardes.**
You do not watch.	**Tu ne regardes pas.**
He prepares.	**Il prépare.**
He does not prepare.	**Il ne prépare pas.**
She sings.	**Elle chante.**
She does not sing.	**Elle ne chante pas.**
I like ...	**J'aime...**
I do not like ...	**Je n'aime pas...**
Jean listens.	**Jean écoute.**
Jean does not listen.	**Jean n'écoute pas.**
That interests me.	**Ça m'intéresse.**
That doesn't interest me.	**Ça ne m'intéresse pas.**

Take It Further

You can form other negatives by substituting different words for pas:

not	ne... pas
never	ne... jamais
no longer, no more, any more, anymore	ne... plus
not yet	ne... pas encore
nothing, anything	ne... rien

Il ne finit jamais ses devoirs.
He never finishes his homework.

Nous ne parlons plus.
We don't speak anymore./We no longer speak.

Je n'arrive pas encore à chanter.
I'm not yet able to sing.

Il n'y a rien ici.
There is nothing here.

Note that the phrase "arriver à + verb" means *to be able to* do something or *to manage to* do something. On the other hand, as you know, "arriver à + destination" simply means *to arrive at* or *to get to* (a destination).

Also notice that pas encore is placed in between arriver and à. This is because pas encore, jamais, and plus must be placed directly after the verb, just like pas.

✎ Sentence Practice 2

Turn the following sentences into negative statements by adding **ne** and **pas** in the correct places.

1. **Il parle italien.** (*He speaks Italian.*) _____

2. **Je danse avec lui.** (*I danse with him.*) _____

3. **Il pleut à Paris.** (*It's raining in Paris.*) _____

4. **Elle marche tous les dimanches.** (*She walks every Sunday.*) _____

_____

5. **Vous êtes dans la cuisine.** (*You are in the kitchen.*) _____

_____

ANSWER KEY:
1. Il ne parle pas italien. 2. Je ne danse pas avec lui. 3. Il ne pleut pas à Paris. 4. Elle ne marche pas tous les dimanches. 5. Vous n'êtes pas dans la cuisine.

✎ Word Recall

Fill in the following table with the correct conjugation of the verb **avoir** (*to have*):

I have	
you have (infml.)	
he has	
she has	
we have	
you have (pl./fml.)	
they have (m.)	
they have (f.)	

ANSWER KEY:
j'ai; tu as; il a; elle a; nous avons; vous avez; ils ont; elles ont

Grammar Builder 2
REFLEXIVE VERBS IN THE NEGATIVE

▶ 7D Lesson 7 Grammar Builder 2 (CD 4, Track 28)

To form a negative statement with a reflexive verb, place **ne** after the subject pronoun (**je**, **tu**, etc.) but before the reflexive pronoun (**me**, **te**, etc.), and then place **pas** immediately after the verb.

subject pronoun + **ne** + reflexive pronoun + verb + **pas**

Je ne me dépêche pas.
I do not hurry. (I'm not hurrying.)

Il ne s'habille pas pour la soirée.
He's not getting dressed for the party.

Vous ne vous réveillez pas avant midi.
You don't get up before noon. (You don't wake up before noon.)

Note that in all of the above cases, **pas** comes directly after the verb and before any additional phrases like **avant midi** (*before noon*) or **pour la soirée** (*for the party*). Remember that this is the case when you negate non-reflexive verbs as well: **Je n'arrive pas avant midi.** (*I don't arrive before noon.*)

⏸

✎ Work Out 2
Turn the following sentences into negative statements by adding **ne** and **pas** in the correct places.

Reflexive Verbs in
the Negative

1. **Elle se lève avant neuf heures.** (*She gets up before 9:00.*) _____

_____

2. **Tu t'amuses en été.** (*You have a good time in the summer.*) _____

_____

3. **Il se dépêche.** (*He hurries.*) _____

4. **Je me trouve devant la Tour Eiffel.** (*I find myself in front of the Eiffel Tower./I'm*

in front of the Eiffel Tower.) _____

_____

5. **Je me demande pourquoi...** (*I wonder why ...*) _____

_____

ANSWER KEY:
1. Elle ne se lève pas avant neuf heures. 2. Tu ne t'amuses pas en été. 3. Il ne se dépêche pas. 4. Je ne me trouve pas devant la Tour Eiffel. 5. Je ne me demande pas pourquoi...

✎ Drive It Home
Fill in the appropriate reflexive pronoun for each sentence.

1. **Nous** _____ habillons pour le travail. (*We get dressed for work.*)

2. **Elle** _____ habille pour le travail. (*She gets dressed for work.*)

3. **Vous** _____ habillez pour le travail. (*You get dressed for work.*)

4. **Je** _____ habille pour le travail. (*I get dressed for work.*)

5. **Ils** _____ habillent pour le travail. (*They get dressed for work.*)

6. **Tu** _____ habilles pour le travail. (*You get dressed for work.*)

ANSWER KEY:
1. nous; 2. s'; 3. vous; 4. m'; 5. s'; 6. t'

Tip

Here are the reflexive verbs you saw in Grammar Builder 1 next to their non-reflexive forms. Notice the differences in meaning.

REFLEXIVE VERBS		REGULAR VERBS	
se laver	*to wash oneself, to wash up*	laver	*to wash*
s'amuser	*to have a good time, to have fun, to enjoy oneself*	amuser	*to entertain*
s'appeler	*to be called*	appeler	*to call*
se blesser	*to hurt oneself*	blesser	*to hurt*
se brosser	*to brush oneself*	brosser	*to brush*
se coucher	*to go to bed, to lie down*	coucher	*to lay down, to put someone to bed*
se demander	*to wonder, to ask oneself*	demander	*to ask, to ask for*
se dépêcher	*to hurry*	dépêcher	*to dispatch*
s'ennuyer	*to get bored, to be bored*	ennuyer	*to annoy, to bore (someone)*
s'habiller	*to dress oneself, to get dressed*	habiller	*to dress*
se lever	*to get up, to rise*	lever	*to lift, to raise*
se promener	*to take a walk*	promener	*to take someone or something for a walk*
se reposer	*to rest (oneself), to relax*	reposer	*to rest*
se réveiller	*to wake up*	réveiller	*to wake (someone)*

REFLEXIVE VERBS		REGULAR VERBS	
se tromper	*to be mistaken, to make a mistake*	tromper	*to deceive*
se trouver	*to be situated, to find oneself somewhere*	trouver	*to find*

Se souvenir (*to remember*) is not listed because it does not have a non-reflexive form.

How Did You Do?

Let's see how you did! By now, you should be able to:

- ☐ Say whether something is *boring*, *bad*, or *perfect*
  (Still unsure? Jump back to page 111)

- ☐ Say *I get dressed* and *I hurry*
  (Still unsure? Jump back to page 114)

- ☐ Say *I don't get dressed* and *I don't hurry*
  (Still unsure? Jump back to page 122)

Lesson 8: Conversations

By the end of this lesson, you will be able to:

☐ Talk about *going*

☐ Talk about *how everything's going*

📣 **Conversation 1**

Marcel and Chantal are planning a night out.

▶ 8A Lesson 8 Conversation 1 (CD 5, Track 1)

Marcel :	Tiens, Chantal ! Tu es libre samedi soir ?
Chantal :	Oui, je suis à la maison samedi soir. Pourquoi ?
Marcel :	Je t'invite à Paris. Tu viens avec moi ?
Chantal :	Où vas-tu ?
Marcel :	Eh bien, il y a une nouvelle discothèque à Paris. Est-ce que tu danses ?
Chantal :	Je ne danse pas très bien. Ça ne me plaît pas.
Marcel :	Est-ce que tu aimes regarder les films ?
Chantal :	Ah oui ! J'adore les westerns. Ça m'intéresse.
Marcel :	C'est bien ! Moi aussi, j'aime bien les westerns. Alors, rendez-vous samedi soir?
Chantal :	D'accord, Marcel. C'est super !

Marcel:	*Say, Chantal! Are you free Saturday night?*
Chantal:	*Yes, I'm at home Saturday night. Why?*
Marcel:	*I'm inviting you to Paris. Are you coming with me?*
Chantal:	*Where are you going?*
Marcel:	*Well, there's a new club in Paris. Do you dance?*
Chantal:	*I don't dance very well. I don't like it. (lit., That doesn't please me.)*

Reflexive Verbs in
the Negative

Expressions
Using *To Go*

Marcel:	*Do you like to watch movies?*
Chantal:	*Oh yes! I love westerns. I find them interesting.*
	(lit., That interests me.)
Marcel:	*That's good! I really like westerns, too. (lit., Me too, I really like*
	Westerns.) So, (it's a) date Saturday night?
Chantal:	*Okay, Marcel. That's great!*

(II)

Take It Further

Here are some words that you saw in Conversation 1, along with some more
vocabulary that you'll see later on in the lesson.

now	maintenant
in general, generally, usually	en général
really	vraiment (remember that it can also be used as a question: **Vraiment ?**)
too (much)	trop
ready	prêt/prête
free	libre
to cook	cuisiner
lunch	le déjeuner*
plants	les plantes (*f.*)
(night)club	la boîte, la discothèque

* In *Essential French*, you saw that déjeuner can also be used as a verb meaning *to have lunch*.

Remember that alors means *so, then,* or *well*.

And speaking of movies, here are a few movie genres:

a western	un western
a drama	un drame

a period drama	un drame d'époque
a comedy	une comédie
a romantic comedy	une comédie romantique
a musical	une comédie musicale
an action movie	un film d'action
a thriller	un film à suspense, un thriller*
a horror movie	un film d'épouvante
a documentary	un documentaire
an animated movie	un film d'animation

* Pronounced [sree-luhr] since the *th* sound doesn't exist in French.

✎ Conversation Practice 1

Re-read Conversation 1. Then say whether each sentence below is vrai (*true*) or faux (*false*). Next to each sentence, write down **V** for vrai or **F** for faux.

1. **Chantal est libre samedi soir.** _____

2. **Il y a une nouvelle discothèque à Paris.** _____

3. **Chantal danse très bien.** _____

4. **Marcel n'aime pas les westerns.** _____

5. **Marcel et Chantal ont rendez-vous samedi soir.** _____

ANSWER KEY:
1. V (Yes, Chantal is free Saturday night.); 2. V (Yes, there is a new club in Paris.); 3. F (No, she does not dance very well.); 4. F (No, Marcel really likes westerns.); 5. V (Yes, Marcel and Chantel do have a date Saturday night.)

✎ Word Recall

Il y a... (*There is .../There are ...*) Translate the following sentences into French using **il y a**.

1. *There is a beautiful garden.* _____

2. *There are ten rooms.* _____

3. *There is a small chair.* _____

4. *There is a new lamp.* _____

5. *There is a big kitchen.* _____

ANSWER KEY:

1. **Il y a un beau jardin.** 2. **Il y a dix pièces.** 3. **Il y a une petite chaise.** 4. **Il y a une nouvelle lampe.** 5. **Il y a une grande cuisine.**

Grammar Builder 1
TO GO

▶ 8B Lesson 8 Grammar Builder 1 (CD 5, Track 2)

Let's review the forms of **aller** (*to go*), which is an important irregular verb in French.

ALLER (*TO GO*) - **PRESENT**			
je vais	*I go*	**nous allons**	*we go*
tu vas	*you go (infml.)*	**vous allez**	*you go (pl./fml.)*
il va	*he goes*	**ils vont**	*they go (m.)*
elle va	*she goes*	**elles vont**	*they go (f.)*

Keep in mind that you can also translate the present tense forms of **aller** as *I'm going, you're going,* etc.

Ⅱ

✎ Work Out 1

Complete the sentences below with the verb aller (*to go*) in the correct form.

1. Il _____ aux États-Unis. (*He goes to the United States.*)

2. Vous _____ à New York. (*You go to New York.*)

3. Pierre _____ à la maison. (*Pierre is going home.*)

4. Luc et Jean _____ dans le jardin. (*Luc and Jean go into the garden.*)

5. Nous _____ dans la salle à manger. (*We go into the dining room.*)

6. Je _____ dans ma chambre. (*I go into my bedroom.*)

7. Est-ce que tu _____ à Paris ? (*Are you going to Paris?*)

8. Elle ne _____ pas à la maison. (*She is not going home.*)

ANSWER KEY:
1. va; 2. allez; 3. va; 4. vont; 5. allons; 6. vais; 7. vas; 8. va

❝ Conversation 2

Martine has invited her friend Claudine to her new home for lunch. Claudine has just arrived at the door.

▶ 8C Lesson 8 Conversation 2 (CD 5, Track 3)

Martine :	Bonjour Claudine. Bienvenue !
Claudine :	Tu es très aimable. Quelle jolie maison !
Martine :	Merci. Entre. Voici le salon et maintenant nous allons dans la cuisine.
Claudine :	Ah, c'est une grande cuisine. Ça m'intéresse parce que j'aime cuisiner.
Martine :	Mon mari aime la cuisine. En général, il prépare le dîner le soir.

Claudine :	Voilà le jardin. C'est super ! Est-ce que tu travailles dans le jardin ?
Martine :	Oui, j'aime travailler avec mes plantes.
Claudine :	C'est parfait ici. Je ne vais pas dans mon jardin. C'est trop petit.
Martine :	Eh bien, est-ce que tu as faim ? Le déjeuner est prêt.
Claudine :	Oui, j'ai vraiment faim.

Martine:	Hello, Claudine. Welcome!
Claudine:	That is very nice of you. (lit., You are very kind.) What a pretty house!
Martine:	Thank you. Come in. Here's the living room and now we're going into the kitchen.
Claudine:	Oh, it's a big kitchen. That interests me because I like to cook.
Martine:	My husband loves the kitchen. Usually, he prepares dinner in the evening.
Claudine:	There's the garden. It's great! Do you work in the garden?
Martine:	Yes, I like working with my plants.
Claudine:	It's perfect here. I don't go into my garden. It's too small.
Martine:	Well, are you hungry? Lunch is ready.
Claudine:	Yes, I'm really hungry.

Take It Further

In Conversation 2, you saw the phrase Quelle jolie maison ! (*What a pretty house!*)

Quel (or quelle, quels, or quelles, depending on the noun) means *which* or *what*, as you know, and it is often used in questions. However, it can also be used to form exclamations. Just start the sentence with the correct form of quel.

Quel soulagement !
What a relief!

Quelle coïncidence !
What a coincidence!

Quelle bonne idée !
What a good idea!

Conversation Practice 2

Unscramble the following sentences from Conversation 2.

1. prépare / dîner / Il / le / soir / le / . _____

2. ce / tu / faim / as / Est / que / ? / - _____

3. ne / pas / mon / Je / vais / dans / jardin / . _____

4. cuisine / mari / la / Mon / aime / . _____

5. Maintenant / allons / la / nous / dans / cuisine / . _____

ANSWER KEY:

1. Il prépare le dîner le soir. 2. Est-ce que tu as faim ? 3. Je ne vais pas dans mon jardin. 4. Mon mari aime la cuisine. 5. Maintenant nous allons dans la cuisine.

✎ Word Recall

Do you remember these avoir expressions? Fill in the table with their French equivalents.

I'm afraid.	
She's sleepy.	
He's hungry.	
They're wrong.	
You're right. (infml.)	

We're hot.	
You're cold. (pl./fml.)	
I'm ashamed.	

ANSWER KEY:

J'ai peur. Elle a sommeil. Il a faim. Ils ont tort. Tu as raison. Nous avons chaud. Vous avez froid. J'ai honte.

Grammar Builder 2
EXPRESSIONS USING *TO GO*

▶ 8D Lesson 8 Grammar Builder 2 (CD 5, Track 4)

Like avoir (*to have*), the verb aller (*to go*) is used in many expressions. You already know a lot of them, but let's review.

Comment vas-tu ?
How are you? (lit., How are you going?)

Comment allez-vous ?
How are you? (lit., How are you going?)

Je vais bien.
I am well. (lit., I am going well.)

Richard va très bien.
Richard is very well. (lit., Richard is going very well.)

Françoise va bien aussi.
Françoise is well, also. (lit., Françoise is going well, also.)

UNIT 2 Lesson 8: Conversations   133

Notice that English sometimes uses the verb *to go* in the same way:

Ça va ?
How's it going? (lit., Is it going?)

✎ Work Out 2

Match the French sentences on the left with the correct English translations on the right.

1. Je vais très bien.	a. *He's going home.*
2. Nous allons dans le salon.	b. *You're well.*
3. Vous allez bien.	c. *She's not well.*
4. Il va à la maison.	d. *She's well.*
5. Elle ne va pas bien.	e. *I'm very well.*
6. Tu vas à la maison.	f. *We're going into the living room.*
7. Elle va dans la cuisine.	g. *You're going home.*
8. Elle va bien.	h. *She's going into the kitchen.*
9. Ils vont à la maison.	i. *It's going well.*
10. Ça va bien.	j. *They're going home.*

ANSWER KEY:
1. e; 2. f; 3. b; 4. a; 5. c; 6. g; 7. h; 8. d; 9. j; 10. i

✎ Drive It Home

Fill in the blanks with the correct form of aller.

1. Nous _____ en vacances. *(We go on vacation.)*

2. Tu _____ en vacances. *(You go on vacation.)*

3. Elle _____ en vacances. *(She goes on vacation.)*

4. Vous _____ en vacances. *(You go on vacation.)*

5. Je _____ en vacances. *(I go on vacation.)*

6. Ils _____ en vacances. *(They go on vacation.)*

7. Il _____ en vacances. *(He goes on vacation.)*

8. Elles _____ en vacances. *(They go on vacation.)*

ANSWER KEY:
1. allons; 2. vas; 3. va; 4. allez; 5. vais; 6. vont; 7. va; 8. vont

How Did You Do?

Let's see how you did! By now, you should be able to:

☐ Talk about *going*
(Still unsure? Jump back to page 129)

☐ Talk about *how everything's going*
(Still unsure? Jump back to page 133)

Unit 2 Essentials

Don't forget to go to **www.livinglanguage.com/languagelab** to access your free online tools for this lesson: audiovisual flashcards and interactive games and quizzes.

Vocabulary Essentials

Remember that if the word has more than one translation, or different masculine and feminine forms, make sure to write them all down.

DAYS OF THE WEEK

Monday		Friday	
Tuesday		Saturday	
Wednesday		Sunday	
Thursday			

[Pg. 85] (If you're stuck, visit this page to review!)

MONTHS OF THE YEAR

January		July	
February		August	
March		September	
April		October	
May		November	
June		December	

[Pg. 86] Remember: If you want to say that something takes place repeatedly or habitually, put le before the day of the week. Use tous (*every, all*) + les + a day of the week in the plural to talk about something that happens *every* week. When giving a date in French, always say: le + number (+ month).

Intermediate French

WEATHER EXPRESSIONS

It's beautiful (out/outside).	
It's sunny (out/outside).	
It's hot.	
It's cold.	
It's windy.	
It's raining./It rains.	
It's snowing./It snows.	

[Pg. 86]

ROOMS AND OBJECTS IN A HOUSE

house, home		*bed*	
room		*chair*	
kitchen		*table*	
dining room		*sofa*	
bedroom		*lamp*	
bathroom		*piece of furniture*	
restroom, toilet		*furniture*	
living room, parlor			

[Pg. 100]

COLORS

blue		*beige, tan*	
black		*yellow*	
green		*pink*	
brown		*white*	
orange		*violet, purple*	
red			

[Pg. 106] Remember: colors come **after** the noun.

PREPOSITIONS

to, at, in		behind	
in, into		in front of	
on		next to	
under		across from, facing	

[Pg. 103]

-ER VERBS

to help		to visit (a place)	
to sing		to speak, to talk	
to decide		to dance	
to dine, to have dinner		to play	
to give		to like, to love	
to wash		to prepare	
to walk		to watch, to look at	
to leave		to listen (to)	
to work			

[Pg. 92]

REFLEXIVE VERBS

to have a good time, to enjoy oneself, to have fun	
to be called (to call oneself)	
to hurt oneself	
to brush oneself (hair, teeth, etc.)	

Intermediate French

to go to bed, to lie down (to lie oneself down)	
to wonder, to ask oneself	
to hurry	
to get bored, to be bored	
to dress oneself, to get dressed	
to get up, to rise (to get oneself up)	
to take a walk	
to rest (oneself), to relax	
to wake up (to wake oneself up)	
to remember	
to be mistaken, to make a mistake	
to be situated, to find oneself somewhere	

[Pg. 117]

Grammar Essentials

REFLEXIVE PRONOUNS

myself	me (m')	ourselves	nous
yourself (infml.)	te (t')	yourselves, yourself (fml.)	vous
himself, herself, itself	se (s')	themselves	se

Remember: To form a negative statement with a reflexive verb, use: subject pronoun + ne + reflexive pronoun + verb + pas

REFLEXIVE VERB CONJUGATION

SE LAVER *(TO WASH ONESELF, TO WASH UP)*			
I wash myself	je me lave	*we wash ourselves*	nous nous lavons
you wash yourself (infml.)	tu te laves	*you wash yourselves (or you wash yourself, fml.)*	vous vous lavez
he washes himself (or it washes itself, m.)	il se lave	*they wash themselves (m.)*	ils se lavent
she washes (or it washes itself, f.)	elle se lave	*they wash themselves (f.)*	elles se lavent

S'APPELER *(TO BE CALLED)*			
I am called	je m'appelle	*we are called*	nous nous appelons
you are called (infml.)	tu t'appelles	*you are called (pl./fml.)*	vous vous appelez
he is called	il s'appelle	*they are called (m.)*	ils s'appellent
she is called	elle s'appelle	*they are called (f.)*	elles s'appellent

-ER VERB CONJUGATION

PRONOUN	ENDING	PRONOUN	ENDING
je	-e	nous	-ons
tu	-es	vous	-ez
il	-e	ils	-ent
elle	-e	elles	-ent

PARLER *(TO SPEAK)*			
I speak	je parle	*we speak*	nous parlons
you speak (infml.)	tu parles	*you speak (pl./fml.)*	vous parlez
he speaks	il parle	*they speak (m.)*	ils parlent
she speaks	elle parle	*they speak (f.)*	elles parlent

OTHER VERBS

ALLER *(TO GO)*			
I go	je vais	*we go*	nous allons
you go (infml.)	tu vas	*you go (pl./fml.)*	vous allez
he goes	il va	*they go (m.)*	ils vont
she goes	elle va	*they go (f.)*	elles vont

Quiz 2

Now let's see how you did in Unit 2!

In this section you'll find a short quiz testing what you learned in Unit 2. After you've answered all of the questions, don't forget to score your quiz to see how you did. If you find that you need to go back and review, please do so before continuing on to Unit 3.

A. Fill in the blanks with the correct form of the reflexive verbs in parentheses.

1. **Les enfants** _____ (s'habiller) à 9h.
   (The children get dressed at 9:00.)

2. **Nous** _____ (se réveiller) à 8h.
   (We wake up at 8:00.)

3. **Est-ce que vous** _____ (s'amuser) à la fête ?
   (Are you having fun at the party?)

4. **Ils** _____ (se coucher) à 22h.
   (They go to bed at 10 p.m.)

5. **Anne** _____ (se reposer) dans le parc.
   (Anne relaxes in the park.)

B. Fill in the blanks with the next logical word in the sequence.

1. **lundi, mardi,** _____

2. **février, mars,** _____

3. **vendredi, samedi,** _____

4. **mai, juin,** _____

5. **octobre, novembre,** _____

C. Match the colors in French on the left to the correct English translations on the right.

1. **noir**   a. *yellow*

2. **jaune**   b. *white*

3. **vert**   c. *black*

4. **blanc**   d. *brown*

5. **marron**   e. *green*

D. Choose the correct word to complete each sentence.

1. Le jardin est _____ (behind) la maison.
   a. devant
   b. derrière
   c. dans
   d. en face de

2. Le salon est _____ (next to) la cuisine.
   a. sous
   b. en face de
   c. à côté de
   d. devant

3. La lampe est _____ (on) la table.
   a. dans
   b. derrière
   c. sur
   d. sous

4. Le journal est _____ (under) la table.
   a. dans
   b. derrière
   c. sur
   d. sous

5. Christine va _____ (to) Paris.
   a. dans
   b. devant
   c. à
   d. en face de

How Did You Do?

Give yourself a point for every correct answer, then use the following key to determine whether or not you're ready to move on:

0-7 points: It's probably best to go back and study the lessons again to make sure you understood everything completely. Take your time; it's not a race! Make sure you spend time reviewing the vocabulary and reading through each grammar note carefully.

8-16 points: If the questions you missed were in Section A or B, you may want to review the vocabulary again; if you missed answers mostly in Section C or D, check the Unit 2 Essentials to make sure you have your conjugations and other grammar basics down.

17-20 points: Feel free to move on to Unit 3! You're doing a great job.

 **Points**

To Eat	On	
	Some	The Near Future (*I'm Going to ...*)

Unit 3:
At a Restaurant

Now let's move on to la nourriture (*food*), which is, of course, one of the most important topics when studying French!

You will see that English has borrowed many expressions from French in this area. For example, you can be a gourmet (*lover of fine food, gourmet*) or a gourmand (*lover of food in general, gourmand*) in both French and English.

Also, so far you have only learned how to talk about the present, but in this unit, you'll learn how to talk about the near future.

By the end of this unit, you should be able to:

☐ Name different types of fruits and vegetables

☐ Talk about what you've had to *eat*

☐ Name different utensils and types of meat

☐ Say that you don't eat something

☐ Name different dishes and desserts

☐ Talk about what *people in general* do

☐ Talk about quantities of food

☐ Say what you're *going to* do in the future

☐ Discuss what you're going to have at a restaurant

☐ Talk to le serveur/la serveuse (*the waiter/the waitress*)

☐ Say what you're having to *drink*

146   Intermediate French

☐ Talk about what someone is *selling*

☐ Indicate what someone else *would like*

☐ Talk about what someone is *finishing*

Now let's go ahead and learn more about la gastronomie (*gastronomy*) in France!

Lesson 9: Words

By the end of this lesson, you will be able to:

☐ Name different types of fruits and vegetables

☐ Talk about what you've had to *eat*

☐ Name different utensils and types of meat

☐ Say that you don't eat something

Word Builder 1

▶ 9A Lesson 9 Word Builder 1 (CD 5, Track 5)

meal	le repas
breakfast	le petit déjeuner
lunch	le déjeuner
dinner	le dîner
fruit	le fruit
apple	la pomme
cherry	la cerise
tomato	la tomate

lemon	le citron
lime	le citron vert
grape	le raisin
vegetable	le légume
potato	la pomme de terre
carrot	la carotte
lettuce	la laitue
corn	le maïs
cucumber	le concombre
celery	le céleri
(green) peas (lit., little peas)	les petits pois (m.)
spinach	les épinards (m.)
green beans	les haricots (m.) verts

Take It Further

Notice similarities between some of the words in Word Builder 1? Let's take a look.

lunch	le déjeuner
breakfast (lit., little lunch)	le petit déjeuner
lemon	le citron
lime (lit., green lemon)	le citron vert
apple	la pomme
potato (lit., apple of earth)	la pomme de terre

Also, do you remember the irregular verb prendre? **Prendre** means *to take* but it can also mean *to have* when talking about food, as in *I'm having the fish* or *What are you having?* You saw the present tense conjugation of prendre in Lesson 8 of *Essential French,* and we'll review its forms later on in this unit, but for now, just keep it in mind and look for examples of it in use throughout the unit.

✎ Word Practice 1

Mme Beaulieu is making her shopping list. Translate her list into French, making sure to write le, la, or les before each item.

1. _____ *apples*

2. _____ *lettuce*

3. _____ *tomatoes*

4. _____ *corn*

5. _____ *celery*

ANSWER KEY:
1. les pommes; 2. la laitue; 3. les tomates; 4. le maïs; 5. le céleri

✎ Word Recall

Numbers are very important when dealing with les recettes *(f.)* *(recipes),* so let's review. Match the French numbers on the left to the correct English translations on the right.

To Eat · On · Some · The Near Future (*I'm Going to ...*)

1. douze	a. *twenty*
2. cinq	b. *eight*
3. huit	c. *twelve*
4. vingt	d. *eleven*
5. onze	e. *five*

ANSWER KEY:
1. c; 2. e; 3. b; 4. a; 5. d

Grammar Builder 1
TO EAT

▶ 9B Lesson 9 Grammar Builder 1 (CD 5, Track 6)

You've seen how to conjugate regular verbs that end in -er: just remove the -er from the infinitive and add the following endings.

PRONOUN	ENDING	PRONOUN	ENDING
je	-e	nous	-ons
tu	-es	vous	-ez
il	-e	ils	-ent
elle	-e	elles	-ent

Unfortunately, there are some exceptions: verbs that end in -er but conjugate irregularly.

You already know about **aller** (*to go*) and **appeler/s'appeler** (*to call/to be called*). **Manger** (*to eat*) is another one. It has an irregular **nous** form.

MANGER (*TO EAT*) - PRESENT			
je mange	*I eat*	**nous mangeons**	*we eat*
tu manges	*you eat*	**vous mangez**	*you eat*
il mange	*he eats*	**ils mangent**	*they eat*
elle mange	*she eats*	**elles mangent**	*they eat*

As you can see, an **e** is added to the **nous** form of the verb: instead of **nous mangons**, it's **nous mangeons**.

All verbs ending in **-ger** write the **nous** form this way. Here are some common **-ger** verbs:

COMMON -GER VERBS	
nager	*to swim*
ranger	*to put away*
voyager	*to travel*
déménager	*to move out*
changer	*to change*
éponger	*to mop, to soak up*
allonger	*to lay down, to lie down*
plonger	*to dive*

So, for example, you would write **nous nageons, nous rangeons, nous voyageons, nous plongeons**, etc.

UNIT 3 Lesson 9: Words   151

A similar spelling change is required for verbs that end in **-cer**, such as **commencer** (*to begin, to start*).

COMMENCER *(TO BEGIN, TO START)*			
je commence	*I begin*	**nous commençons**	*we begin*
tu commences	*you begin*	**vous commencez**	*you begin*
il commence	*he begins*	**ils commencent**	*they begin*
elle commence	*she begins*	**elles commencent**	*they begin*

Notice that the final **c** is changed to a **ç** in the **nous** form.

Here are a few other verbs ending in **-cer**:

COMMON -CER VERBS	
avancer	*to advance*
annoncer	*to announce*
menacer	*to threaten*

So you would write **nous avançons**, **nous annonçons**, and **nous menaçons**.

Ⅱ

✎ Work Out 1

Fill in the blanks with the correct form of the verb in parentheses.

1. **Je** _____ (manger) une salade.

2. **Nous** _____ (manger) un dessert.

3. **Nous** _____ (commencer) le dîner.

To Drink		*Would Like*	
	Verbs Ending in **-RE**		Verbs Ending in **-IR**

4. **Tu** _____ (voyager) en France.

5. **Nous** _____ (voyager) aux États-Unis.

ANSWER KEY:
1. mange (*I'm eating a salad.*); 2. mangeons (*We're eating a dessert.*); 3. commençons (*We're beginning/starting dinner.*); 4. voyages (*You're traveling to/in France.*); 5. voyageons (*We're traveling to/in the United States.*)

Word Builder 2

As in the U.S., a meal in France often begins with une entrée/un hors-d'œuvre (*an appetizer*), followed by un plat (principal) (*a main course*). Here are some common French appetizers, types of meat and fish that you might see in main courses, and words for table settings.

▶ 9C Lesson 9 Word Builder 2 (CD 5, Track 7)

APPETIZERS	
soup	la soupe, le potage
raw vegetables – a French appetizer of raw, mixed vegetables	les crudités (*f. pl.*)
goose liver pâté – a spreadable purée of goose liver	le pâté de foie gras
cantaloupe (melon)	le melon

MEAT AND FISH	
meat	la viande
steak	le steak
beef	le bœuf
ham	le jambon
pork	le porc
chicken	le poulet

MEAT AND FISH	
duck	le canard
veal	le veau
fish	le poisson
lobster	le homard

TABLE SETTING	
table setting	le couvert
fork	la fourchette
plate	l'assiette (*f.*)
knife	le couteau
spoon	la cuiller, la cuillère
tablecloth	la nappe
napkin	la serviette
glass	le verre
cup	la tasse

Take It Further

Now let's review some of the dishes and drinks you saw in *Essential French*.

APPETIZERS (LES ENTRÉES *[f.]*/LES HORS-D'ŒUVRES *[m.]*)	
onion soup	la soupe à l'oignon
sardines in tomato sauce	les sardines (*f.*) sauce tomate
noodle soup *(vermicelli pasta consommé)*	le consommé aux vermicelles

MAIN COURSES (LES PLATS PRINCIPAUX)	
lobster bisque	la bisque de homard
pork chop	la côte de porc
roast rack of lamb	le carré d'agneau rôti
trout cooked in wine (and vinegar)	la truite au bleu
roast beef	le rôti de bœuf
duck à l'orange, duck with orange sauce	le canard à l'orange

SIDES (LES PLATS [m.pl.] D'ACCOMPAGNEMENT)	
rice	le riz
bread	le pain
butter	le beurre

DESSERTS (LES DESSERTS)	
cheese	le fromage
pastry	la pâtisserie
crêpe – a tissue-thin pancake	la crêpe
crêpe Suzette – a crêpe with sugar, orange, and liqueur	la crêpe Suzette
peaches with ice cream	la pêche Melba
fruit salad	la salade de fruits
creamy dessert made with caramel	la crème caramel

DRINKS (LES BOISSONS)	
wine	le vin
red wine	le vin rouge
white wine	le vin blanc
rosé wine	le vin rosé

DRINKS (LES BOISSONS)	
coffee (black coffee)	le café
coffee with cream	le café-crème
tea	le thé

And here are some more useful words related to food and drinks. You'll see all of these words in use (and with audio) in Grammar Builder 2.

water	l'eau (*f.*)
ice cream	la glace
chocolate	le chocolat
chocolate ice cream	la glace au chocolat
banana	la banane
strawberry	la fraise
snails, escargots	les escargots (*m.*)

✎ Word Practice 2

Fill in the following table setting with the correct French word for each item. Make sure to include le or la (or l') before each word.

1. _____

2. _____

3. _____

4. _____

To Drink		Would Like	
	Verbs Ending in **-RE**		Verbs Ending in **-IR**

ANSWER KEY:
1. la fourchette (*fork*); 2. l'assiette (*plate*); 3. le couteau (*knife*); 4. la cuiller/la cuillère (*spoon*)

✎ Word Recall

Let's review some of the basic vocabulary that you saw in Lesson 1. Translate the following words and phrases into French.

1. *thank you* _____

2. *please (fml.)* _____

3. *also* _____

4. *okay* _____

5. *pardon me*

ANSWER KEY:
1. merci; 2. s'il vous plaît; 3. aussi; 4. d'accord; 5. pardon

Grammar Builder 2
SOME

▶ 9D Lesson 9 Grammar Builder 2 (CD 5, Track 8)

You know that de (*of, from, for*) combines with the definite article in the following way:

de + le = du

de + la = de la

de + l' = de l'

de + les = des

In technical terms, this set of words is known as the "partitive."

De la, de l', du, and **des** can mean *some* or *of the*, and also *any*. In addition, you know that **des** is the plural form of **un/une** (*a, an*).

Here are some examples. Remember that while it is usually optional to use *some* in English, it is required in French.

Je mange de la glace.
I eat (some) ice cream.

Je mange des fraises.
I eat (some) strawberries.

Elle a des bananes.
She has (some) bananas.

Il mange de la salade.
He eats (some) salad.

However, note that **du, de la,** etc. are ***not*** used when talking in general about things you like or dislike. Instead, the definite article (**le, la,** etc.) is usually used.

J'aime la glace au chocolat.
I like chocolate ice cream.

Elle adore la salade.
She loves salad.

Mon mari aime le vin.
My husband likes wine.

Philippe aime l'eau.
Philippe likes water.

Nous aimons les escargots comme hors-d'œuvre.
We like snails as an hors d'œuvre.

In a negative sentence, **de la, de l', du**, and **des** change to **de/d'**.

Il mange de la salade.
He eats salad.

Il ne mange pas de salade.
He doesn't eat salad.

Of course, this just applies to the partitive. The definite article doesn't change in a negative sentence: **Philippe aime l'eau. Philippe n'aime pas l'eau.**

Ⅱ

✎ Work Out 2

Fill in the blanks with **de, la**, or **de la**.

1. **Je mange** _____ **soupe.** (*I eat soup.*)

2. **Je ne mange pas** _____ **soupe.** (*I don't eat soup.*)

3. **Je n'aime pas** _____ **soupe.** (*I don't like soup.*)

4. **Tu as** _____ **pommes.** (*You have apples.*)

5. **Elle n'a pas** _____ **pommes.** (*She doesn't have apples.*)

ANSWER KEY:
1. **de la**; 2. **de**; 3. **la**; 4. **des**; 5. **de**

✎ Drive It Home

A. Fill in the blanks with the **nous** form of each verb in parentheses.

1. Nous _____ (manger) une pomme. *(We eat an apple.)*

2. Nous _____ (manger) au restaurant. *(We eat at the restaurant.)*

3. Nous _____ (manger) le petit déjeuner avant l'école.

   (We eat breakfast before school.)

4. Nous _____ (commencer) le film. *(We start the movie.)*

5. Nous _____ (commencer) nos vacances samedi.

   (We start our vacation on Saturday.)

6. Nous _____ (commencer) le repas. *(We start the meal.)*

B. Rewrite each French sentence in the negative.

1. Je mange de la salade. *(I'm eating some salad.)* _____

   _____

2. Je mange du jambon. *(I'm eating some ham.)* _____

   _____

3. Je mange des épinards. *(I'm eating some spinach.)* _____

   _____

4. Je mange du poisson. *(I'm eating some fish.)* _____

   _____

5. Je mange de la viande. *(I'm eating some meat.)* _____

   _____

6. **Je mange des cerises.** (*I'm eating some cherries.*) _____

_____

ANSWER KEY:

A. 1. mangeons; 2. mangeons; 3. mangeons; 4. commençons; 5. commençons; 6. commençons

B. 1. Je ne mange pas de salade. 2. Je ne mange pas de jambon. 3. Je ne mange pas d'épinards. 4. Je ne mange pas de poisson. 5. Je ne mange pas de viande. 6. Je ne mange pas de cerises.

🌐 Culture

The French are well known for their food. Think of all the famous French dishes that have made their way onto American menus, such as **quiche, soufflé, parfait,** and **fondue,** just to name a few!

Mealtimes are very important to the French, and they eat them more slowly than Americans do. Let's start with the first meal of the day, which is breakfast. **Le petit déjeuner** (*breakfast*) is light and often consists of **le café (noir)** (*black coffee*), **le café-crème** (*coffee with cream*), or **le café au lait** (*coffee with milk*), consumed from a large cup or bowl. Children might drink **le chocolat chaud** (*hot chocolate*). A flaky **croissant** (*croissant*), **brioche** (*sweet bun*), or **tartine** (*bread with butter and jelly*) frequently accompanies the coffee or hot chocolate.

Le déjeuner (*lunch*) used to be the most important meal of the day. Families would gather at home for an hour and a half to two hours to share a meal. However, lunch is losing its place as the main meal, especially in large cities where people are too busy to take such a long break in the middle of the day. A quick meal at a fast food restaurant or a **baguette** sandwich at a nearby **café** or **brasserie** (*a casual type of French restaurant*) is now a common substitute.

Le dîner (*dinner*) has therefore become the most important meal in some areas, and families who do not share a leisurely meal at lunch will make sure that everyone is together in the evening. **Le dîner** is served around seven, eight, or even nine in the evening. When the French are going out in the evening—for example, to a concert or play—a late meal is eaten afterwards, around eleven or midnight. This is called **le souper** (*late dinner*) because very often soup is on the menu. The verb **souper** means *to have a late dinner*.

How Did You Do?

Let's see how you did! By now, you should be able to:

☐ Name different types of fruits and vegetables
(Still unsure? Jump back to page 147)

☐ Talk about what you've had to *eat*
(Still unsure? Jump back to page 150)

☐ Name different utensils and types of meat
(Still unsure? Jump back to page 153)

☐ Say that you don't eat something
(Still unsure? Jump back to page 157)

Lesson 10: Phrases

By the end of this lesson, you will be able to:

☐ Name different dishes and desserts

☐ Talk about what *people in general* do

☐ Talk about quantities of food

☐ Say what you're *going to* do in the future

Phrase Builder 1

Here are more words and phrases for French nourriture (*food*), plats (*dishes*), and desserts (*desserts*).

▶ 10A Lesson 10 Phrase Builder 1 (CD 5, Track 9)

a poached egg	un œuf poché
a fried egg (an over easy egg)	un œuf au plat, un œuf sur le plat
a soft-boiled egg	un œuf à la coque
a grilled ham and cheese sandwich	un croque-monsieur
rosette-cut radishes served with butter on top (lit., radishes in butter)	les radis (*m.*) au beurre
scallops	les coquilles (*f.*) Saint-Jacques
(some) sausages	des saucisses (*f.*)
mashed potatoes	la purée de pommes de terre
boiled potatoes in their skins (or baked potatoes)	les pommes (*f.*) de terre en robe des champs
french fries	les frites (*f.*)
Dijon mustard	la moutarde de Dijon
(an) apple pie	une tarte aux pommes
(a) pumpkin pie	une tarte à la citrouille
(a) chocolate cake	un gâteau au chocolat
(a) chocolate mousse	une mousse au chocolat
whipped cream (that is flavored and sweetened)	la crème chantilly
vanilla ice cream	la glace à la vanille
strawberry ice cream	la glace à la fraise

| chocolate ice cream | la glace au chocolat |
| herbal tea | la tisane |

Take It Further

The names of many French dishes are proper names or expressions and can't necessarily be translated directly. For example, here are some literal translations of the phrases you saw:

PHRASE	LITERAL TRANSLATION
un croque-monsieur	a crunch-sir
les pommes de terre en robe des champs	potatoes in jackets
les coquilles Saint-Jacques	shells of Saint James
la crème chantilly	Chantilly cream (the town of Chantilly is supposedly where this type of whipped cream was invented)
un œuf à la coque	an egg in the shell
un œuf au plat, un œuf sur le plat	a flat egg

Now let's look at some of the individual words that you saw in Phrase Builder 1:

cream	la crème
mousse	la mousse
cake	le gâteau
pie, tart	la tarte
pumpkin	la citrouille
vanilla	la vanille
mustard	la moutarde
purée	la purée

Notice that French often uses **à la, à l', au,** or **aux** in food expressions to indicate a flavor or main ingredient. For example:

strawberry pie	la tarte aux fraises
apple pie	la tarte aux pommes
vanilla ice cream	la glace à la vanille
onion soup	la soupe à l'oignon

 Phrase Practice 1

M. Beaulieu is planning a dinner party. Use the words from the word bank below to create the menu. There will be two items for each course and any meat or fish should be used as a main course.

le homard	les carottes
la tisane	le potage
les coquilles Saint-Jacques	la glace à la fraise
les pommes de terre	le vin
les crudités	le gâteau au chocolat

LE MENU

1. **Les entrées** _____

2. **Les plats principaux** _____

3. **Les légumes** _____

4. **Les desserts** _____

5. **Les boissons** _____

ANSWER KEY:
1. **Les entrées : les crudités, le potage** (*Appetizers: crudités, soup*); 2. **Les plats principaux : le homard, les coquilles Saint-Jacques** (*Main courses: lobster, scallops*); 3. **Les légumes : les carottes, les pommes de terre** (*Vegetables: carrots, potatoes*); 4. **Les desserts : la glace à la fraise, le gâteau au chocolat** (*Desserts: strawberry ice cream, chocolate cake*); 5. **Les boissons : la tisane, le vin** (*Drinks: herbal tea, wine*)

✎ Word Recall

Let's review the survival expressions from *Essential French*, which may come in very handy at a restaurant if you don't understand what the waiter is saying. Translate the following phrases into French.

1. *What did you say?* _____

2. *Repeat that, please (fml.).* _____

3. *Speak more slowly, please (fml.).* _____

4. *I don't understand.* _____

ANSWER KEY:
1. Comment ? 2. Répétez, s'il vous plaît. 3. Parlez plus lentement, s'il vous plaît. 4. Je ne comprends pas.

Grammar Builder 1
ON

▶ 10B Lesson 10 Grammar Builder 1 (CD 5, Track 10)

You first learned about the subject pronoun **on** in *Essential French*. It's commonly used and a useful pronoun to know, so let's review.

In casual conversation, **on** is often used instead of **nous** to mean *we*. For instance, the sentences **on va à une soirée** (*we're going to a party*) and **nous allons à une soirée** (*we're going to a party*) are essentially interchangeable, although the sentence using **on** is more casual.

On can also mean *one* or *people in general*. Furthermore, **on** can be translated as the "general" *you* or *they*. For example: *You can't look directly at an eclipse.* or *They say it can't be done.*

In other words, **on** can be translated as *we, one, people (in general), you,* or *they* depending on context.

Dans un café, on mange.
In a café, one eats.

Le dimanche, on mange des croissants pour le petit déjeuner à la maison.
On Sundays, we eat croissants for breakfast at home.

Keep in mind that the **on** form of the verb is the same as the **il** and **elle** form: **il est, elle est, on est,** for instance.

Work Out 1

Write the correct form of each verb in parentheses.

1. **Dans un parc, on** _____ (marcher). (*In a park, one walks.*)

2. **On** _____ (dîner) **dans un restaurant.** (*You dine in a restaurant.*)

3. **On** _____ (aller) **en ville.** (*We're going into town.*)

4. **Le soir, on** _____ (préparer) **le dîner.** (*In the evening, people prepare dinner.*)

5. **On** _____ (avoir) **beaucoup de livres.** (*We have a lot of books.*)

ANSWER KEY:
1. marche; 2. dîne; 3. va; 4. prépare; 5. a

Phrase Builder 2

▶ 10C Lesson 10 Phrase Builder 2 (CD 5, Track 11)

a carton of orange juice	une boîte de jus d'orange
a bottle of champagne	une bouteille de champagne
a cup of tea	une tasse de thé
a glass of milk	un verre de lait
a slice of cheese	une tranche de fromage
a basket of plums	un panier de prunes
a kilo of ... *	un kilo de...
a pound of butter	une livre de beurre
a pitcher of wine	une carafe de vin
a dozen eggs	une douzaine d'œufs
too much sauce	trop de sauce
a little spinach	un peu d'épinards
a lot of ice cream	beaucoup de glace
less vegetables	moins de légumes
more candy	plus de bonbons

⏸ * 1 kilo(gram) = approximately 2.2 pounds

Take It Further

Now let's quickly review each of those quantity expressions on its own:

a carton of	une boîte de (un carton de, une brique de)
a bottle of	une bouteille de
a cup of	une tasse de
a glass of	un verre de

a slice of (bread, cheese)	**une tranche de**
a basket of	**un panier de**
a kilo of	**un kilo de**
a pound of	**une livre de**
a pitcher of	**une carafe de**
a dozen of	**une douzaine de**
too much of	**trop de**
a little of	**un peu de**
a lot of	**beaucoup de**
less of, fewer of	**moins de***
more of	**plus de**

* By itself, **moins** means *minus* or *less*.

Note that all expressions of quantity are followed by the preposition **de/d'**, and *not* the partitive (**du, de la, de l', des**). For example, look at the differences in the sentences below.

Je prends du vin.	**Je prends un peu de vin.**
I'm having some wine.	*I'm having a little wine.*
Nous prenons de l'eau.	**Nous prenons un verre d'eau.**
We're having some water.	*We're having a glass of water.*

Speaking of water, you learned how to say *a pitcher of wine* (**une carafe de vin**), but another useful expression is **une carafe d'eau** (*a pitcher of water*). This is the standard way to ask for tap water at a French restaurant. For example:

Une carafe d'eau, s'il vous plaît.
A pitcher of water, please./Tap water, please.

To Eat	On	

Some   The Near Future
                                                  (*I'm Going to ...*)

And finally, here are some more quantity expressions that might come in handy:

a slice of (cake, pie, pizza)	une part de
a (round) slice of (cucumber, banana, sausage, etc.)	une rondelle de
a piece of, a bite of	un morceau de
a gram of	un gramme de
two dozen of	deux douzaines de

✎ Phrase Practice 2

Match the French words on the left to the English translations on the right.

1. une tranche de   a. *a little of*

2. un peu de   b. *a dozen of*

3. une douzaine de   c. *a slice of*

4. un verre de   d. *a pound of*

5. une livre de   e. *a glass of*

ANSWER KEY:

1. c; 2. a; 3. b; 4. e; 5. d

✎ Word Recall

Fill in the blanks with the correct form of the verb **aller** (*to go*).

1. je _____

2. tu _____

3. il _____

4. elle _____

5. on _____

6. nous _____

7. vous _____

8. ils _____

9. elles _____

ANSWER KEY:
1. **vais**; 2. **vas**; 3. **va**; 4. **va**; 5. **va**; 6. **allons**; 7. **allez**; 8. **vont**; 9. **vont**

Grammar Builder 2
THE NEAR FUTURE (*I'M GOING TO …*)

▶ 10D Lesson 10 Grammar Builder 2 (CD 5, Track 12)

By now, you should be pretty familiar with the verb **aller** (*to go*). It was introduced in *Essential French*, reviewed in Lesson 8 of this course, and reviewed again in the Word Recall just before this section.

Je vais à Paris.
I'm going to Paris.

Marc va à la maison.
Marc is going home.

And you know that aller can be used in certain expressions, particularly related to greetings:

Je vais bien.
I'm doing well. (lit., I'm going well.)

However, aller can also be used to talk about something that will happen in the future, equivalent to the use of *going to* in English: *I'm going to prepare some soup.* This use of aller, known as the "near future," is frequently used in French conversation, and is important to know.

Fortunately, it's very simple to learn. Just combine the present tense of aller with a verb in the infinitive, such as manger (*to eat*):

MANGER (*TO EAT*) - NEAR FUTURE			
je vais manger	*I'm going to eat*	**nous allons manger**	*we're going to eat*
tu vas manger	*you're going to eat*	**vous allez manger**	*you're going to eat*
il va manger	*he's going to eat*	**ils vont manger**	*they're going to eat*
elle va manger	*she's going to eat*	**elles vont manger**	*they're going to eat*

See? Very straightforward, and now you know one way to talk about the future!

Je vais prendre des crudités comme hors-d'œuvre.
I'm going to have some raw vegetables as an hors d'œuvre.

Qu'est-ce que tu vas prendre ?
What are you going to have?

Nous allons dîner à la maison.
We're going to dine at home. (We're going to have dinner at home.)

Je vais préparer de la soupe à l'oignon.
I'm going to prepare some onion soup.

✎ Work Out 2

Rewrite the following French sentences in the near future.

1. **Tu dînes au restaurant.** *(You're dining at the restaurant.)*

_____

2. **Est-ce que ma mère prépare le déjeuner ?** *(Is my mother preparing lunch?)*

_____

3. **Nous mangeons ensemble.** *(We're eating together.)*

_____

4. **Mes parents sont au café.** *(My parents are at the café.)*

_____

ANSWER KEY:
1. **Tu vas dîner au restaurant.** *(You're going to dine at the restaurant.)* 2. **Est-ce que ma mère va préparer le déjeuner ?** *(Is my mother going to prepare lunch?)* 3. **Nous allons manger ensemble.** *(We're going to eat together.)* 4. **Mes parents vont être au café.** *(My parents are going to be at the café.)*

✎ Drive It Home

A. Conjugate the verbs in parentheses in the present tense.

1. **On** _____ **(aller) au restaurant.**

2. **On** _____ **(manger) au restaurant.**

Some   The Near Future
(I'm Going to ...)

3. On _____ (arriver) au restaurant.

4. On _____ (être) au restaurant.

5. On _____ (travailler) au restaurant.

6. On _____ (jouer) au restaurant.

7. On _____ (parler) au restaurant.

8. On _____ (chanter) au restaurant.

B. Great! Now write the following verbs in the near future.

1. j'étudie _____

2. tu vas _____

3. il parle _____

4. elle danse _____

5. nous avons _____

6. vous êtes _____

7. ils regardent _____

8. elles quittent _____

ANSWER KEY:
A. 1. va (*We go to the restaurant.*); 2. mange (*We eat at the restaurant.*); 3. arrive (*We arrive at the restaurant.*); 4. est (*We are at the restaurant.*); 5. travaille (*We work at the restaurant.*); 6. joue (*We play at the restaurant.*); 7. parle (*We speak at the restaurant.*); 8. chante (*We sing at the restaurant.*)
B. 1. je vais étudier (*I'm going to study*); 2. tu vas aller (*you're going to go*); 3. il va parler (*he's going to speak*); 4. elle va danser (*she's going to dance*); 5. nous allons avoir (*we're going to have*); 6. vous allez être (*you're going to be*); 7. ils vont regarder (*they're going to watch*); 8. elles vont quitter (*they're going to leave*)

🌐 Culture Note

In contrast to the many cocktails that Americans order in the United States, the French usually order simple drinks in a café or restaurant. For example, they might order a glass of **vin** (*wine*), **bière** (*f.*) (*beer*), or often, **eau** (*f.*) **minérale** (*mineral water*), which has its source in many of the natural springs found in France, such as Évian, Vichy, Volvic, and Perrier. Quite often, flavored syrup, such as **menthe** (*mint*), is mixed into the water.

They might also order **le vin mousseux** (*sparkling wine*), such as **le champagne**, which comes from the Champagne region in the northeast of France, or **le crémant**, another type of French sparkling wine.

How Did You Do?

Let's see how you did! By now, you should be able to:

☐ Name different dishes and desserts
(Still unsure? Jump back to page 163)

☐ Talk about what *people in general* do
(Still unsure? Jump back to page 166)

☐ Talk about quantities of food
(Still unsure? Jump back to page 168)

☐ Say what you're *going to* do in the future
(Still unsure? Jump back to page 171)

Lesson 11: Sentences

By the end of this lesson, you will be able to:

☐ Discuss what you're going to have at a restaurant

☐ Talk to **le serveur/la serveuse** (*the waiter/the waitress*)

☐ Say what you're having to *drink*

☐ Talk about what someone is *selling*

Sentence Builder 1

(▶) 11A Lesson 11 Sentence Builder 1 (CD 5, Track 13)

What is there to eat?	**Qu'est-ce qu'il y a à manger ?**
What is there to drink?	**Qu'est-ce qu'il y a à boire ?**
Let's have a drink. (infml.) *(We're going to have a drink.)*	**On va prendre un pot.**
What are you going to drink?	**Qu'est-ce que tu vas boire ?**
As a drink, I'm going to have (a) red wine.	**Comme boisson, je vais prendre un vin rouge.**
What are you having?	**Qu'est-ce que tu prends ?**
For the main course, I'm having chicken cooked in wine.	**Comme plat principal, je prends du coq au vin.**
For dessert, I'm having an éclair.	**Comme dessert, je prends un éclair.**
Bring me some salt, please.	**Apportez-moi du sel, s'il vous plaît.**
Enjoy your meal!	**Bon appétit !**
It's delicious!	**C'est délicieux !**
I'm hungry.	**J'ai faim.**

Intermediate French

| *I'm not hungry anymore.* | **Je n'ai plus faim.** |
| *The check, please. (The bill, please.)* | **L'addition, s'il vous plaît.** |

Take It Further

A related sentence is:

| *I'm starving./I'm so hungry I could eat a horse.* *(lit., I have the hunger of a wolf.)* | **J'ai une faim de loup.** |

And of course, we can't do this unit without the following vocabulary:

a reservation	**une réservation**
to make a reservation	**faire une réservation**
to reserve	**réserver**

You'll learn more about making reservations in French in the next unit, which deals with appointments and phone calls.

Now let's break down some of the foods and drinks mentioned in Sentence Builder 1:

drink	**la boisson**
drink (infml.)	**le pot**
rooster	**le coq**
chicken/rooster cooked in wine	**le coq au vin**
éclair – a type of cream-filled pastry	**l'éclair** (*m.*)

Finally, don't forget that **comme** means *like* or *as*, but it can also mean *for* in phrases like **comme dessert**, which can be translated as *for (a) dessert* or *as (a) dessert*.

We'll look at the verb **boire** (*to drink*) in Grammar Builder 1.

To Eat	On	
	Some	The Near Future *(I'm Going to ...)*

✎ Sentence Practice 1

Complete the following conversation based on the English translations.

1. **Alors, Marie,** _____

   _____ ? *(So, Marie, what are you going to drink?)*

2. _____ ,

   Paul ? Moi, je prends un vin blanc. *(What are you having, Paul? Me, I'm having a white wine.)*

3. _____ **, je vais prendre un vin rouge.**

   (As a drink, I'm going to have a red wine.)

4. _____ ? *(What is there to eat?)*

5. _____ **! Je prends le coq au vin.**

   (I'm hungry! I'm having the chicken cooked in wine.)

ANSWER KEY:
1. qu'est-ce que tu vas boire; 2. Qu'est-ce que tu prends; 3. Comme boisson; 4. Qu'est-ce qu'il y a à manger; 5. J'ai faim

✎ Word Recall

Give the correct form of the -er verb in parentheses.

1. **Nous** _____ **(voyager) en France avec nos cousins.**

   (We're traveling in France with our cousins.)

2. **Nous** _____ **(commencer) un nouveau livre demain.**

   (We're starting a new book tomorrow.)

Intermediate French

3. Nous ne _____ (manger) pas de viande. *(We don't eat meat.)*

4. Nous _____ (changer) le menu ? *(We're changing the menu?)*

5. Nous n' _____ (annoncer) rien. *(We're not announcing anything.)*

ANSWER KEY:

1. voyageons; 2. commençons; 3. mangeons; 4. changeons; 5. annonçons

Grammar Builder 1
TO DRINK

▶ 11B Lesson 11 Grammar Builder 1 (CD 5, Track 14)

Boire means *to drink*. It is, unfortunately, completely irregular, but it's a useful verb to learn.

BOIRE *(TO DRINK)* - PRESENT			
je bois	*I drink*	**nous buvons**	*we drink*
tu bois	*you drink*	**vous buvez**	*you drink*
il boit	*he drinks*	**ils boivent**	*they drink*
elle boit	*she drinks*	**elles boivent**	*they drink*

Qu'est-ce que tu bois avec le dîner ce soir ?
What are you drinking with dinner tonight?

Il boit de l'eau.
He's drinking water.

Nous buvons du vin rouge.
We're drinking red wine.

To Eat		On
	Some	
		The Near Future *(I'm Going to …)*

Mes amis boivent du champagne.
My friends are drinking champagne.

Je bois du thé.
I'm drinking tea.

✎ Work Out 1

Fill in the blanks with the correct form of the verb boire.

1. **Il** _____ **du vin.** *(He drinks wine.)*

2. **Nous** _____ **du café.** *(We drink coffee.)*

3. **Je** _____ **du café le matin.** *(I drink coffee in the morning.)*

4. _____-**vous du vin rouge ou du vin blanc ?**

   (Do you drink red wine or white wine?)

5. **Tu** _____ **de l'eau minérale.** *(You drink mineral water.)*

   ANSWER KEY:
   1. **boit**; 2. **buvons**; 3. **bois**; 4. **Buvez**; 5. **bois**

Sentence Builder 2

▶ 11C Lesson 11 Sentence Builder 2 (CD 5, Track 15)

The menu, please.	**Le menu/La carte, s'il vous plaît.**
What is the specialty of the house?	**Quelle est la spécialité de la maison ?**
What do you recommend?	**Qu'est-ce que vous recommandez ?**
He's having a grilled ham and cheese sandwich.	**Il prend un croque-monsieur.**

My friend is having (a) chicken and fries.	**Mon ami prend un poulet frites.**
We are out of steak and fries. (We don't have any more steak and fries.)	**Nous n'avons plus de steak frites.**
Are you having a ham sandwich, a cheese sandwich, or ham and cheese? (lit., Are you having a sandwich of ham, of cheese, or ham-cheese?)	**Prenez-vous un sandwich au jambon, au fromage, ou jambon-fromage ?**
I'm having a mushroom omelette.	**Je prends une omelette aux champignons.**
Are you having (a) dessert?	**Est-ce que tu prends un dessert ?**
I'm drinking (a) white wine with cassis.	**Je bois un kir.**
(a) champagne with cassis	**un kir royal**
You're having mint water (a water with mint syrup).	**Tu prends une menthe à l'eau.**
Dinner's ready!/The food is ready! (lit., To the table!)	**À table !**
To your health! (a toast)	**À votre santé !**

Take It Further

If you visit France, you'll see a lot of foods flavored with **cassis**. **Cassis** is *black currant*—a very tart, intensely flavored berry—and it's a popular flavor in France. You'll see it in everything from **la glace** (*ice cream*) to **le macaron**, which is kind of like a meringue cookie sandwich (and ***not*** related to the coconut macaroons that you see in the U.S.).

You'll also see **cassis** liqueur in drinks. So when you saw in Sentence Builder 2 that **un kir** is *a white wine with cassis*, that means it's a drink containing white wine and black currant liqueur. A **kir royal** contains champagne and black currant liqueur. If you see **cassis** served with **l'eau** (*water*), it's usually non-alcoholic, black currant-flavored syrup added to water.

Now let's look at some of the new dishes you saw, and introduce a few others as well.

DISHES WITH FRIES	
chicken and fries (lit., chicken fries)	poulet frites
steak and fries	steak frites
mussels and fries	moules frites

As you can see, **les moules** (*f.*) are *mussels*. Speaking of mussels, *clams* are **les palourdes** (*f.*) or **les clams** (*m.*) and *oysters* are **les huîtres** (*f.*).

SANDWICHES	
a sandwich	un sandwich
a ham sandwich	un sandwich au jambon
a cheese sandwich	un sandwich au fromage
a ham and cheese sandwich	un sandwich jambon-fromage
a grilled ham and cheese sandwich	un croque-monsieur
a grilled ham and cheese sandwich with an egg on top	un croque-madame

And you already know:

EGGS	
an egg	un œuf
a poached egg	un œuf poché
a fried egg, an over easy egg	un œuf au plat, un œuf sur le plat
a soft-boiled egg	un œuf à la coque

But here are some new terms for egg dishes:

an omelet	**une omelette**
a hard-boiled egg (lit., a hard egg)	**un œuf dur**
scrambled eggs	**les œufs brouillés**
egg whites	**les blancs** *(m.)* **(d'œufs)**

Finally, here are two different types of salad:

SALADS	
a niçoise salad – usually lettuce, tomatoes, green beans, hard-boiled eggs, olives, tuna, anchovies, and mustard vinaigrette	**une salade niçoise**
a green salad	**une salade verte**

Speaking of vegetables, **un champignon** is *a mushroom*.

✎ Sentence Practice 2

Translate each sentence into French.

1. *What do you recommend?* _____

2. *The menu, please (fml.).* _____

3. *To your health!* _____

4. *What is the specialty of the house?* _____

5. *Dinner's ready!* _____

ANSWER KEY:

1. **Qu'est-ce que vous recommandez ?** 2. **Le menu, s'il vous plaît./La carte, s'il vous plaît.** 3. **À votre santé !** 4. **Quelle est la spécialité de la maison ?** 5. **À table !**

✎ Word Recall

Match the French foods on the left to the correct English translations on the right.

1. la crème chantilly	a. *poached egg*
2. la tisane	b. *pumpkin pie*
3. la tarte aux pommes	c. *sweetened, flavored whipped cream*
4. l'œuf poché	d. *apple pie*
5. l'œuf au plat	e. *fried egg*
6. la tarte à la citrouille	f. *herbal tea*

ANSWER KEY:
1. c; 2. f; 3. d; 4. a; 5. e; 6. b

Grammar Builder 2
VERBS ENDING IN -RE

▶ 11D Lesson 11 Grammar Builder 2 (CD 5, Track 16)

Now let's look at verbs that end in -re.

To conjugate a regular -re verb, cut off the -re from the infinitive form and then add the following endings:

PRONOUN	ENDING	PRONOUN	ENDING
je	-s	nous	-ons
tu	-s	vous	-ez
il	-	ils	-ent
elle	-	elles	-ent

The symbol - means that nothing is added. In other words, you cut off the **-re** and that's it. You don't add anything to that.

Note that the **nous, vous,** and **ils/elles** endings for -re verbs are the same as they are for **-er** verbs: **-ons, -ez,** and **-ent.**

Let's look at an example. Here's the verb vendre (*to sell*):

VENDRE *(TO SELL)* - **PRESENT**			
je vends	*I sell*	**nous vendons**	*we sell*
tu vends	*you sell*	**vous vendez**	*you sell*
il vend	*he sells*	**ils vendent**	*they sell*
elle vend	*she sells*	**elles vendent**	*they sell*

Elles ne vendent pas de pommes.
They don't sell apples.

Here are some other regular -re verbs:

REGULAR -RE **VERBS**	
attendre	*to wait (for), to expect*
défendre	*to defend*
descendre	*to go down, to come down*
entendre	*to hear*
perdre	*to lose*
rendre	*to give back, to return*
répondre	*to answer, to respond*

Est-ce que Jean descend ?
Is Jean coming down?

You know that there are some -er verbs with irregular spelling changes, such as appeler (*to call*), manger (*to eat*), and commencer (*to begin, to start*). Well, there are some -re verbs with irregular spelling changes as well. For example, the il and elle forms of the verbs rompre (*to break*) and interrompre (*to interrupt*) end in -t.

elle rompt
she breaks

il interrompt
he interrupts

Also remember that although it does end in -re, prendre (*to take, to have*) is irregular and does not conjugate like other -re verbs. To review:

PRENDRE *(TO TAKE, TO HAVE)* - **PRESENT**			
je prends	*I take*	**nous prenons**	*we take*
tu prends	*you take*	**vous prenez**	*you take*
il prend	*he takes*	**ils prennent**	*they take*
elle prend	*she takes*	**elles prennent**	*they take*

Verbs that follow the same pattern as prendre include:

comprendre	*to understand*
apprendre	*to learn*
surprendre	*to surprise*

Je comprends le français.
I understand French.

Ils prennent des œufs.
They have eggs. (They're having eggs.)

Verbs Ending in **-RE** · · · · · · · · · · · · · · · · · Verbs Ending in **-IR**

Les enfants apprennent à lire.
The children are learning to read.

Nous apprenons l'anglais.
We're learning English.

✎ Work Out 2

Complete the following sentences with the correct form of the verb in parentheses.

1. Tu _____ (prendre) un sandwich au restaurant.

   (*You're having a sandwich at the restaurant.*)

2. Vous _____ (comprendre) le menu en français ?

   (*Do you understand the menu in French?*)

3. Pourquoi _____ (attendre)-vous ? (*Why are you waiting?*)

4. Nous ne _____ (répondre) pas. (*We don't respond.*)

5. Mes amis _____ (attendre) le bus.

   (*My friends are waiting for the bus.*)

6. Il _____ (vendre) sa voiture. (*He's selling his car.*)

7. Ils _____ (apprendre) à cuisiner. (*They're learning to cook.*)

   ANSWER KEY:
   1. prends; 2. comprenez; 3. attendez; 4. répondons; 5. attendent; 6. vend; 7. apprennent

✎ Drive It Home

A. Fill in the blanks with the correct form of the verb **boire** (*to drink*).

1. **Ils** _____ de l'eau. (*They drink some water.*)

2. **Je** _____ de l'eau. (*I drink some water.*)

3. **Elles** _____ de l'eau. (*They drink some water.*)

4. **Tu** _____ de l'eau. (*You drink some water.*)

5. **Nous** _____ de l'eau. (*We drink some water.*)

6. **Elle** _____ de l'eau. (*She drinks some water.*)

7. **Vous** _____ de l'eau. (*You drink some water.*)

8. **Il** _____ de l'eau. (*He drinks some water.*)

B. Now fill in the blanks with the correct form of the verb **vendre** (*to sell*).

1. **Tu** _____ la maison. (*You sell the house.*)

2. **Vous** _____ la maison. (*You sell the house.*)

3. **Elles** _____ la maison. (*They sell the house.*)

4. **Nous** _____ la maison. (*We sell the house.*)

5. **Ils** _____ la maison. (*They sell the house.*)

6. **Je** _____ la maison. (*I sell the house.*)

7. **Il** _____ la maison. (*He sells the house.*)

8. **Elle** _____ la maison. (*She sells the house.*)

ANSWER KEY:
A. 1. **boivent**; 2. **bois**; 3. **boivent**; 4. **bois**; 5. **buvons**; 6. **boit**; 7. **buvez**; 8. **boit**
B. 1. **vends**; 2. **vendez**; 3. **vendent**; 4. **vendons**; 5. **vendent**; 6. **vends**; 7. **vend**; 8. **vend**

Tip

We mentioned at the very beginning of this unit that English borrowed many food expressions from French. So you actually know a good amount of French food terms already! Here are some of them, beyond what you've already seen in this unit. Can you think of more?

à la carte	phrase used in dining for when dishes are individually ordered instead of being part of a fixed menu (lit., on the menu)
apéritif	drink served before the meal
bistro	casual French restaurant or café
cuisine	style of cooking (in French, cuisine can also mean *kitchen* or the act of *cooking*)
quiche	baked dish made with eggs and cream, and usually another ingredient such as meat, cheese, etc.
sauté in French, sautéed in English	quickly fried in a pan with little or no oil
gratin or gratiné/gratinée	topped with browned cheese (and possibly also breadcrumbs)

Finally, did you know that *R.S.V.P.* is an acronym of a French phrase? *R.S.V.P.* stands for Répondez, s'il vous plaît (*Respond, please*).

How Did You Do?

Let's see how you did! By now, you should be able to:

□ Discuss what you're going to have at a restaurant
(Still unsure? Jump back to page 176)

□ Talk to **le serveur/la serveuse** (*the waiter/the waitress*)
(Still unsure? Jump back to page 180)

□ Say what you're having to *drink*
(Still unsure? Jump back to page 179)

□ Talk about what someone is *selling*
(Still unsure? Jump back to page 184)

Lesson 12: Conversations

By the end of this lesson, you will be able to:

□ Indicate what someone else *would like*

□ Talk about what someone is *finishing*

Conversation 1

Paul and Thomas are colleagues eating lunch together at a café.

12A Lesson 12 Conversation 1 (CD 5, Track 17)

Paul : Qu'est-ce que tu prends comme hors-d'œuvre ?
Thomas : Je pense que je vais prendre des crudités et après, un croque-monsieur. Et toi, qu'est-ce que tu prends ?
Paul : Je ne sais pas. Peut-être une salade verte et un poulet frites.
Thomas : La soupe à l'oignon gratinée dans ce café est délicieuse.

Paul :	Ah bon, alors je voudrais une soupe à l'oignon gratinée et un poulet frites.
Thomas :	Comme boisson, je prends une bière. J'ai soif.
Paul :	Je vais commander un Perrier cassis.

Paul:	*What are you having as an appetizer?*
Thomas:	*I think that I'm going to have some crudités and after, a grilled ham and cheese sandwich. And you, what are you having?*
Paul:	*I don't know. Maybe a green salad and (a) chicken and fries.*
Thomas:	*The French onion soup in this café is delicious.*
Paul:	*Oh good, then I would like a French onion soup and (a) chicken and fries.*
Thomas:	*For a drink, I'm having a beer. I'm thirsty.*
(▮▮) Paul:	*I'm going to order a Perrier cassis.*

Take It Further

You saw a few important verbs in Conversation 1:

to think	penser
I think (that)	je pense (que)
to know	savoir
I know	je sais
I don't know	je ne sais pas
to order	commander
I order	je commande
I'm going to order	je vais commander

Penser and **commander** conjugate like regular **-er** verbs. However, **savoir** is an irregular verb. You'll learn its full conjugation in *Advanced French*, but for now, just remember its **je** form: **je sais**. As you can imagine, it's a good phrase to know.

You know that **la soupe à l'oignon** is onion soup and **gratinée** means *topped with browned cheese (and breadcrumbs)*, so **la soupe à l'oignon gratinée** is literally *onion soup topped with browned cheese*, or as it's commonly known in English, *French onion soup*!

Finally, remember that **peut-être** means *maybe*. As with **je sais**, it's a good phrase to know.

✎ Conversation Practice 1

Complete the following sentences based on Conversation 1.

1. **Thomas va prendre des** _____

   et un _____ .

2. **La** _____ **dans le café est délicieuse.**

3. **Paul va prendre une** _____

   et un _____ .

4. **Thomas va boire une** _____ .

5. **Paul va boire un** _____ .

ANSWER KEY:
1. **crudités, croque-monsieur** (*Thomas is going to have some crudités and a grilled ham and cheese sandwich.*) 2. **soupe à l'oignon gratinée** (*The French onion soup in the café is delicious.*) 3. **soupe à l'oignon gratinée, poulet frites** (*Paul is going to have a French onion soup and a chicken and fries.*) 4. **bière** (*Thomas is going to drink a beer.*) 5. **Perrier cassis** (*Paul is going to drink a Perrier cassis.*)

✎ Word Recall

Try to translate the following paragraph into English.

Le dimanche, nous mangeons des œufs pochés pour le petit déjeuner. À midi, nous déjeunons. Nous nous promenons dans le parc. Après, je me repose. Nous mangeons du poisson pour le dîner.

_____

_____

_____

_____

_____

ANSWER KEY:
On Sundays, we eat (some) poached eggs for breakfast. At noon, we have lunch. We take a walk in the park. After(wards), I relax/rest. We eat (some) fish for dinner.

Grammar Builder 1
WOULD LIKE

▶ 12B Lesson 12 Grammar Builder 1 (CD 5, Track 18)

You already know how to say *I would like*: je voudrais.

Je voudrais un bonbon.
I would like a candy.

Je voudrais danser.
I would like to dance.

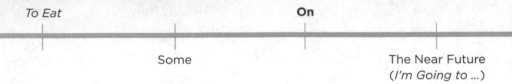

However, it's also helpful to know how to say what someone else would like. Here are all of the forms:

VOULOIR (*TO WANT, TO WISH*) - CONDITIONAL			
je voudrais	*I would like*	nous voudrions	*we would like*
tu voudrais	*you would like*	vous voudriez	*you would like*
il voudrait	*he would like*	ils voudraient	*they would like*
elle voudrait	*she would like*	elles voudraient	*they would like*

In technical terms, that was the full conjugation of the verb vouloir (*to want, to wish*) in what's known as the "conditional" tense. You'll learn about the conditional in Unit 5, so don't worry about that tense right now. Just focus on remembering the forms of would like.

Speaking of vouloir, let's review it in the ***present*** tense. You first saw its full conjugation in Lesson 10 of *Essential French*:

VOULOIR (*TO WANT, TO WISH*) - PRESENT			
je veux	*I want*	nous voulons	*we want*
tu veux	*you want*	vous voulez	*you want*
il veut	*he wants*	ils veulent	*they want*
elle veut	*she wants*	elles veulent	*they want*

✎ Work Out 1

Complete the sentences with the correct form of *would like* in French.

1. Nous _____ des pommes. (*We would like some apples.*)

2. Ils _____ prendre un dessert. (*They would like to have a dessert.*)

3. Jean _____ un croque-monsieur.

   (*Jean would like a grilled ham and cheese sandwich.*)

To Drink		Would Like

Verbs Ending in **-RE**   Verbs Ending in **-IR**

4. Qu'est-ce que tu _____ boire ? (*What would you like to drink?*)

5. Je _____ un verre d'eau. (*I would like a glass of water.*)

ANSWER KEY:

1. voudrions; 2. voudraient; 3. voudrait; 4. voudrais; 5. voudrais

Conversation 2

Mireille and her husband Étienne are in a crêperie, which is a restaurant that specializes in various kinds of crêpes for dinner or dessert.

▶ 12C Lesson 12 Conversation 2 (CD 5, Track 19)

Étienne :	Qu'est-ce que tu vas prendre ce soir, chérie ?
Mireille :	Il y a beaucoup de crêpes au menu. C'est difficile de se décider.
Étienne :	Eh bien, moi, je voudrais une crêpe au poulet.
Mireille :	J'ai envie de prendre un dessert. On prépare de bons desserts ici.
Étienne :	Quel parfum prends-tu ?
Mireille :	Alors, je pense que je prends une crêpe aux marrons.
Étienne :	Est-ce que tu voudrais boire du cidre ce soir ?
Mireille :	Bonne idée ! Je voudrais bien du cidre doux.
Étienne :	D'accord, nous allons prendre une bouteille de cidre doux.

Étienne:	What are you going to have tonight, honey?
Mireille:	There are a lot of crêpes on the menu. It's difficult to make up my mind.
Étienne:	Well, me, I would like a chicken crêpe.
Mireille:	I feel like having a dessert. They prepare good desserts here.
Étienne:	What flavor are you having?
Mireille:	Well, I think that I'm having a chestnut crêpe.
Étienne:	Would you like to drink some cider tonight?
Mireille:	Good idea! I would really like some sweet cider.
Étienne:	Okay, we're going to have a bottle of sweet cider.

Take It Further

Le cidre (*cider*) is produced in various regions of France, especially in Normandy (the combined area of Basse-Normandie and Haute-Normandie), which is famous for growing apples. However, cider in France is not the same as cider in the United States. It contains l'alcool (*m.*) (*alcohol*) and it comes in several varieties, including doux (*sweet*), brut (*dry*), and sparkling.

Conversation 2 also talked about crêpes, which are tissue-thin pancakes. As you know, a crêperie is a restaurant that mainly produces various types of crêpes, both sucrées (*sweet*) and salées (*savory*).

Crêpes salées are usually made of sarrasin (*buckwheat*) flour and could be stuffed with anything from poulet (*chicken*) or champignons (*mushrooms*) to œufs (*eggs*) and fromage (*cheese*). Crêpes sucrées are made of sweetened wheat flour and might be filled with la confiture (*jelly, jam, marmalade*), a chocolat (*chocolate*) or marron (*chestnut*) spread or cream, or even just sucre (*sugar*) and beurre (*butter*). There are also well-known combinations of fillings, like the crêpe Suzette, which is filled with orange, sugar, and liqueur.

Le parfum (*flavor*) is a useful word to know when ordering dessert. For example, if you're ordering ice cream, the server might ask you:

Quel parfum ?
Which flavor?/What flavor?

Parfum also means *fragrance* and, not surprisingly, *perfume*.

Finally, you saw the following new words in Conversation 2:

honey, dear, darling	chéri/chérie
to make up one's mind, to be decided, to be resolved (to do something)	se décider

Remember that décider, the non-reflexive form of se décider, means *to decide*.

Verbs Ending in **-RE**   Verbs Ending in **-IR**

✎ Conversation Practice 2

Translate the following phrases and sentences into English based on Conversation 2.

1. **C'est difficile.** _____

2. **Bonne idée !** _____

3. **Quel parfum ?** _____

4. **Tu voudrais boire du cidre.** _____

5. **J'ai envie de...** _____

ANSWER KEY:
1. *It's difficult.* 2. *Good idea!* 3. *Which/What flavor?* 4. *You would like to drink some cider.* 5. *I feel like ...*

✎ Word Recall

Match the quantity expressions in English on the left to the correct French translations on the right.

1. *a glass of*	a. trop de
2. *a little of*	b. une carafe de
3. *more of*	c. moins de
4. *less of, fewer of*	d. un verre de
5. *too much of*	e. plus de
6. *a pitcher of*	f. un peu de

ANSWER KEY:
1. d; 2. f; 3. e; 4. c; 5. a; 6. b

Grammar Builder 2
VERBS ENDING IN -IR

▶ 12D Lesson 12 Grammar Builder 2 (CD 5, Track 20)

Let's review the last group of French verbs: verbs ending in -ir.

To conjugate a regular -ir verb in the present tense, just cut off the -ir from the infinitive and add the following endings:

PRONOUN	ENDING	PRONOUN	ENDING
je	-is	nous	-issons
tu	-is	vous	-issez
il	-it	ils	-issent
elle	-it	elles	-issent

For example, here's the full conjugation of finir (*to finish*) in the present tense:

FINIR (*TO FINISH*) - PRESENT			
je finis	*I finish*	nous finissons	*we finish*
tu finis	*you finish*	vous finissez	*you finish*
il finit	*he finishes*	ils finissent	*they finish*
elle finit	*she finishes*	elles finissent	*they finish*

Le bébé finit son petit déjeuner.
The baby finishes his breakfast.

Je finis mon croissant.
I'm finishing my croissant.

Here are some other regular -ir verbs:

REGULAR -IR VERBS	
bâtir	to build
choisir	to choose
obéir	to obey
punir	to punish
rougir	to blush (to redden)
agir	to act (to behave)
désobéir	to disobey
nourrir	to feed
réfléchir	to think, to reflect
réussir	to succeed, to do well
remplir	to fill (in)
maigrir	to lose weight
grossir	to gain weight
grandir	to grow

✎ Work Out 2

Fill in the correct, present tense form of the verb in parentheses.

1. Nous _____ (finir) à dix heures. (*We finish at 10:00.*)

2. La fille _____ (rougir) devant ses amis.
   (*The girl is blushing in front of her friends.*)

3. Il _____ (bâtir) la maison. (*He's building the house.*)

To Eat		On	
	Some		The Near Future *(I'm Going to ...)*

4. Est-ce que vous _____ (obéir) à vos parents ?

   (Do you obey your parents?)

5. Le garçon _____ (finir) le sandwich. *(The boy is finishing the sandwich.)*

   ANSWER KEY:
   1. finissons; 2. rougit; 3. bâtit; 4. obéissez (Wondering why obéir is followed by à? You'll learn more in *Advanced French.*); 5. finit

✎ Drive It Home

A. Fill in the blanks with the correct form of *would like* in French.

1. Sophie _____ aller au cinéma. *(Sophie would like to go to the movies.)*

2. Nous _____ aller au cinéma. *(We would like to go to the movies.)*

3. Tu _____ aller au cinéma. *(You would like to go to the movies.)*

4. Ils _____ aller au cinéma. *(They would like to go to the movies.)*

5. Marc _____ aller au cinéma. *(Marc would like to go to the movies.)*

6. Je _____ aller au cinéma. *(I would like to go to the movies.)*

B. Fill in the blanks with the correct form of **choisir** *(to choose)*.

1. Je _____ le plat principal. *(I choose the main course.)*

2. Les enfants _____ le plat principal.

   (The children choose the main course.)

3. Vous _____ le plat principal. *(You choose the main course.)*

4. Tu _____ le plat principal. *(You choose the main course.)*

5. Nous _____ le plat principal. (*We choose the main course.*)

6. Elle _____ le plat principal. (*She chooses the main course.*)

ANSWER KEY:
A. 1. voudrait; 2. voudrions; 3. voudrais; 4. voudraient; 5. voudrait; 6. voudrais
B. 1. choisis; 2. choisissent; 3. choisissez; 4. choisis; 5. choisissons; 6. choisit

 Tip

You learned *a lot* of food vocabulary in this unit. Don't forget to use the free online tools—flashcards, games and quizzes, etc.—to help you review everything you've learned. Of course, you can also create your own flash cards. But don't just write the vocabulary words on note cards. Instead, find images of the food items online or in magazines and paste each one on one side of a note card. Then write the French translation on the other side. Visual association is an excellent way to reinforce vocabulary.

Also, now that you've reviewed all three types of French verbs, remember to practice them as much as possible—via the online tools, your own flashcards, listening to the audio on the go, reviewing the lesson, or whatever method works best for you.

Go to *www.livinglanguage.com/languagelab* to access the online tools.

How Did You Do?

Let's see how you did! By now, you should be able to:

☐ Indicate what someone else *would like*
(Still unsure? Jump back to page 193)

☐ Talk about what someone is *finishing*
(Still unsure? Jump back to page 198)

Unit 3 Essentials

Don't forget to go to **www.livinglanguage.com/languagelab** to access your free online tools for this lesson: audiovisual flashcards, and interactive games and quizzes.

Vocabulary Essentials

MEALS AND DISHES

meal		lunch	
breakfast		dinner	

[Pg. 147] (If you're stuck, visit this page to review!)

FRUIT

fruit		lime	
apple		grape	
lemon		tomato	

[Pg. 147]

VEGETABLES

vegetable		corn	
potato		cucumber	
carrot		spinach	
lettuce		green beans	

[Pg. 148]

APPETIZER

soup	

[Pg. 153]

MEAT AND FISH

meat		chicken	
steak		duck	
beef		veal	
ham		fish	
pork		lobster	

[Pg. 153]

TABLE SETTING

fork		napkin	
knife		glass	
spoon		cup	
plate			

[Pg. 154]

DISHES

a poached egg	
a grilled ham and cheese sandwich	
(some) sausages	
scallops	
mashed potatoes	
french fries	

[Pg. 163]

DESSERTS

an apple pie	
a chocolate cake	
a chocolate mousse	
vanilla ice cream	
chocolate ice cream	

[Pg. 163]

DRINKS

herbal tea	

[Pg. 164]

QUANTITY EXPRESSIONS

a carton of		a pitcher of	
a bottle of		a dozen of	
a cup of		too much of	
a glass of		a little of	
a slice of (bread, cheese)		a lot of	
a kilo of		less of	
a pound of		more of	

[Pg. 168]

FOOD EXPRESSIONS

What are you having?	
Bring me some salt, please.	
Enjoy your meal!	
It's delicious!	
I'm hungry.	
The check, please./The bill, please.	

[Pg. 176]

MORE FOOD EXPRESSIONS

The menu, please.	
What do you recommend?	
Dinner's ready!/The food is ready!	
To your health! (a toast)	

[Pg. 180]

REGULAR -ER VERBS (G SPELLING)

to swim		*to change*	
to put away		*to lay down, to lie down*	
to travel		*to dive*	

[Pg. 151]

REGULAR -ER VERBS (C SPELLING)

to advance		to threaten	
to announce			

[Pg. 152]

REGULAR -RE VERBS

to wait (for), to expect		to lose	
to defend		to give back, to return	
to go down, to come down		to answer, to respond	
to hear			

[Pg. 185]

REGULAR -IR VERBS

to build		to feed	
to choose		to think, to reflect	
to obey		to succeed, to do well	
to punish		to fill (in)	
to blush, to redden		to lose weight	
to act, to behave		to gain weight	
to disobey		to grow	

[Pg. 199]

Grammar Essentials

THE PARTITIVE

de + le = du

de + la = de la

de + l' = de l'

de + les = des

In a negative sentence, de la, de l', du, and des change to de/d'.

THE SUBJECT PRONOUN ON

The subject pronoun on can be translated as:

a. *we* (in casual conversation)

b. *one* or *people in general*

c. the "general" *you* or *they*

The on form of the verb is the same as the il and elle form.

-RE VERB ENDINGS

PRONOUN	ENDING	PRONOUN	ENDING
je	-s	nous	-ons
tu	-s	vous	-ez
il	-	ils	-ent
elle	-	elles	-ent

PRENDRE *(TO TAKE)* - PRESENT			
I take	je prends	*we take*	nous prenons
you take	tu prends	*you take*	vous prenez
he takes	il prend	*they take*	ils prennent
she takes	elle prend	*they take*	elles prennent

VENDRE *(TO SELL)* - **PRESENT**			
I sell	je vends	*we sell*	nous vendons
you sell	tu vends	*you sell*	vous vendez
he sells	il vend	*they sell*	ils vendent
she sells	elle vend	*they sell*	elles vendent

Remember the spelling change in the il and elle form of interrompre (*to interrupt*).

INTERROMPRE *(TO INTERRUPT)* - **PRESENT**			
I interrupt	j'interromps	*we interrupt*	nous interrompons
you interrupt (infml.)	tu interromps	*you interrupt (pl./fml.)*	vous interrompez
he interrupts	il interrompt	*they interrupt (m.)*	ils interrompent
she interrupts	elle interrompt	*they interrupt (f.)*	elles interrompent

-IR **VERB ENDINGS**

PRONOUN	ENDING	PRONOUN	ENDING
je	-is	nous	-issons
tu	-is	vous	-issez
il	-it	ils	-issent
elle	-it	elles	-issent

CHOISIR (TO CHOOSE) - PRESENT			
I choose	je choisis	we choose	nous choisissons
you choose (infml.)	tu choisis	you choose (pl./fml.)	vous choisissez
he chooses	il choisit	they choose (m.)	ils choisissent
she chooses	elle choisit	they choose (f.)	elles choisissent

FINIR (TO FINISH) - PRESENT			
I finish	je finis	we finish	nous finissons
you finish	tu finis	you finish	vous finissez
he finishes	il finit	they finish	ils finissent
she finishes	elle finit	they finish	elles finissent

THE NEAR FUTURE

To form the near future, combine the present tense of aller with a verb in the infinitive.

MANGER (TO EAT) - NEAR FUTURE			
I'm going to eat	je vais manger	we're going to eat	nous allons manger
you're going to eat	tu vas manger	you're going to eat	vous allez manger
he's going to eat	il va manger	they're going to eat	ils vont manger
she's going to eat	elle va manger	they're going to eat	elles vont manger

OTHER VERBS

BOIRE *(TO DRINK)* - **PRESENT**			
I drink	je bois	*we drink*	nous buvons
you drink	tu bois	*you drink*	vous buvez
he drinks	il boit	*they drink*	ils boivent
she drinks	elle boit	*they drink*	elles boivent

COMMENCER *(TO START, TO BEGIN)* - **PRESENT**			
I begin	je commence	*we begin*	nous commençons
you begin	tu commences	*you begin*	vous commencez
he begins	il commence	*they begin*	ils commencent
she begins	elle commence	*they begin*	elles commencent

MANGER *(TO EAT)* - **PRESENT**			
I eat	je mange	*we eat*	nous mangeons
you eat	tu manges	*you eat*	vous mangez
he eats	il mange	*they eat*	ils mangent
she eats	elle mange	*they eat*	elles mangent

VOULOIR *(TO WANT)* - **PRESENT**			
I want	je veux	*we want*	nous voulons
you want	tu veux	*you want*	vous voulez
he wants	il veut	*they want*	ils veulent
she wants	elle veut	*they want*	elles veulent

VOULOIR *(TO WANT)* - **CONDITIONAL**			
I would like	je voudrais	*we would like*	nous voudrions
you would like	tu voudrais	*you would like*	vous voudriez
he would like	il voudrait	*they would like*	ils voudraient
she would like	elle voudrait	*they would like*	elles voudraient

Unit 3 Quiz

Now let's see how you did in Unit 3!

After you've answered all of the questions, don't forget to score your quiz to see how you did. If you find that you need to go back and review, please do so before continuing on to Unit 4.

A. Translate the following phrases into French.

1. *a bottle of wine*_____

2. *a glass of milk*_____

3. *a dozen eggs*_____

4. *a pound of apples*_____

5. *a little lemon*_____

B. Fill in the blanks with the correct form of each verb.

1. **Tu ne** _____ **(répondre) pas.** *(You're not responding.)*

2. **Elle** _____ **(attendre) son père.** *(She's waiting for her father.)*

3. **Ils** _____ **(vendre) leur télévision.** *(They're selling their television.)*

4. **Est-ce que vous** _____ **(comprendre) ?** *(Do you understand?)*

5. **Nous** _____ **(apprendre) le français.** *(We're learning French.)*

C. Choose the correct word to complete each sentence.

1. **Nous avons** _____ **crudités.** (*We have some crudités.*)
   a. **des**   c. **d'**
   b. **de**   d. **de l'**

2. **Je voudrais manger** _____ **glace à la vanille.**
   (*I would like to eat some vanilla ice cream.*)
   a. **du**   c. **des**
   b. **de la**   d. **de**

3. **Je n'ai pas** _____ **fraises.** (*I don't have strawberries.*)
   a. **des**   c. **d'**
   b. **du**   d. **de**

4. **Elle voudrait une carafe** _____ **eau.** (*She would like a pitcher of water.*)
   a. **de la**   c. **des**
   b. **de l'**   d. **d'**

5. **Est-ce que tu prends** _____ **potage ?** (*Are you having some soup?*)
   a. **des**   c. **de la**
   b. **du**   d. **de**

D. MATCH THE FOODS ON THE LEFT TO THE CORRECT FRENCH TRANSLATIONS ON THE RIGHT.

1. *chicken*	a. **le jambon**
2. *fish*	b. **la viande**
3. *meat*	c. **le canard**
4. *ham*	d. **le poisson**
5. *duck*	e. **le poulet**

ANSWER KEY:

A. 1. une bouteille de vin; 2. un verre de lait; 3. une douzaine d'œufs; 4. une livre de pommes; 5. un peu de citron

B. 1. réponds; 2. attend; 3. vendent; 4. comprenez; 5. apprenons

C. 1. a. des; 2. b. de la; 3. d. de; 4. d. d'; 5. b. du

D. 1. e; 2. d; 3. b; 4. a; 5. c

How Did You Do?

Give yourself a point for every correct answer, then use the following key to determine whether or not you're ready to move on:

0-7 points: It's probably best to go back and study the lessons again to make sure you understood everything completely. Take your time; it's not a race! Make sure you spend time reviewing the vocabulary and reading through each grammar note carefully.

8-16 points: If the questions you missed were in Section A or B, you may want to review the vocabulary again; if you missed answers mostly in Section C or D, check the Unit 3 Essentials to make sure you have your conjugations and other grammar basics down.

17-20 points: Feel free to move on to the next unit! You're doing a great job.

 Points

Unit 4: Using the Telephone and Making Appointments

You're more than halfway through *Intermediate French*! **Bravo !**

In Unit 4, you'll learn lots of useful vocabulary and expressions for talking on the phone and making appointments. You'll also learn how to talk about the past and another way to talk about the future.

By the end of this unit, you should be able to:

☐ Say whether you're *early* or *late*

☐ Talk about something that happened in the past

☐ Use words like *soon* and *often*

☐ Talk about something that didn't happen in the past

☐ Ask whether something happened

☐ Tell someone that *it's twenty to three*

☐ Answer the phone

☐ Say what you *had*, where you *have been*, and whether you *understood*

☐ Talk to someone on the phone

☐ Say what you *have to* or *must* do

☐ Make an appointment

☐ Talk about what you *did* or *made*

☐ Say what you *will* do in the future

☐ Say where you *will go*, what you *will have*, and where you *will be*

Lesson 13: Words

By the end of this lesson, you will be able to:

☐ Say whether you're *early* or *late*

☐ Talk about something that happened in the past

☐ Use words like *soon* and *often*

☐ Talk about something that didn't happen in the past

☐ Ask whether something happened

Word Builder 1

▶ 13A Lesson 13 Word Builder 1 (CD 5, Track 21)

at what time? (lit., at what hour?)	à quelle heure ?
exactly at noon (at noon sharp)	à midi précis
at 1:00 sharp (exactly at 1:00)	à une heure précise
at 10:00 sharp (exactly at 10:00)	à dix heures précises
3:00 in the morning	trois heures du matin
3:00 in the afternoon	trois heures de l'après-midi
8:00 in the evening	huit heures du soir
around 9:00	vers neuf heures
in a quarter of an hour	dans un quart d'heure
a half hour	une demi-heure
late	en retard, tard
on time	à l'heure
early	en avance, tôt
next week	la semaine prochaine

| last year | l'année (*f.*) dernière |
| in one month (next month) | dans un mois |

Take It Further

Notice that *half* is spelled demi when it comes before heure (*hour, o'clock*), as in une demi-heure (*a half hour*), but it's spelled demie when it comes after heure, as in une heure et demie (1:30). This is because when demi/demie (*half*) follows the noun it's being used as an adjective and therefore must agree with the feminine noun heure (although it only agrees in gender, not number).

The adjective précis/précise (*sharp, exact, precise*) must agree with the noun in gender and number, so you say à une heure précise, à dix heures précises, and à midi précis (midi is a masculine noun).

Finally, remember that France generally uses the 24-hour clock, so *1 p.m.* is 13h, *2 p.m.* is 14h, and so on. However, the 24-hour clock isn't always used, especially in informal conversation, so you will also hear huit heures du soir (*8:00 in the evening*) instead of vingt heures (*8 p.m.*), or trois heures de l'après-midi (*3:00 in the afternoon*) instead of quinze heures (*3 p.m.*). French doesn't have any direct equivalent to *a.m.* and *p.m.*

Word Practice 1

Translate the following words into French. If there are two possible translations, be sure to give both.

1. *early* _____

2. *late* _____

3. *on time* _____

4. *next week* _____

5. *last year* _____

ANSWER KEY:

1. en avance, tôt; 2. en retard, tard; 3. à l'heure; 4. la semaine prochaine; 5. l'année dernière

Word Recall

Fill in the blanks with the correct present tense form of avoir.

1. Étienne _____ deux sœurs. (*Étienne has two sisters.*)

2. Nous _____ un appartement à Paris. (*We have an apartment in Paris.*)

3. _____ -vous du vin ? (*Do you have some wine?*)

4. Je n' _____ pas de vin. (*I don't have any wine.*)

5. Nos cousins _____ une très belle maison.

(*Our cousins have a very beautiful home.*)

ANSWER KEY:

1. a; 2. avons; 3. Avez; 4. ai; 5. ont

Grammar Builder 1
THE PAST TENSE (*I DANCED*)

▶ 13B Lesson 13 Grammar Builder 1 (CD 5, Track 22)

So far, you've learned the present tense—*I sell, I'm dancing, I finish*, etc.—and the near future tense—*I'm going to sell, I'm going to dance, I'm going to finish*, etc.—of French verbs.

Now let's talk about the past: *I sold, I danced, I finished*, etc. To form the past tense, or passé composé, of a verb in French, all you need to do is the following:

present tense of avoir or être + the past participle of the verb.

Most verbs use avoir to form the past, and we'll focus on those verbs for now. You'll learn about verbs that use être in Unit 5.

The past participle is a special form of the verb that is used to create certain tenses, like the past tense. Here is how the past participle is formed:

1. **-ER** VERBS: to form the past participle of an **-er** verb, cut off the **-er** from the infinitive and add é.

For example, the past participle of the verb danser (*to dance*) would therefore be dansé. So:

DANSER *(TO DANCE)* - **PAST**			
j'ai dansé	*I danced*	nous avons dansé	*we danced*
tu as dansé	*you danced*	vous avez dansé	*you danced*
il a dansé	*he danced*	ils ont dansé	*they danced*
elle a dansé	*she danced*	elles ont dansé	*they danced*

There are three ways to translate the French past tense into English: *I danced, I have danced,* and *I did dance.*

2. **-RE** VERBS: to form the past participle of an **-re** verb, cut off the **-re** and add **u**.

For example:

VERB		PAST PARTICIPLE	
vendre	*to sell*	vendu	*sold (have sold, did sell)*

So the past tense of vendre would be **j'ai vendu** (*I sold*), **tu as vendu** (*you sold*), etc.

3. **-IR** VERBS: to form the past participle of an **-ir** verb, cut off the **-ir** and add **i**.

For example:

VERB		PAST PARTICIPLE	
finir	*to finish*	fini	*finished (have finished, did finish)*

So the past tense of **finir** would be **j'ai fini** (*I finished*), **tu as fini** (*you finished*), etc.

Ⅱ

✎ Work Out 1

Conjugate the verbs in the past tense.

1. **Nous** _____ **(finir) le dessert.** (*We finished the dessert.*)

2. **J'** _____ **(entendre) mes amis.** (*I heard my friends.*)

3. **Ma famille** _____ (vendre) la maison. (*My family sold the house.*)

4. **Tu** _____ (choisir) ce film. (*You chose this movie.*)

5. **Elles** _____ (parler) en français. (*They spoke in French.*)

ANSWER KEY:
1. avons fini; 2. ai entendu; 3. a vendu; 4. as choisi; 5. ont parlé

Word Builder 2
Note that many of the words below are "adverbs of frequency," describing how often something happened or is happening.

▶ 13C Lesson 13 Word Builder 2 (CD 5, Track 23)

always, still	toujours
still, more	encore
ever, never	jamais
often	souvent
now	maintenant
rarely	rarement
long, (for a) long time	longtemps
soon	bientôt
formerly, in the past	autrefois
the day before yesterday	avant-hier
the day after tomorrow	après-demain

Take It Further

Another helpful time phrase to know is tout de suite, which means *right away* or *immediately*.

Now let's look at different ways to talk about previous or upcoming days and months. So far, you already know:

next week	la semaine prochaine
last year	l'année (*f.*) dernière
in one month, next month	dans un mois
the day before yesterday	avant-hier
the day after tomorrow	après-demain

You can use dernier/dernière (*last*) for almost any time frame: lundi dernier (*last Monday*), le mois dernier (*last month*), l'été (*m.*) dernier (*last summer*), la nuit dernière (*last night*), etc. (Although you can also say hier soir for *last night*. It literally means *yesterday evening*.)

You can use prochain/prochaine (*next*) to say samedi prochain (*next Saturday*), le mois prochain (*next month*), etc. You can sometimes also use dans (*in*) to say *next*, as in dans un mois (*in one month, next month*), dans une semaine (*in one week, next week*), etc.

However, there is actually a special word for *the next day*: le lendemain.

Here are a few other related expressions:

before	auparavant, avant
two months before	deux mois auparavant
two months before	deux mois avant

To say *the day before*, you say **la veille de**, as in **la veille de Noël** (*the day before Christmas, Christmas Eve*).

Finally:

before last	précédent/précédente, d'avant
the week before last	la semaine précédente
the week before last	la semaine d'avant
after next	suivant/suivante, d'après
the week after next	la semaine suivante
the week after next	la semaine d'après

Two weeks is sometimes expressed as *15 days*:

the week after next, in two weeks	dans deux semaines/dans quinze jours

Pas l'année prochaine, mais l'année d'après.
Not next year, but the year after that/after next.

✎ Word Practice 2

Complete the following sentences.

1. **Tu travailles** _____ (*always*). (*You're always working.*)

2. **Je vais** _____ (*often*) **au restaurant.** (*I often go to the restaurant.*)

3. **Il parle** _____ (*rarely*) **avec Sophie.** (*He rarely speaks with Sophie.*)

4. **Elle n'étudie** _____ (*never*). (*She never studies.*)

5. **Je voudrais partir** _____ (*now*). (*I would like to leave now.*)

ANSWER KEY:

1. **toujours**; 2. **souvent**; 3. **rarement**; 4. **jamais**; 5. **maintenant**

✎ Word Recall

Translate each sentence into French using **C'est...** (*This is ...*).

1. *This is our car.* _____

2. *This is her house.* _____

3. *This is their kitchen.* _____

4. *This is your (infml.) computer.* _____

5. *This is my bedroom.* _____

ANSWER KEY:
1. C'est notre voiture. 2. C'est sa maison. 3. C'est leur cuisine. 4. C'est ton ordinateur. 5. C'est ma chambre (à coucher).

Grammar Builder 2
THE PAST TENSE: NEGATIVE AND QUESTIONS

▶ 13D Lesson 13 Grammar Builder 2 (CD 5, Track 24)

To form the negative of the past tense, place **ne (n')** and **pas** around the present tense form of **avoir**. In other words:

ne (n') + form of **avoir** + **pas** + past participle

Nous n'avons pas chanté.
We didn't sing.

Vous n'avez pas parlé.
You haven't spoken.

Je n'ai pas regardé la télévision.
I didn't watch TV.

Tu n'as pas mangé à neuf heures.
You didn't eat at 9:00.

It's not difficult to ask a question in the past tense. Just use the forms of asking questions that you've already learned.

Vous avez parlé ?
Did you speak?/Have you spoken?/You spoke?

Est-ce que vous avez parlé ?
Did you speak?/Have you spoken?

To form a question by switching the verb and subject (inversion), just put the form of **avoir** before the pronoun, followed by the past participle.

Avez-vous parlé ?
Did you speak?/Have you spoken?

You need to add -t- if the pronoun is **il**, **elle**, or **on**:

A-t-il parlé ?
Did he speak?/Has he spoken?

Of course, you can also use a question word:
Pourquoi avez-vous parlé ? (Why did you speak?)

✎ Work Out 2

Change the following questions from the **est-ce que** form to the inversion form.

1. **Est-ce qu'elle a mangé à six heures ?** (*Did she eat at 6:00?*)

2. **Est-ce que nous avons fini ?** (*Did we finish?*)

3. **Est-ce que vous avez regardé la télévision ?** (*Did you watch television?*)

4. **Est-ce que tu as préparé le dîner ?** (*Did you prepare dinner?*)

5. **Est-ce qu'ils ont répondu ?** (*Did they respond?*)

ANSWER KEY:
1. A-t-elle mangé à six heures ? 2. Avons-nous fini ? 3. Avez-vous regardé la télévision ? 4. As-tu préparé le dîner ? 5. Ont-ils répondu ?

🖊 Drive It Home

A. Complete each sentence by putting the -er verb in the past tense.

1. **Est-ce que tu** _____ (parler) français ?
   (*Did you speak French?*)

2. **Est-ce que nous** _____ (parler) français ?
   (*Did we speak French?*)

3. **Est-ce qu'elle** _____ (parler) français ?
   (*Did she speak French?*)

4. **Est-ce qu'ils** _____ (parler) français ?
   (*Did they speak French?*)

The Past Tense:
Negative and Questions

B. Complete each sentence by putting the **-re** verb in the past tense.

1. **Est-ce que nous** _____ **(perdre) notre vélo ?**

   (Did we lose our bike?)

2. **Est-ce qu'il** _____ **(perdre) son vélo ?**

   (Did he lose his bike?)

3. **Est-ce que j'**_____ **(perdre) mon vélo ?**

   (Did I lose my bike?)

4. **Est-ce qu'elles** _____ **(perdre) leur vélo ?**

   (Did they lose their bike?)

C. Complete each sentence by putting the **-ir** verb in the past tense.

1. **Est-ce que vous** _____ **(finir) vos devoirs ?**

   (Did you finish your homework?)

2. **Est-ce que j'**_____ **(finir) mes devoirs ?**

   (Did I finish my homework?)

3. **Est-ce qu'elle** _____ **(finir) ses devoirs ?**

   (Did she finish her homework?)

4. **Est-ce que tu** _____ **(finir) tes devoirs ?**

   (Did you finish your homework?)

ANSWER KEY:
A. 1. as parlé; 2. avons parlé; 3. a parlé; 4. ont parlé
B. 1. avons perdu; 2. a perdu; 3. ai perdu; 4. ont perdu
C. 1. avez fini; 2. ai fini; 3. a fini; 4. as fini

How Did You Do?

Let's see how you did! By now, you should be able to:

☐ Say whether you're *early* or *late*
(Still unsure? Jump back to page 217)

☐ Talk about something that happened in the past
(Still unsure? Jump back to page 220)

☐ Usc words like *soon* and *often*
(Still unsure? Jump back to page 222)

☐ Talk about something that didn't happen in the past
(Still unsure? Jump back to page 225)

☐ Ask whether something happened
(Still unsure? Jump back to page 225)

Lesson 14: Phrases

By the end of this lesson, you will be able to:

☐ Tell someone that *it's twenty to three*

☐ Answer the phone

☐ Say what you *had,* where you *have been,* and whether you *understood*

Phrase Builder 1

You learned how to say what time it is in *Essential French*, and saw a few phrases using **heure** (*hour*) earlier in this unit. Now let's review, and expand upon what you already know about telling time.

▶ 14A Lesson 14 Phrase Builder 1 (CD 5, Track 25)

What time is it? (lit., What hour is it?)	Quelle heure est-il ?
It is 1:00.	Il est une heure.
It is 2:00.	Il est deux heures.
It is five minutes after two. *(It is 2:05.)*	Il est deux heures cinq.
It is ten minutes after two. *(It is 2:10.)*	Il est deux heures dix.
It is a quarter after two.	Il est deux heures et quart.*
It is twenty minutes after two. *(It is 2:20.)*	Il est deux heures vingt.
It is twenty-five minutes after two. *(It is 2:25.)*	Il est deux heures vingt-cinq.
It is half past two.	Il est deux heures et demie.
It is twenty-five minutes to three. *(lit., It is three hours minus twenty-five.)*	Il est trois heures moins vingt-cinq.
It is twenty minutes to three.	Il est trois heures moins vingt.
It is a quarter to three. *(lit., It is three hours minus the quarter.)*	Il est trois heures moins le quart.
It is ten minutes to three.	Il est trois heures moins dix.
It is five minutes to three.	Il est trois heures moins cinq.

| It is noon. | Il est midi.** |
| It is midnight. | Il est minuit. |

* Et (*and*) is only used with quart (*quarter*) and demi/demie (*half*).

** Note that midi (*noon*) and minuit (*midnight*) are masculine words, so you would say Il est minuit et demi (*It is half past midnight*) and not Il est minuit et demie.

Take It Further

In the previous lesson, you learned that you can use dernier/dernière to mean *last*, as in la nuit dernière (*last night*).

However, you can actually also say la dernière nuit, in which case it means *final* night.

Dernier/dernière is a special adjective that can be placed before *or* after a noun, but its placement changes the meaning. If it's after the noun it means *last*, but if it's before the noun it means *final* or *latest*.

Other adjectives like dernier/dernière include:

ADJECTIVE	MEANING BEFORE THE NOUN	MEANING AFTER THE NOUN
cher/chère	*dear*	*expensive*
pauvre	*unfortunate, poor* (as in, *that poor woman!*)	*poor, impoverished*
seul/seule	*on one's own, only, alone*	*lonely*
ancien/ancienne	*former*	*old, antique*
vieux/vieil/vieille	*old* (as in, *known a long time*)	*old* (as in, *age*)
propre	*own*	*clean*
brave	*good*	*courageous, brave*

mon cher ami
my dear friend

un plat cher
an expensive dish

une pauvre amie
an unfortunate friend

une amie pauvre
an impoverished friend

la seule femme
the only woman

la femme seule
the lonely woman

mon ancien patron
my former boss

ma table ancienne
my antique table

un vieil ami
an old friend (a longtime friend)

un ami vieux
an old friend (a friend who is old in age)

ma propre voiture
my own car

ma voiture propre
my clean car

un brave homme
a good man

un homme brave
a brave man, a courageous man

Note that **vieil** is used before **ami**, but **vieux** is used after **ami**. This is because you must use **vieil** if the adjective comes *before* a masculine noun that begins with a vowel or silent **h**. However, if the adjective comes *after* that kind of masculine noun, then you just use **vieux**.

Finally, there are also some adjectives that can be placed before or after a noun *without* a change in meaning. There are not many of them. One example is **charmant/charmante** (*charming*). For instance, the following two phrases are interchangeable:

mes charmants enfants	*my charming children*
mes enfants charmants	*my charming children*

✎ Phrase Practice 1

Rewrite the following phrases in French.

1. *It is twenty minutes after four.* _____

2. *It is half past noon.* _____

3. *It is seven minutes to two.* _____

4. *It is a quarter to five.* _____

5. *It is thirty-five minutes after six.* _____

ANSWER KEY:
1. Il est quatre heures vingt. 2. Il est midi et demi. 3. Il est deux heures moins sept. 4. Il est cinq heures moins le quart. 5. Il est six heures trente-cinq.

✎ Word Recall

Now let's practice the 24-hour clock. Write the following times in English using *a.m.* and *p.m.* For example, if you saw **Il est quatorze heures**, you would write *It is 2 p.m.*

1. **Il est quinze heures.** _____

2. **Il est vingt heures.** _____

3. **Il est dix-sept heures.** _____

4. **Il est vingt-trois heures.** _____

5. **Il est seize heures.** _____

ANSWER KEY:
1. *It is 3 p.m.* 2. *It is 8 p.m.* 3. *It is 5 p.m.* 4. *It is 11 p.m.* 5. *It is 4 p.m.*

Grammar Builder 1
REVIEW OF THE PAST TENSE

▶ 14B Lesson 14 Grammar Builder 1 (CD 5, Track 26)

Let's review what you've learned about forming the **passé composé** (*past tense*).

Here are verbs from each verb group (**-er**, **-ir**, and **-re**) in the past tense:

PARLER (*TO SPEAK*) - **PAST**	FINIR (*TO FINISH*) - **PAST**	RÉPONDRE (*TO ANSWER*) - **PAST**
j'ai parlé (*I spoke*)	j'ai fini (*I finished*)	j'ai répondu (*I answered*)
tu as parlé	tu as fini	tu as répondu
il a parlé	il a fini	il a répondu
elle a parlé	elle a fini	elle a répondu
nous avons parlé	nous avons fini	nous avons répondu
vous avez parlé	vous avez fini	vous avez répondu
ils ont parlé	ils ont fini	ils ont répondu
elles ont parlé	elles ont fini	elles ont répondu

And remember that to negate a verb in the past tense, you place **ne** (**n'**) and **pas** around the present tense form of **avoir**.

✎ Work Out 1

Translate the following sentences into French using the verbs below:

travailler	maigrir	attendre	manger

1. *He lost weight.* _____

2. *We didn't eat.* _____

3. *She worked.* _____

4. *I didn't wait.* _____

ANSWER KEY:
1. Il a maigri. 2. Nous n'avons pas mangé./On n'a pas mangé. 3. Elle a travaillé. 4. Je n'ai pas attendu.

Phrase Builder 2

▶ 14C Lesson 14 Phrase Builder 2 (CD 5, Track 27)

telephone	le téléphone
phone number	le numéro de téléphone
to make a phone call (to call)	téléphoner
to make a phone call (infml.) (lit., to give/pass a hit of the wire)	donner (or passer) un coup de fil
to consult a phone book	consulter l'annuaire
extension 224 (lit., extension two hundred twenty-four)	le poste 224 (deux cent vingt-quatre)
Hello? (only used when answering the phone)	Allô ?
Who is it?	Qui est-ce ?
Wait, please.	Attendez, s'il vous plaît.
Hold on, please. (lit., Don't leave, please.)	Ne quittez pas, s'il vous plaît.

Can you hear me? (*lit., You hear me?*)	**Vous m'entendez ?**
I can't hear you. (*lit., I don't hear you.*)	**Je ne vous entends pas.**
Hang up, please.	**Raccrochez, s'il vous plaît.**

Take It Further

In addition to **téléphoner** (*to make a phone call, to call*), you saw some other helpful verbs:

| raccrocher | *to hang up* |
| passer | *to pass, to go past, to spend (time)* |

Some more verbs and phrases related to the telephone include:

le (téléphone) portable	*cell phone*
Qui est à l'appareil ?	*Who's calling?* (*lit., Who is at the device?*)
appeler	*to call*
rappeler	*to call back*
décrocher	*to pick up (the phone)*
répondre au téléphone	*to answer the phone*
sonner	*to ring*

Rappeler (*to call back*) conjugates in the same irregular way as **appeler** (*to call*). For example: **je rappelle** (*I call back*), **nous rappelons** (*we call back*), etc.

Also, notice that the phrases **Attendez, Raccrochez,** and **Ne quittez pas** have similar forms. You've seen this form before, in phrases like **Apportez-moi** (*Bring me*) and **Entrez** (*Come in/Enter*). It's known as the imperative or command form. Essentially, it's how you tell people what to do in French. You'll learn more about it in the next unit.

Finally, you saw a new question phrase: est-ce ? (*is it?*), pronounced [ehs].

Qui est-ce ?
Who is it?

Est-ce possible ?
Is it possible?

Est-ce le bon restaurant ?
Is it the right restaurant? (lit., Is it the good restaurant?)

 ## Phrase Practice 2

Match the English phrases on the left to the correct French translations on the right.

1. *Hello?* (only on the phone)	a. **Qui est-ce ?**
2. *Who is it?*	b. **Vous m'entendez ?**
3. *Hold on, please.*	c. **Allô ?**
4. *Can you hear me?*	d. **Raccrochez, s'il vous plaît.**
5. *Hang up, please.*	e. **Ne quittez pas, s'il vous plaît.**

ANSWER KEY
1. c; 2. a; 3. e; 4. b; 5. d

✎ Word Recall

Fill in the blanks with **le petit déjeuner**, **le déjeuner**, or **le dîner**.

1. À 7h du matin, je prends _____ .

2. À 8h du soir, nous allons au restaurant pour _____ .

3. À midi, elle mange toujours un sandwich pour _____ .

4. À 20h, je prépare _____ .

ANSWER KEY:
1. le petit déjeuner (*At 7:00 in the morning, I have breakfast.*); 2. le dîner (*At 8:00 in the evening, we go to the restaurant for dinner.*); 3. le déjeuner (*At noon, she always eats a sandwich for lunch.*), 4. le dîner (*At 8:00 p.m., I prepare dinner.*)

Grammar Builder 2
IRREGULAR PAST TENSE

▶ 14D Lesson 14 Grammar Builder 2 (CD 5, Track 28)

Some verbs have irregular past participles. Unfortunately, they just need to be memorized.

Here are a few important verbs that have irregular past participles:

VERB	PAST PARTICIPLE
avoir (*to have*)	eu
être (*to be*)	été
boire (*to drink*)	bu
comprendre (*to understand*)	compris
prendre (*to take*)	pris
apprendre (*to learn*)	appris

Also, the past participle of **vouloir** (*to want*) is **voulu**.

As an example, here's the full conjugation of prendre in the past tense:

PRENDRE (*TO TAKE*) - PAST			
j'ai pris	*I took*	nous avons pris	*we took*
tu as pris	*you took*	vous avez pris	*you took*
il a pris	*he took*	ils ont pris	*they took*
elle a pris	*she took*	elles ont pris	*they took*

Remember that the past tense in French can be translated into English in different ways. So, for example, pris could mean *took, have taken*, or *did take*, bu could mean *drank, have drunk*, or *did drink*, été could mean *was/were* or *have been*, etc.

Ⓘ

✎ Work Out 2

Fill in the blanks with the past tense form of the verb.

1. **Paul** _____ (boire) un verre de vin rouge. (*Paul drank a glass of red wine.*)

2. **Mes amis** _____ (être) en France. (*My friends were in France.*)

3. **J'** _____ (comprendre) le film. (*I understood the film.*)

4. **Nous** _____ (avoir) une maison. (*We had a house.*)

5. **Vous** _____ (être) aux États-Unis. (*You have been to the United States.*)

6. **Elle** _____ (prendre) mon livre. (*She took my book.*)

ANSWER KEY:
1. a bu; 2. ont été; 3. ai compris; 4. avons eu; 5. avez été; 6. a pris

✎ Drive It Home

A. Let's practice the verb **être**. Rewrite the following phrases in the past tense.

1. **je suis** _____ _____

2. **elle est** _____

3. **nous sommes** _____

4. **ils sont** _____

5. **tu es** _____

6. **vous êtes** _____

7. **elles sont** _____

8. **il est** _____

B. Great! Now let's practice the verb **vouloir**. Rewrite the following phrases in the past tense.

1. **tu veux** _____

2. **il veut** _____

3. **nous voulons** _____

4. **je veux** _____

5. **elles veulent** _____

6. **vous voulez** _____

7. **elle veut** _____

8. **ils veulent** _____

ANSWER KEY:
A. 1. j'ai été; 2. elle a été; 3. nous avons été; 4. ils ont été; 5. tu as été; 6. vous avez été; 7. elles ont été;
8. il a été
B. 1. tu as voulu; 2. il a voulu; 3. nous avons voulu; 4. j'ai voulu; 5. elles ont voulu; 6. vous avez voulu;
7. elle a voulu; 8. ils ont voulu

How Did You Do?

Let's see how you did! By now, you should be able to:

☐ Tell someone that *it's twenty to three*
(Still unsure? Jump back to page 230)

☐ Answer the phone
(Still unsure? Jump back to page 236)

☐ Say what you *had*, where you *have been*, and whether you *understood*
(Still unsure? Jump back to page 239)

Lesson 15: Sentences

By the end of this lesson, you will be able to:

☐ Talk to someone on the phone

☐ Say what you *have to* or *must* do

☐ Make an appointment

☐ Talk about what you *did* or *made*

I Must	The Future Tense (*I Will Dance*)
To Do	Irregular Future Tense

Sentence Builder 1

15A Lesson 15 Sentence Builder 1 (CD 6, Track 1)

I would like to make a phone call.	Je voudrais téléphoner.
I would like to speak to …	Je voudrais parler à…
Who's calling, please? (lit., *This is on behalf of who, please?*)	C'est de la part de qui, s'il vous plaît ?
I am sorry.	Je suis désolé/désolée.
He/She isn't here. (lit., *He/She isn't there.*)	Il/Elle n'est pas là.
Do you want to leave a message?	Voulez-vous laisser un message ?
I would like to leave a message.	Je voudrais laisser un message.
Can you tell him/her that I called?	Pouvez-vous lui dire que j'ai appelé ?
Speak slower (more slowly), please.	Parlez plus lentement, s'il vous plaît.
What is your telephone number?	Quel est votre numéro de téléphone ?
I'm getting him/her for you. (lit., *I'm passing him/her to you.*)	Je vous le/la passe.
The line is busy.	La ligne est occupée.
I'm going to call back.	Je vais rappeler.

Take It Further

You just saw the new phrase **de la part de**, which means *on behalf of* or *from* (*someone*). You can also say:

de ma part	*on my behalf, from me, on my part*
de sa part	*on his/her behalf, from him/her, on his/her part*

UNIT 4 Lesson 15: Sentences   243

And so on.

You also saw some new verbs:

| laisser | to leave, to let (someone do something), to let go |
| dire | to say, to tell |

Dire is an irregular verb. You'll learn more about it in *Advanced French*.

In the sentence **Pouvez-vous lui dire que j'ai appelé ?**, the word **pouvez** is a form of the irregular verb **pouvoir** (*can, to be able to*). You learned its present tense forms in *Essential French*, but here's a review:

POUVOIR *(CAN, TO BE ABLE TO)* - **PRESENT**			
je peux	*I can*	**nous pouvons**	*we can*
tu peux	*you can*	**vous pouvez**	*you can*
il peut	*he can*	**ils peuvent**	*they can*
elle peut	*she can*	**elles peuvent**	*they can*

Notice that the forms of **pouvoir** are fairly similar to the forms of **vouloir**.

The past participle of **pouvoir** is irregular: **pu**. For example: **J'ai pu aller en France.** (*I was able to go to France.*)

Finally, notice that both **le/la** and **lui** were used to mean *him/her* in the sentences **Je vous le/la passe.** and **Pouvez-vous lui dire que j'ai appelé ?**. So far, you've learned that **le** and **la** mean *the*, and you've seen **lui** used to mean *him* but not *her*. Well, **le/la** and **lui** can also mean *him/her* when they're used in a specific way; in technical terms, when they're used as direct or indirect object pronouns. You'll learn more about this in *Advanced French*, so don't worry about it for now. Just try to remember those sentences as a whole.

✎ Sentence Practice 1

Translate this short telephone conversation into English.

- Allô ?
- Bonjour. Je voudrais parler à Marie, s'il vous plaît.
- Je suis désolé. Elle n'est pas là. Voulez-vous laisser un message ?
- Non, merci. Je vais rappeler.

_____

_____

_____

_____

ANSWER KEY:
- *Hello?*
- *Hello. I would like to speak to Marie, please.*
- *I am sorry. She isn't here. Do you want to leave a message?*
- *No, thank you. I'm going to call back.*

✎ Word Recall

Let's practice reflexive verbs. Transform the following verbs into reflexive verbs in the present tense, and then translate the new phrases into English.

1. **je lave** (*I wash*) _____

2. **elle demande** (*she asks*) _____

3. **il trompe** (*he deceives*) _____

4. **tu dépêches** (*you dispatch*) _____

5. **nous amusons** (*we entertain*) _____

Grammar Builder 1
I MUST

▶ 15B Lesson 15 Grammar Builder 1 (CD 6, Track 2)

You already know a lot of irregular verbs in French: avoir, être, aller, prendre, boire, pouvoir, vouloir, etc.

Here is another irregular verb to add to your list: devoir.

Devoir has several meanings. If it's followed by a verb in the infinitive (such as parler, finir, etc.), then it usually means *to have to, must,* or *should*. If it isn't followed by a verb, then it typically means *to owe*.

Here are its forms in the present tense:

DEVOIR (*TO HAVE TO, MUST, SHOULD*)			
je dois	*I have to*	nous devons	*we have to*
tu dois	*you have to*	vous devez	*you have to*
il doit	*he has to*	ils doivent	*they have to*
elle doit	*she has to*	elles doivent	*they have to*

Let's look at some examples:

Je dois appeler le restaurant pour faire des réservations.
I have to call the restaurant to make reservations.

Tu dois être prêt à cinq heures.
You must be ready by 5:00.

Combien est-ce que je dois ?
How much do I owe?

Il doit dix dollars.
He owes ten dollars.

The past participle of **devoir** is **dû: J'ai dû aller aux États-Unis.** (*I had to go to the United States.*)

✎ Work Out 1

Fill in the blanks with the correct form of the verb **devoir** in the present tense.

1. **Tu ne** _____ **pas travailler.** (*You shouldn't work.*)

2. **Est-ce que nous** _____ **aller à New York ?** (*Should we go to New York?*)

3. **Vous** _____ **être au café à l'heure.** (*You must be at the café on time.*)

4. **Elle** _____ **beaucoup à ses parents.** (*She owes a lot to her parents.*)

5. **À quelle heure est-ce que je** _____ **partir ?** (*At what time do I have to leave?*)

   ANSWER KEY:
   1. dois; 2. devons; 3. devez; 4. doit; 5. dois

Sentence Builder 2

Now let's look at how to **prendre rendez-vous**, or *make appointments (lit., to take appointment)*. We'll also look at some expressions that use the word *time*.

▶ 15C Lesson 15 Sentence Builder 2 (CD 6, Track 3)

I would like to make an appointment.	Je voudrais prendre un rendez-vous.
Are you free at 9:00? (*infml.*)	Est-ce que tu es libre à neuf heures ?
Are you free at a quarter past seven? (*fml.*)	Êtes-vous libre à sept heures et quart ?
Do you have time to go with me? (*fml.*)	Avez-vous le temps d'aller avec moi ?
Do you have time to go with me? (*infml.*)	As-tu le temps d'aller avec moi ?
I don't have (the) time.	Je n'ai pas le temps.
He's wasting his time. (*lit., He's losing his time.*)	Il perd son temps.
It's time for you to relax.	Il est temps de te reposer.

Take It Further

The term **le temps** can mean both *time* and *weather*.

Je n'ai pas le temps.
I don't have (the) time.

Quel temps fait-il ?
What's the weather today?

However, when you're talking about a specific time of day, and not just time in general, don't forget to use **heure** to mean *time*, and not **temps**.

Quelle heure est-il ?
What time is it?

Sentence Practice 2

Translate the following sentences into English.

1. **Est-ce que Marie est libre à huit heures et demie ?**

_____

2. **Est-ce que nous sommes libres à quatre heures moins le quart ?**

_____

3. **Est-ce que je suis libre à midi moins dix ?**

_____

4. **Est-ce qu'il est libre à cinq heures quarante ?**

_____

5. **Est-ce qu'elles sont libres à une heure ?**

_____

ANSWER KEY:
1. Is Marie free at half past eight? 2. Are we free at a quarter to four? 3. Am I free at ten (minutes) to noon? 4. Is he free at forty minutes after five?/Is he free at 5:40? 5. Are they free at 1:00?

✎ Word Recall

Match the English sentences on the left to the correct French translations on the right.

1. *You should think.*	a. **Tu dois descendre.**
2. *You should study.*	b. **Tu dois écouter.**
3. *You should come down.*	c. **Tu dois réussir.**
4. *You should walk.*	d. **Tu dois marcher.**
5. *You should listen.*	e. **Tu dois réfléchir.**
6. *You should succeed.*	f. **Tu dois étudier.**

ANSWER KEY:
1. e; 2. f; 3. a; 4. d; 5. b; 6. c

Grammar Builder 2
TO DO

▶ 15D Lesson 15 Grammar Builder 2 (CD 6, Track 4)

You're already familiar with the irregular verb **faire** (*to do, to make*). You learned its full conjugation in Lesson 8 of *Essential French*. However, **faire** is used *a lot* in French, so let's review:

FAIRE *(TO DO, TO MAKE)* - **PRESENT**			
je fais	*I do, I make*	**nous faisons**	*we do, we make*
tu fais	*you do, you make*	**vous faites**	*you do, you make*
il fait	*he does, he makes*	**ils font**	*they do, they make*
elle fait	*she does, she makes*	**elles font**	*they do, they make*

You know that faire is used in a wide variety of set expressions, such as faire la queue (*to wait in line*), faire le ménage (*to clean the house, to do the house cleaning*), and faire de la natation (*to go swimming*). Note that, in these expressions, faire doesn't always translate as *to do* or *to make*.

Here are some other examples:

Il fait froid.	*It's cold. (lit., It makes cold.)*
Je fais du sport.	*I play sports. (lit., I do sport.)*
Je fais du ski.	*I ski. (lit., I do skiing.)*
Je fais du ski nautique.	*I water-ski. (lit., I do water-skiing.)*
Je fais la cuisine.	*I'm cooking. (lit., I do cooking.)*
Je fais des courses./ Je fais du shopping.	*I'm shopping. (lit., I do shopping.)*
Je fais des achats.	*I'm running errands. (lit., I do purchases.)*
Je fais une promenade.	*I'm taking a walk. (lit., I do a walk.)*

Ça fait is another common expression that uses faire. It can mean *that makes, it is,* or *that is.* For example, if you're counting the number of people in a group, you could conclude by saying: Ça fait six personnes. (*That makes six people./That's six people.*)

Ça fait can also mean *it has been*, as in ça fait six mois (*it's been six months*) or ça fait longtemps (*it's been a long time*). Furthermore, you can use ça fait in the expression ça fait du bien, which literally means *that does one good*.

Note that the past participle of faire is fait.

J'ai fait des achats.
I ran some errands. (lit., I did some purchases.)

✎ Work Out 2

Fill in the blank with the correct form of the verb faire in the present or past tense, depending on the English translation.

1. Tu _____ une omelette. (*You're making an omelet.*)

2. Tu _____ une omelette. (*You made an omelet.*)

3. Qu'est-ce que vous _____ ? (*What are you doing?/What are you making?*)

4. Nous _____ un grand dîner. (*We're making a big dinner.*)

5. Les filles _____ du ski. (*The girls are skiing.*)

6. Est-ce qu'il _____ du shopping ? (*Is he shopping?*)

7. Ils _____ le ménage. (*They cleaned the house.*)

ANSWER KEY:
1. fais; 2. as fait; 3. faites; 4. faisons; 5. font; 6. fait; 7. ont fait

✎ Drive It Home

A. Fill in the blanks with the correct form of devoir in the present tense.

1. Nous _____ finir notre dîner. (*We must finish our dinner.*)

2. Elle _____ finir son dîner. (*She must finish her dinner.*)

3. Je _____ finir mon dîner. (*I must finish my dinner.*)

4. Ils _____ finir leur dîner. (*They must finish their dinner.*)

5. Vous _____ finir votre dîner. (*You must finish your dinner.*)

6. Tu _____ finir ton dîner. (*You must finish your dinner.*)

7. Elles _____ finir leur dîner. (*They must finish their dinner.*)

8. Il _____ finir son dîner. (*He must finish his dinner.*)

B. Fill in the blanks with the correct form of faire in the present tense.

1. Nathalie _____ la cuisine. (*Nathalie is cooking.*)

2. Pierre et Marc _____ la cuisine. (*Pierre and Marc are cooking.*)

3. Tu _____ la cuisine. (*You are cooking.*)

4. Marc _____ la cuisine. (*Marc is cooking.*)

5. Nous _____ la cuisine. (*We are cooking.*)

6. Nathalie et Sophie _____ la cuisine. (*Nathalie and Sophie are cooking.*)

7. Je _____ la cuisine. (*I am cooking.*)

8. Vous _____ la cuisine. (*You are cooking.*)

ANSWER KEY:
A. 1. devons; 2. doit; 3. dois; 4. doivent; 5. devez; 6. dois; 7. doivent; 8. doit
B. 1. fait; 2. font; 3. fais; 4. fait; 5. faisons; 6. font; 7. fais; 8. faites

Tip

The **nous** and **vous** forms of an irregular verb in the present tense are often similar to that verb's infinitive form, even if the rest of the forms (je, tu, etc.) are very different.

For example:

INFINITIVE FORM	NOUS FORM	VOUS FORM
avoir	avons	avez
aller	allons	allez
pouvoir	pouvons	pouvez

INFINITIVE FORM	NOUS FORM	VOUS FORM
vouloir	voulons	voulez
devoir	devons	devez

Obviously, this isn't true of all irregular verbs, including être and faire, but you will see more examples of this as you continue to learn other irregular verbs.

How Did You Do?

Let's see how you did! By now, you should be able to:

☐ Talk to someone on the phone
(Still unsure? Jump back to page 243)

☐ Say what you *have to* or *must* do
(Still unsure? Jump back to page 246)

☐ Make an appointment
(Still unsure? Jump back to page 248)

☐ Talk about what you *did* or *made*
(Still unsure? Jump back to page 250)

Lesson 16: Conversations

By the end of this lesson, you will be able to:

☐ Say what you *will* do in the future

☐ Say where you *will go*, what you *will have*, and where you *will be*

⟨⟨ Conversation 1

In this dialogue, Jean-Claude is trying to reach his friend Marc at home.

▶ 16A Lesson 16 Conversation 1 (CD 6, Track 5)

Mme Soubrié :	Allô ?
Jean-Claude :	Bonjour madame. Je voudrais parler à Marc, s'il vous plaît.
Mme Soubrié :	Qui est à l'appareil ?
Jean-Claude :	C'est Jean-Claude DuLac. Je suis un ami de Marc.
Mme Soubrié :	Ne quittez pas, s'il vous plaît, je vais le chercher.

(She returns to the line after a few moments.)

Mme Soubrié :	Je regrette, mais Marc n'est plus ici. Il a quitté la maison il y a deux minutes.
Jean-Claude :	Je vais laisser un message pour lui.
Mme Soubrié :	Bien sûr. Il va revenir à cinq heures et quart.
Jean-Claude :	D'accord. Je vais téléphoner ce soir vers sept heures, madame.
Mme Soubrié :	Bon. Je vais donner le message à Marc.

Mrs. Soubrié:	*Hello?*
Jean-Claude:	*Hello, ma'am. I would like to speak to Marc, please.*

Mrs. Soubrié:	Who's calling?
Jean-Claude:	It's Jean-Claude DuLac. I'm a friend of Marc's.
Mrs. Soubrié:	Hold on, please, I'm going to look for him.

(She returns to the line after a few moments.)

Mrs. Soubrié:	I'm sorry, but Marc is no longer here. He left the house two minutes ago.
Jean-Claude:	I'm going to leave a message for him.
Mrs. Soubrié:	Of course. He's going to come back at a quarter after five.
Jean-Claude:	Okay. I'm going to call tonight around 7:00, ma'am.
Mrs. Soubrié:	Good. I'm going to give the message to Marc.

Take It Further

You're already familiar with the common expression il y a, which means *there is* or *there are*. However, il y a can also mean *ago* when used with an expression of time.

il y a trois heures	*three hours ago*
il y a deux minutes	*two minutes ago*
il y a longtemps	*a long time ago*

In Conversation 1, you also saw another way to say *I'm sorry*:

| je regrette | *I'm sorry, I regret* |
| regretter | *to be sorry, to regret* |

Also, you already know the verb chercher (*to look for*) from *Essential French*, but it's important to keep in mind that chercher means *to look **for***, so it should not be followed by a word like pour (*for*). For example, you would say je cherche mon livre (*I'm looking for my book*) and not je cherche pour mon livre.

Finally, notice that she said **je vais le chercher** (*I'm going to look for him*). This is another example of **le** being used to mean *him*. Again, you'll learn more in *Advanced French*.

 # Conversation Practice 1

Unscramble these sentences based on Conversation 1.

1. Marc / voudrait / à / Jean-Claude / parler / .

_____

2. a quitté / il y a / maison / minutes / Marc / la / deux / .

_____

3. revenir / à / heures / va / cinq / Marc / quart / et / .

_____

4. message / pour / va / un / Jean-Claude / lui / laisser / .

_____

ANSWER KEY:
1. Jean-Claude voudrait parler à Marc. (*Jean-Claude would like to speak to Marc.*) 2. Marc a quitté la maison il y a deux minutes. (*Marc left the house two minutes ago.*) 3. Marc va revenir à cinq heures et quart. (*Marc is going to come back at a quarter after five.*) 4. Jean-Claude va laisser un message pour lui. (*Jean-Claude is going to leave a message for him.*)

✎ Word Recall

Complete the following sentences using the verb forms below.

avons	buvons	devons
allons	voulons	prenons

1. Nous _____ du thé. (*We're drinking tea.*)

2. Nous _____ en ville samedi soir.

   (*We're going into town Saturday night.*)

3. Nous ne _____ pas aller au restaurant.

   (*We don't want to go to the restaurant.*)

4. Nous _____ une sœur et deux frères.

   (*We have one sister and two brothers.*)

5. Nous _____ le petit déjeuner. (*We're having breakfast.*)

6. Nous _____ vingt dollars. (*We owe twenty dollars.*)

ANSWER KEY:
1. buvons; 2. allons; 3. voulons; 4. avons; 5. prenons; 6. devons

Grammar Builder 1
THE FUTURE TENSE (*I WILL DANCE*)

▶ 16B Lesson 16 Grammar Builder 1 (CD 6, Track 6)

You already know how to form the "near future" tense. You just take the present tense of <u>aller</u> and add an infinitive. For example: je vais aller (*I'm going to go*).

Now let's look at the future tense, which is the equivalent of *will* or *will be* + verb in English: *I will dance, I will finish, I will be dancing, I will be finishing*, etc.

To form the future tense:

1. For **-er** and **-ir** verbs, add the following endings onto the infinitive form of the verb.

2. For **-re** verbs, drop the final e from the infinitive form and then add the following endings.

PRONOUN	ENDING	PRONOUN	ENDING
je	-ai	nous	-ons
tu	-as	vous	-ez
il	-a	ils	-ont
elle	-a	elles	-ont

Here are examples of each type of verb in the future tense:

DANSER (*TO DANCE*) - FUTURE	FINIR (*TO FINISH*) - FUTURE	VENDRE (*TO SELL*) - FUTURE
je danserai (*I will dance*)	je finirai (*I will finish*)	je vendrai (*I will sell*)
tu danseras	tu finiras	tu vendras
il dansera	il finira	il vendra
elle dansera	elle finira	elle vendra
nous danserons	nous finirons	nous vendrons
vous danserez	vous finirez	vous vendrez
ils danseront	ils finiront	ils vendront
elles danseront	elles finiront	elles vendront

Je marcherai au parc avec toi.
I will walk in the park with you.

Ils inviteront tout le monde.
They will invite everyone.

✎ Work Out 1

Fill in the blanks by conjugating each verb in the future tense.

1. Les enfants _____ (obéir) à leurs parents.

   (Children will obey their parents.)

2. Elles _____ (parler) en français. *(They will speak in French.)*

3. Est-ce que tu _____ (répondre) ? *(Will you respond?)*

4. J' _____ (accompagner) mes amis au restaurant.

   (I will accompany my friends to the restaurant.)

5. Vous ne _____ (regarder) pas la télévision.

   (You will not watch television.)

   ANSWER KEY:
   1. obéiront; 2. parleront; 3. répondras; 4. accompagnerai; 5. regarderez

❝ Conversation 2

Carole calls a restaurant to make reservations for dinner on Saturday evening.
The **maître d'hôtel** (*maître d'*) answers.

▶ 16C Lesson 16 Conversation 2 (CD 6, Track 7)

Le maître d'hôtel :	Allô, bonsoir. Puis-je vous aider ?
Carole :	Je voudrais faire des réservations pour dîner samedi soir.
Le maître d'hôtel :	Vous serez combien de personnes, madame ?
Carole :	Nous serons quatre personnes.
Le maître d'hôtel :	À quelle heure est-ce que vous désirez réserver une table ?
Carole :	Nous arriverons vers sept heures et demie, monsieur.

Le maître d'hôtel :	Très bien, madame. La réservation sera sous quel nom ?
Carole :	C'est pour la famille Rigaud.
Le maître d'hôtel :	Entendu. Quatre personnes pour le dîner samedi soir à sept heures et demie.

Maître d':	*Hello, good evening. Can I help you?*
Carole:	*I would like to make reservations to have dinner Saturday evening.*
Maître d':	*How many people will you be, ma'am?*
Carole:	*We will be four people.*
Maître d':	*At what time do you want to reserve a table?*
Carole:	*We will be arriving around half past seven, sir.*
Maître d':	*Very well, ma'am. The reservation will be under what name?*
Carole:	*It's for the Rigaud family.*
Maître d':	*All right. Four people for dinner on Saturday evening at half past seven.*

Take It Further

You heard some useful polite phrases in that dialogue. For example:

Puis-je vous aider ?
Can I help you?

This is a very good expression to know. You will most likely hear it when you enter a store, a restaurant, etc. Note that **je puis** comes from the verb **pouvoir** (*to be able to, can*). In other words, **pouvoir** actually has two different **je** forms in the present tense: **je puis** and **je peux**. **Je peux** is the most commonly used; **je puis** is mostly used when asking formal questions.

If you're in a store, and you're just looking around, you can respond with:

Non, merci. Je regarde seulement.
No, thank you. I'm just looking (lit., I'm only watching).

If you're looking for something specific, you can say: **Oui, je voudrais...** (*Yes, I would like ...*) or **Oui, je cherche...** (*Yes, I'm looking for ...*).

In Conversation 2, you also saw the verb **désirer**, which means *to want* or *to wish*. As you know, the verb **vouloir** also means *to want* or *to wish*. **Désirer** is generally a more formal way of talking about what you want.

Finally, let's review reservation expressions, and also introduce a few new ones:

a reservation	une réservation
to reserve	réserver
to make a reservation	faire une réservation
under what name?	sous quel nom ?
name	le nom
a table for two	une table pour deux
four people for dinner	quatre personnes pour le dîner
for a party of four	pour quatre personnes

✎ Conversation Practice 2

Match the French phrases to the correct English translations.

1. Puis-je vous aider ?	a. *How many people will you be?*
2. Vous serez combien de personnes ?	b. *At what time?*
3. La réservation sera sous quel nom ?	c. *Can I help you?*
4. À quelle heure ?	d. *The reservation will be under what name?*

ANSWER KEY:
1. c; 2. a; 3. d; 4. b

✎ Word Recall

Now that you've translated questions using combien, quel, and à quelle heure, let's practice matching other question words.

Match the English question words to the correct French translations.

1. *why*	a. quand
2. *when*	b. comment
3. *who*	c. où
4. *how*	d. pourquoi
5. *where*	e. qui

ANSWER KEY:
1. d; 2. a; 3. e; 4. b; 5. c

Grammar Builder 2
IRREGULAR FUTURE TENSE

16D Lesson 16 Grammar Builder 2 (CD 6, Track 8)

You've learned that the future tense is formed by taking a verb's infinitive form, or the infinitive minus e, and adding the appropriate ending. The infinitive or infinitive minus e component of the future tense is known as the "stem."

Unfortunately, some irregular verbs also have irregular stems. In other words, they don't use the infinitive or the infinitive minus e to form the future tense. There isn't a pattern; you will have to memorize them.

Here are some common examples. Just add the regular future tense endings to the following stems to form the future tense:

VERB	FUTURE STEM
aller	ir-
avoir	aur-
être	ser-
faire	fer-
devoir	devr-

J'irai à Paris.
I will go to Paris.

Il devra dix dollars.
He will owe ten dollars.

I Must	The Future Tense (*I Will Dance*)
	To Do	Irregular Future Tense

Nous serons en retard.
We will be late.

Il fera soleil demain.
It will be sunny tomorrow.

Elle aura trente ans.
She will be thirty years old.

✎ Work Out 2

Complete the sentences by putting the verb in parentheses in the future tense.

1. **Vous** _____ **(être) combien de personnes ?**

   (How many people will you be?)

2. **Nous** _____ **(être) au restaurant à midi.**

   (We will be at the restaurant at noon.)

3. **Ils** _____ **(avoir) une fête ce soir.**

   (They will have a party tonight.)

4. **Est-ce que vous** _____ **(aller) en France ?** *(Will you go to France?)*

5. **Je** _____ **(devoir) finir.** *(I will have to finish.)*

6. **Jeudi, il** _____ **(faire) beau.** *(It will be beautiful outside on Thursday.)*

   ANSWER KEY:
   1. **serez**; 2. **serons**; 3. **auront**; 4. **irez**; 5. **devrai**; 6. **fera**

✎ Drive It Home

A. Fill in the blanks with the future tense of the verb vendre.

1. Je _____ ma voiture. (*I'll sell my car.*)

2. Nous _____ ma voiture. (*We'll sell my car.*)

3. Elle _____ ma voiture. (*She'll sell my car.*)

4. Martin et Anne _____ ma voiture.

   (*Martin and Anne will sell my car.*)

5. Tu _____ ma voiture. (*You'll sell my car.*)

6. Paul _____ ma voiture. (*Paul will sell my car.*)

7. Vous _____ ma voiture. (*You'll sell my car.*)

8. Anne et Sophie _____ ma voiture.

   (*Anne and Sophie will sell my car.*)

B. Great! Now fill in the blanks with the future tense of the verb aller.

1. _____ -vous en vacances en septembre ?

   (*Will you go on vacation in September?*)

2. _____ -je en vacances en septembre ?

   (*Will I go on vacation in September?*)

3. _____ -tu en vacances en septembre ?

   (*Will you go on vacation in September?*)

4. _____ -t-elle en vacances en septembre ?

(Will she go on vacation in September?)

5. _____ -elles en vacances en septembre ?

(Will they go on vacation in September?)

6. _____ -t-il en vacances en septembre ?

(Will he go on vacation in September?)

7. _____ -nous en vacances en septembre ?

(Will we go on vacation in September?)

8. _____ -ils en vacances en septembre ?

(Will they go on vacation in September?)

ANSWER KEY:
A. 1. vendrai; 2. vendrons; 3. vendra; 4. vendront; 5. vendras; 6. vendra; 7. vendrez; 8. vendront
B. 1. Irez; 2. Irai; 3. Iras; 4. Ira; 5. Iront; 6. Ira; 7. Irons; 8. Iront

How Did You Do?

Let's see how you did! By now, you should be able to:

☐ Say what you *will* do in the future
(Still unsure? Jump back to page 258)

☐ Say where you *will go*, what you *will have*, and where you *will be*
(Still unsure? Jump back to page 264)

Unit 4 Essentials

Don't forget to go to **www.livinglanguage.com/languagelab** to access your free online tools for this lesson: audiovisual flashcards and interactive games and quizzes.

Vocabulary Essentials

AT WHAT TIME?

at what time?		a quarter of an hour	
at noon sharp, exactly at noon		around (as in, around 9:00)	
in the morning		late	
in the afternoon		on time	
in the evening		early	
a half hour			

[Pg. 217] (If you're stuck, visit this page to review!)

ADVERBS

always, still		rarely	
still, more		long, (for a) long time	
ever, never		soon	
often		formerly, in the past	
now			

[Pg. 222]

TELLING TIME

What time is it?	
It's 1:00.	
It's five (minutes) after two.	
It's a quarter after two.	
It's half past two.	
It's twenty minutes to three.	
It's a quarter to three.	
It's noon.	
It's midnight.	

[Pg. 230]

TELEPHONE EXPRESSIONS

telephone	
phone number	
to make a phone call, to call	
to make a phone call (infml.)	
extension	
Hello?	
Who is it?	
Hold on, please.	
Can you hear me?	
I can't hear you.	
Hang up, please.	

[Pg. 236]

MORE TELEPHONE EXPRESSIONS

I would like to speak to ...	
I'm sorry.	
He/She isn't here.	
Do you want to leave a message?	
I would like to leave a message.	
Can you tell him/her that I called?	
Speak slower, please./ *Speak more slowly, please.*	
What is your telephone number?	
The line is busy.	

[Pg. 243]

APPOINTMENTS

I would like to make an appointment.	
Are you free at ... ? (infml.)	
Are you free at ... ? (fml.)	
Do you have time ... ? (infml.)	
Do you have time ... ? (fml.)	
I don't have (the) time.	

[Pg. 248]

EXPRESSIONS USING FAIRE

to wait in line	
to clean the house, *to do the house cleaning*	
to go swimming	
to play sports, to do sports	
to ski	

to water-ski	
to cook	
to shop	
to run errands	
to take a walk	
that makes, that does, it is, that is, it has been	

[Pg. 251]

Grammar Essentials

THE PAST TENSE

The past tense is formed as follows:

the present tense of avoir or être + the past participle of the verb

The negative past tense is formed as follows:

ne (n') + form of avoir or être + pas + past participle

To form a question by switching the verb and subject (inversion), just put the form of avoir before the pronoun, followed by the past participle.

PAST PARTICIPLES

1. -ER VERBS: to form the past participle of an -er verb, cut off the -er from the infinitive and add é.
2. -RE VERBS: to form the past participle of an -re verb, cut off the -re and add u.
3. -IR VERBS: to form the past participle of an -ir verb, cut off the -ir and add i.

FINIR (TO FINISH) - PAST

I finished	j'ai fini	we finished	nous avons fini
you finished (infml.)	tu as fini	you finished (pl./fml.)	vous avez fini
he finished	il a fini	they finished (m.)	ils ont fini
she finished	elle a fini	they finished (f.)	elles ont fini

PARLER (TO SPEAK) - PAST

I spoke	j'ai parlé	we spoke	nous avons parlé
you spoke (infml.)	tu as parlé	you spoke (pl./fml.)	vous avez parlé
he spoke	il a parlé	they spoke (m.)	ils ont parlé
she spoke	elle a parlé	they spoke (f.)	elles ont parlé

IRREGULAR PAST PARTICIPLES

VERB	PAST PARTICIPLE
avoir (to have)	eu
être (to be)	été
boire (to drink)	bu
comprendre (to understand)	compris
prendre (to take)	pris
apprendre (to learn)	appris
vouloir (to want)	voulu
devoir (to have to, must, should)	dû
faire (to do, to make)	fait

PRENDRE *(TO TAKE)* - **PAST**			
I took	**j'ai pris**	*we took*	**nous avons pris**
you took (infml.)	**tu as pris**	*you took (pl./fml.)*	**vous avez pris**
he took	**il a pris**	*they took (m.)*	**ils ont pris**
she took	**elle a pris**	*they took (f.)*	**elles ont pris**

RÉPONDRE *(TO RESPOND)* - **PAST**			
I responded	**j'ai répondu**	*we responded*	**nous avons répondu**
you responded (infml.)	**tu as répondu**	*you responded (pl./fml.)*	**vous avez répondu**
he responded	**il a répondu**	*they responded (m.)*	**ils ont répondu**
she responded	**elle a répondu**	*they responded (f.)*	**elles ont répondu**

FORMING THE FUTURE TENSE

1. For **-er** and **-ir** verbs, add the following endings onto the infinitive form of the verb.

2. For **-re** verbs, drop the final **e** from the infinitive form and then add the following endings.

PRONOUN	ENDING	PRONOUN	ENDING
je	-ai	nous	-ons
tu	-as	vous	-ez
il	-a	ils	-ont
elle	-a	elles	-ont

DANSER (*TO DANCE*) - **FUTURE**

I will dance	je danserai	*we will dance*	nous danserons
you will dance (infml.)	tu danseras	*you will dance (pl./fml.)*	vous danserez
he will dance	il dansera	*they will dance (m.)*	ils danseront
she will dance	elle dansera	*they will dance (f.)*	elles danseront

FINIR (*TO FINISH*) - **FUTURE**

I will finish	je finirai	*we will finish*	nous finirons
you will finish (infml.)	tu finiras	*you will finish (pl./fml.)*	vous finirez
he will finish	il finira	*they will finish (m.)*	ils finiront
she will finish	elle finira	*they will finish (f.)*	elles finiront

VENDRE (*TO SELL*) - **FUTURE**

I will sell	je vendrai	*we will sell*	nous vendrons
you will sell (infml.)	tu vendras	*you will sell (pl./fml.)*	vous vendrez
he will sell	il vendra	*they will sell (m.)*	ils vendront
she will sell	elle vendra	*they will sell (f.)*	elles vendront

IRREGULAR STEMS IN THE FUTURE TENSE

VERB	FUTURE STEM
aller	ir-
avoir	aur-
être	ser-
faire	fer-
devoir	devr-

ALLER *(TO GO)* - FUTURE

I will go	j'irai	we will go	nous irons
you will go (infml.)	tu iras	you will go (pl./fml.)	vous irez
he will go	il ira	they will go (m.)	ils iront
she will go	elle ira	they will go (f.)	elles iront

AVOIR *(TO HAVE)* - FUTURE

I will have	j'aurai	we will have	nous aurons
you will have (infml.)	tu auras	you will have (pl./fml.)	vous aurez
he will have	il aura	they will have (m.)	ils auront
she will have	elle aura	they will have (f.)	elles auront

ÊTRE *(TO BE)* - FUTURE

I will be	je serai	we will be	nous serons
you will be (infml.)	tu seras	you will be (pl./fml.)	vous serez
he will be	il sera	they will be (m.)	ils seront
she will be	elle sera	they will be (f.)	elles seront

OTHER VERBS

DEVOIR *(TO HAVE TO, MUST, SHOULD)* - **PRESENT**			
I have to	je dois	*we have to*	nous devons
you have to (infml.)	tu dois	*you have to (pl./fml.)*	vous devez
he has to	il doit	*they have to (m.)*	ils doivent
she has to	elle doit	*they have to (f.)*	elles doivent

FAIRE *(TO DO, TO MAKE)* - **PRESENT**			
I do	je fais	*we do*	nous faisons
you do (infml.)	tu fais	*you do (pl./fml.)*	vous faites
he does	il fait	*they do (m.)*	ils font
she does	elle fait	*they do (f.)*	elles font

Unit 4 Quiz

A. Translate the following telephone expressions into French.

1. *Hello?* _____

2. *Speak more slowly, please.* _____

3. *I would like to speak to ...* _____

4. *I'm sorry.* _____

5. *What is your telephone number?* _____

B. Match the following English words to their correct French translations.

1. *late*   a. **toujours**

2. *early*   b. **maintenant**

3. *always*   c. **tôt**

4. *often*   d. **en retard**

5. *now*   e. **souvent**

C. Put the following verbs in the future tense.

1. Ma sœur _____ (dîner) à 8h du soir.
   (*My sister will have dinner at 8:00 at night.*)

2. Vous _____ (répondre) à midi précis.
   (*You will respond at noon sharp.*)

3. Mes parents _____ (finir) le dîner à 20h.
   (*My parents will finish dinner at 8 p.m.*)

4. Est-ce que tu _____ (être) libre à 5h ?
   (*Will you be free at 5:00?*)

5. Elle n' _____ (avoir) pas le temps.
   (*She will not have time.*)

D. Now put those same verbs in the past tense.

1. Ma sœur _____ (dîner) à 8h du soir.
   (*My sister had dinner at 8:00 at night.*)

2. Vous _____ (répondre) à midi précis.
   (*You responded at noon sharp.*)

3. Mes parents _____ (finir) le dîner à 20h.
   (*My parents finished dinner at 8 p.m.*)

4. Est-ce que tu _____ (être) libre à 5h ?
   (*Were you free at 5:00?*)

5. Elle n' _____ pas _____ (avoir) le temps. (*She didn't have time.*)

How Did You Do?

Give yourself a point for every correct answer, then use the following key to determine whether or not you're ready to move on:

0-7 points: It's probably best to go back and study the lessons again to make sure you understood everything completely. Take your time; it's not a race! Make sure you spend time reviewing the vocabulary and reading through each grammar note carefully.

8-16 points: If the questions you missed were in Section A or B, you may want to review the vocabulary again; if you missed answers mostly in Section C or D, check the Unit 4 Essentials to make sure you have your conjugations and other grammar basics down.

17-20 points: Feel free to move on to the last unit of *Intermediate French*! You're doing great!

 **Points**

Unit 5:
Asking for Directions

In this last unit of *Intermediate French*, you will learn how to make commands, talk about events in the recent past, and say whether you *would* do something. In other words, you're going to learn more about verb forms and tenses. You will also learn vocabulary for **le transport** (*transportation*) and **l'argent** (*m.*) (*money, cash*).

By the end of this unit, you should be able to:

☐ Name different types of buildings and shops

☐ Talk about *driving*

☐ Name different types of transportation

☐ Make commands and requests

☐ Talk more about location

☐ Say *I'm going there*

☐ Say whether something is *everywhere* or *nowhere*

☐ Talk about doing something *slowly*, *happily*, or *easily*

☐ Ask for directions

☐ Tell someone where you *went* or if you *fell*

☐ Get around a train station

☐ Say what you *just* did

☐ Say what you *would* finish

☐ Say where you *would go* and who you *would be*

Lesson 17: Words

By the end of this lesson, you will be able to:

☐ Name different types of buildings and shops

☐ Talk about *driving*

☐ Name different types of transportation

☐ Make commands and requests

Word Builder 1

Let's get started with the names of **les bâtiments** (*m.*) (*buildings*).

▶ 17A Lesson 17 Word Builder 1 (CD 6, Track 9)

apartment building, office building	l'immeuble (*m.*)
museum	le musée
store	le magasin
small shops	les boutiques (*f.*)
city hall, town hall, municipal building	l'hôtel (*m.*) de ville
school	l'école (*f.*)
high school	le lycée
church	l'église (*f.*)
cathedral	la cathédrale
synagogue	la synagogue
mosque	la mosquée
bank	la banque
movie theater	le cinéma

theater	le théâtre
train station	la gare
airport	l'aéroport (m.)
library	la bibliothèque
bookstore	la librairie
supermarket	le supermarché
bakery	la boulangerie
pastry shop	la pâtisserie*
candy store	la confiserie
butcher shop	la boucherie
delicatessen (store that sells prepared meats)	la charcuterie
grocery store	l'épicerie (f.)
hardware store	la quincaillerie
beauty parlor (beauty salon)	l'institut (m.) de beauté

Ⅱ   * Remember that pâtisserie can also mean *pastry*.

Take It Further

There are many different types of stores or shops in France, so let's look at them more in detail.

Store is magasin, while un grand magasin is *a department store*. You will also find un centre commercial (*a mall*) in many cities. Une boutique is a small store specializing in gifts, clothing, or accessories.

In addition, there are smaller shops specializing in various items. For example, you would go to a boucherie (*butcher shop*) for various cuts of raw viande (*meat*) and volaille (*poultry*). On the other hand, you would go to a charcuterie (*delicatessen*) to buy prepared meats, many of which are from **porc** (*pork*). You can buy **pain** (*bread*) in a **boulangerie** (*bakery*), but also in a **pâtisserie** (*pastry shop*). Sometimes you will find a combination shop called **la pâtisserie-confiserie** (*pastry and candy store*) that sells candies, cakes, and a variety of breads.

Remember that **librairie** is a "false" similar word. As you've seen, it means *bookstore*, not *library*. *Library* is **bibliothèque**. Another "false" similar word is **l'hôtel de ville**. Some visitors to France have tried to book a room in the **hôtel de ville**, only to find that it's *city hall*, not a hotel. Instead, you can book a room at **un hôtel** (*a hotel*) or **une auberge** (*an inn*).

✎ Word Practice 1

Match the French words on the left to the English translations on the right.

1. la gare	a. *hardware store*
2. la librairie	b. *train station*
3. la boucherie	c. *bookstore*
4. la quincaillerie	d. *library*
5. l'aéroport	e. *butcher shop*
6. la bibliothèque	f. *airport*

ANSWER KEY:
1. b; 2. c; 3. e; 4. a; 5. f; 6. d

✎ Word Recall

Let's practice possessives. Choose the correct word to complete each sentence.

1. C'est _____ (my) maison.
   a. ma
   b. mon
   c. sa
   d. son

2. C'est _____ (her) livre.
   a. ma
   b. mon
   c. sa
   d. son

3. C'est _____ (their) film.
   a. notre
   b. votre
   c. leur
   d. sa

4. C'est _____ (your, infml.) amie.
   a. ta
   b. ton
   c. votre
   d. sa

ANSWER KEY:
1. a (*That's my house.*); 2. d (*That's her book.*); 3. c (*That's their movie.*); 4. b (*That's your friend.*)

Grammar Builder 1
TO DRIVE

▶ 17B Lesson 17 Grammar Builder 1 (CD 6, Track 10)

This unit is devoted to transportation and getting around town, so here is a good verb to know for that topic: **conduire** (*to drive*).

Conduire is an irregular verb, but it's not difficult to learn. Here are its forms in the present tense:

CONDUIRE (TO DRIVE) - PRESENT			
je conduis	I drive	nous conduisons	we drive
tu conduis	you drive	vous conduisez	you drive

CONDUIRE *(TO DRIVE)* - **PRESENT**			
il conduit	*he drives*	ils conduisent	*they drive*
elle conduit	*she drives*	elles conduisent	*they drive*

Verbs that are conjugated like **conduire** include **construire** (*to construct*) and **produire** (*to produce*).

Now let's look at some examples of **conduire** in use.

Remember how to combine **à** with **la, le, l', and les**? Those combinations are very useful when forming sentences with **conduire** and a location that you're driving *to*.

à + la = à la
à + le = au
à + l' = à l'
à + les = aux

Elle conduit les enfants à la bibliothèque.
She's driving the children to the library.

Nous conduisons ma fille à l'école.
We're driving my daughter to school.

The past participle of **conduire** is **conduit**.

Ils ont conduit pendant quatre heures.
They drove for four hours.

Pendant is a good word to know when talking about duration. It means *during* or *for* a period of time. You'll learn more about it in *Advanced French*.

Ⅱ

✎ Work Out 1

Complete each sentence with the correct conjugation of conduire in the present tense.

1. Pour regarder un film, on _____ les enfants au cinéma.

   (To watch a movie, we drive the children to the movie theater.)

2. Marc voudrait acheter un steak, donc je _____ Marc à la boucherie.

   (Marc would like to buy a steak, so I drive Marc to the butcher shop.)

3. Elle _____ son mari à l'aéroport. (She drives her husband to the airport.)

4. Elles voudraient du pâté, donc vous _____ les filles à la charcuterie.

   (They would like some pâté, so you drive the girls to the delicatessen.)

5. Ils _____ Sophie à l'hôtel de ville. (They drive Sophie to city hall.)

   ANSWER KEY:
   1. conduit; 2. conduis; 3. conduit; 4. conduisez; 5. conduisent

Word Builder 2

Now let's look at forms of le transport (transportation).

▶ 17C Lesson 17 Word Builder 2 (CD 6, Track 11)

car	l'automobile (f.), l'auto (f.), la voiture
bicycle	la bicyclette
bike	le vélo
motorcycle	la motocyclette, la moto
moped	le solex, le vélomoteur
truck	le camion
boat, ship	le bateau

cruise ship, ocean liner	**le paquebot**
train	**le train**
subway (metro)	**le métro**
airplane	**l'avion** (*m.*)

Take It Further

Instead of taking a form of transportation, you can always go à pied (*on foot, by foot*). Many French people, especially in the big cities, walk to various destinations or ride a bike instead of driving.

✎ Word Practice 2

Translate each sentence into French.

1. *I drive a car.* _____

2. *She drives a truck.* _____

3. *They (m.) drive a truck.* _____

4. *Do you (pl./fml.) have a bike?* _____

5. *I like his motorcycle.* _____

6. *I don't like airplanes.* _____

ANSWER KEY:

1. **Je conduis une voiture/auto/automobile.** 2. **Elle conduit un camion.** 3. **Ils conduisent un camion.** 4. **Avez-vous un vélo ?/Est-ce que vous avez un vélo ?/Vous avez un vélo ?** 5. **J'aime sa motocyclette/moto.** 6. **Je n'aime pas les avions.**

Word Recall

Now translate the following paragraph into French. If you need to go back and review, re-read Conversation 2 in Unit 4 before doing the exercise below.

I would like to make reservations to have dinner Friday evening, sir. We will be two people. We will be arriving around 8:00 in the evening. It's for the Benoît family. Thank you.

_____

_____

_____

_____

ANSWER KEY:
Je voudrais faire des réservations pour dîner vendredi soir, monsieur. Nous serons deux personnes. Nous arriverons vers huit heures du soir. C'est pour la famille Benoît. Merci.

Grammar Builder 2
GIVING COMMANDS: THE IMPERATIVE

▶ 17D Lesson 17 Grammar Builder 2 (CD 6, Track 12)

If you want to give a command or make a strong request, you use what's known as the "imperative."

For most verbs, forming the imperative is pretty simple: just use the **tu**, **nous**, or **vous** form of the verb in the present tense, but without the pronoun. For instance, **tu finis** (*you finish*) becomes **Finis !** (*Finish!*) and **vous finissez** becomes **Finissez !** (*Finish!*)

Note, however, that for the **tu** form of **-er** verbs, you also need to drop the final **s**. For example, **tu danses** (*you dance*) becomes:

Danse !
Dance!

This only applies to **-er** verbs.

Here are all of the imperative forms of **danser** and **finir**, along with **répondre**:

	DANSER (TO DANCE) - IMPERATIVE	FINIR (TO FINISH) - IMPERATIVE	RÉPONDRE (TO ANSWER) - IMPERATIVE
tu	Danse ! (*Dance!*)	Finis ! (*Finish!*)	Réponds ! (*Answer!*)
nous	Dansons ! (*Let's dance!*)	Finissons ! (*Let's finish!*)	Répondons ! (*Let's answer!*)
vous	Dansez ! (*Dance!*)	Finissez ! (*Finish!*)	Répondez ! (*Answer!*)

So, use the **tu** form of the imperative when you're commanding a friend or someone informally, use the **nous** form when you want to say *let's* do something, and use the **vous** form when you're addressing a superior or someone formally, or when you're addressing a group of people.

Of course, the exclamation point is optional; we're just using it here to emphasize that it's a command.

Here are a few more examples:

Écoute !
Listen!

Mange.
Eat.

Verbs that are irregular in the present tense, such as aller (*to go*), generally keep the same irregular forms in the imperative. For example, you say tu vas, nous allons, and vous allez in the present tense, so the imperative of aller is:

ALLER *(TO GO)* - IMPERATIVE	
tu	Va ! (*Go!*)
nous	Allons ! (*Let's go!*)
vous	Allez ! (*Go!*)

Note that, even though it's irregular, aller still counts as an -er verb, so you need to drop the final s in the tu form. In other words, tu vas (*you go*) becomes Va ! (*Go!*).

Va au lit.
Go to bed.

Unfortunately, the irregular verbs avoir and être are also irregular in the imperative.

	AVOIR *(TO HAVE)* - IMPERATIVE	ÊTRE *(TO BE)* - IMPERATIVE
tu	Aie ! (*Have!*)	Sois ! (*Be!*)
nous	Ayons ! (*Let's have!*)	Soyons ! (*Let's be!*)
vous	Ayez ! (*Have!*)	Soyez ! (*Be!*)

Soyez patients.
Be patient.

Sois sage !
Be good! (Be well-behaved!)

Ds that Use **Être** in the Past Tense   The Conditional (*I Would* ...)

- - - - - - - - - -|- - - - - - - - - - - -|- - - - - - - - - -|- - - - - - - - - -|- - - - - - - - - -

                        The Recent Past (*I Just* ...)   Irregular Conditional

Ayons (de la) patience. / Soyons patients
Let's have patience.

Note that **donc** (*then, so*) is often used with the imperative for emphasis.

Pensez donc !
Just think! (So think!)

Entrez donc !
Come on in! (So come in!)

If you want to command someone *not* to do something, just place ne before the verb and pas after it.

Ne danse pas.
Don't dance.

Ne dansez pas.
Don't dance.

Ne répondons pas !
Don't answer! (Let's not answer!)

⏸

✎ Work Out 2

Translate the following imperative sentences into English.

1. **Va au magasin.** _____

2. **Soyez sérieux !** _____

3. **Parlons français !** _____

4. **Allons au cinéma !** _____

5. **Ne regardez pas un film.** _____

ANSWER KEY:
1. *Go to the store.* 2. *Be serious!* 3. *Let's speak French!* 4. *Let's go to the movie theater/the movies!* 5. *Don't watch a movie.*

✎ Drive It Home

A. Give the correct form of the verb **conduire** in the present tense.

1. **Je** _____ **Marc à la gare.** (*I'm driving Marc to the train station.*)

2. **Tu** _____ **Marc à la gare.** (*You're driving Marc to the train station.*)

3. **Elle** _____ **Marc à la gare.** (*She's driving Marc to the train station.*)

4. **Nous** _____ **Marc à la gare.** (*We're driving Marc to the train station.*)

5. **Ils** _____ **Marc à la gare.** (*They're driving Marc to the train station.*)

B. Put the following verbs in the imperative **tu** form and then translate the phrases into English. Use exclamation points.

1. **manger** _____

2. **finir** _____

3. **vendre** _____

4. **avoir** _____

5. **être** _____

6. **aller** _____

s that Use **Être** in the Past Tense   The Conditional (*I Would* ...)

The Recent Past (*I Just ...*)   Irregular Conditional

7. prendre _____

8. choisir _____

C. Now put the following verbs in the **negative** imperative **tu** form and translate the phrases into English. Use exclamation points.

1. manger _____

2. finir _____

3. vendre _____

4. avoir _____

5. être _____

6. aller _____

7. prendre _____

8. choisir _____

ANSWER KEY:
A. 1. conduis; 2. conduis; 3. conduit; 4. conduisons; 5. conduisent
B. 1. Mange ! (*Eat!*) 2. Finis ! (*Finish!*) 3. Vends ! (*Sell!*) 4. Aie ! (*Have!*) 5. Sois ! (*Be!*) 6. Va ! (*Go!*) 7. Prends ! (*Take!/Have!*) 8. Choisis ! (*Choose!*)
C. 1. Ne mange pas ! (*Don't eat!*) 2. Ne finis pas ! (*Don't finish!*) 3. Ne vends pas ! (*Don't sell!*) 4. N'aie pas ! (*Don't have!*) 5. Ne sois pas ! (*Don't be!*) 6. Ne va pas ! (*Don't go!*) 7. Ne prends pas ! (*Don't take!/Don't have!*) 8. Ne choisis pas ! (*Don't choose!*)

🌐 Culture Note

The French **TGV** trains, or **les trains à grande vitesse** (*high-speed trains*), link many cities within France. They also link France to neighboring countries. If you want to book a trip on a **TGV** train, you will need a reservation, so make sure to plan ahead!

How Did You Do?

Let's see how you did! By now, you should be able to:

☐ Name different types of buildings and shops
(Still unsure? Jump back to page 281)

☐ Talk about *driving*
(Still unsure? Jump back to page 284)

☐ Name different types of transportation
(Still unsure? Jump back to page 286)

☐ Make commands and requests
(Still unsure? Jump back to page 288)

Lesson 18: Phrases

By the end of this lesson, you will be able to:

☐ Talk more about location

☐ Say *I'm going there*

☐ Say whether something is *everywhere* or *nowhere*

☐ Talk about doing something *slowly, happily,* or *easily*

Phrase Builder 1

When looking at the phrases below, keep in mind that **de** can mean *of, from,* or *for,* and **à** can mean *to, at,* or *in.* As a result, phrases like **à gauche** can mean *on the left, to the left,* or *at the left.* However, only one of the translations is listed below.

▶ 18A Lesson 18 Phrase Builder 1 (CD 6, Track 13)

around	autour de
at someone's house	chez (+ person's name)
on the other side of	de l'autre côté de
upstairs (up above)	en haut
downstairs (down below)	en bas
this way	par ici
that way	par là
at the end of	au bout de
on the left	à gauche
on the right	à droite
at the foot of	au pied de
through, across	à travers
at the edge of (at the border of)	au bord de
in the middle of	au milieu de
there	y

Take It Further

Chez can actually refer to anybody's place, not just a house or home. For example, **chez le médecin** means *at the doctor's.*

You can also use pronouns like **moi, toi, lui,** etc. with **chez.** You first saw those pronouns in *Essential French* and then periodically here in this course. Let's review.

me	moi
you (infml.)	toi
him	lui

her	elle
us	nous
you (pl./fml.)	vous
them (m.)	eux
them (f.)	elles

So you can say:

at my house, at home	chez moi
at your house	chez toi
at his house	chez lui
at her house	chez elle
at our house	chez nous
at your house	chez vous
at their house	chez eux
at their house	chez elles

These pronouns can follow pretty much any preposition, not just chez.

for me	pour moi
with you	avec toi
behind him	derrière lui
like us	comme nous
without them	sans eux

They can also be used in other phrases like:

you and me	toi et moi

os that Use **Être** in the Past Tense   The Conditional (*I Would* ...)

The Recent Past (*I Just* ...)   Irregular Conditional

✏ Phrase Practice 1

Match the French location phrases on the left to the correct English translations on the right.

1. **chez**	a. *around*
2. **en haut**	b. *at the end of*
3. **autour de**	c. *through*
4. **à travers**	d. *at someone's house/place*
5. **au bout de**	e. *upstairs*

ANSWER KEY:
1. d; 2. e; 3. a; 4. c; 5. b

✏ Word Recall

Now let's do a quick review of the vocabulary from earlier in the unit. Translate the following words into French. Don't forget to include **le**, **la**, or **l'** before each word.

1. *grocery store* _____

2. *hardware store* _____

3. *train station* _____

4. *high school* _____

5. *city hall* _____

6. *store* _____

Giving Commands:
The Imperative

Adverbs

7. *apartment building, office building* _____

8. *bank* _____

ANSWER KEY:
1. l'épicerie; 2. la quincaillerie; 3. la gare; 4. le lycée; 5. l'hôtel de ville; 6. le magasin; 7. l'immeuble; 8. la banque

Grammar Builder 1
Y (*THERE*)

▶ 18B Lesson 18 Grammar Builder 1 (CD 6, Track 14)

Y is a very flexible word. It is usually translated as *there*, but it can also mean any of the following:

to it	to them
in it	in them
on it	on them

Essentially, **y** is used to replace a location word or phrase. For example, **y** lets you say *I'm going there* instead of *I'm going to Paris*. In other words, **y** replaces **à Paris** (*to Paris*).

In French, **y** often replaces **à** + noun, but it can also replace **dans** (*in*) + noun, **sur** (*on*) + noun, **chez** (*at someone's house/place*) + noun, and other similar words and phrases. Furthermore, it can replace a location that was mentioned earlier on.

This can be confusing, so let's take a look at a variety of examples.

Look at the table below. On the left is a sentence that uses a location, and on the right is that same sentence with the location replaced by **y**. Keep in mind that **y** is placed *before* the verb in sentences.

Je vais à l'épicerie.	J'y vais.
I'm going to the grocery store.	*I'm going there. (lit., I'm there going.)*
Elle va à Paris au printemps.	Elle y va au printemps.
She's going to Paris in the spring.	*She's going there in the spring.*
Je vais chez mon ami.	J'y vais.
I'm going to my friend's house.	*I'm going there.*

Now here are some examples of **y** replacing a location that was already mentioned. In the answer, **y** replaces the location mentioned in the question.

QUESTION	ANSWER
Qui va au parc ?	Charles y va.
Who's going to the park?	*Charles is going there.*
Ils sont sur la chaise ?	Non, ils n'y sont pas.
Are they on the chair?	*No, they are not on it.*

Notice that, in the negative, **y** is placed in between **ne (n')** and the verb: **ils n'y sont pas.**

Y can also replace certain phrases that use prepositions even when they don't deal with location. Note that, in the imperative, **y** is placed *after* the verb.

Répondons au téléphone.	Répondons-y.
Let's answer the phone.	*Let's answer it.*
(lit., Let's respond to the phone.)	*(lit., Let's respond to it.)*

Giving Commands:
The Imperative

You've actually seen y before. Remember the following phrases?

| On y va ! | Let's go! |
| Allons-y ! | Let's go! |

Now you know that those phrases literally translate as *We go there!* and *Let's go there!*, respectively. As you can see, allons-y is an imperative phrase. Another related imperative phrase is:

Vas-y !
Go there!

Vas-y is also frequently used to mean *Go on!* or *Go ahead!*

Note the difference between Va au lit ! (*Go to bed!*) and Vas-y ! They both use the imperative tu form of aller, but one is spelled va and the other is spelled vas. This is because the final s is **not** removed from the imperative tu form of an -er verb when the verb is followed by y.

✎ Work Out 1

Rewrite the following sentences using y.

1. Allons chez moi ! (*Let's go to my house!*)

   _____

2. Elle va au restaurant. (*She goes to the restaurant.*)

   _____

3. Nous arrivons à l'aéroport. (*We arrive at the airport.*)

   _____

4. **Vous restez à l'hôtel ?** (*Are you staying at the hotel?*)

   _____

5. **Le livre n'est pas sur la table.** (*The book is not on the table.*)

   _____

ANSWER KEY:
1. Allons-y ! 2. Elle y va. 3. Nous y arrivons. 4. Vous y restez ? 5. Le livre n'y est pas.

Phrase Builder 2

Let's look at some more location phrases, both old and new.

(▶) 18C Lesson 18 Phrase Builder 2 (CD 6, Track 15)

here	ici
there	là
over there	là-bas
at the side	à côté
between (in between)	entre
behind	derrière
in front of, before	devant
on top	dessus
underneath	dessous
outside	dehors
everywhere	partout
nowhere (anywhere)	nulle part
elsewhere	ailleurs
far	loin
near (close)	près

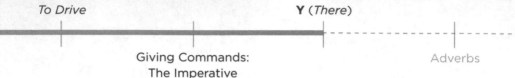
Take It Further

Remember the location phrases that you learned in Lesson 6 of Unit 2? Some of them were included in the list above, but let's review the ones that weren't mentioned.

to, at, in	à
in, into	dans
on	sur
under	sous
next to	à côté de
across from, facing	en face de

Notice some similarities between those phrases and the new phrases in Phrase Builder 2?

under	sous
underneath	dessous
next to	à côté de
at the side, on the side, to the side	à côté

Finally, note the resemblance between these two French words:

on top	dessus
underneath	dessous

As you can see, they're exact opposites in meaning, despite the similarity in spelling. This is an example of why pronunciation is so important. In French, ou is pronounced like the *oo* in *boot*. However, you pronounce u by keeping your lips rounded as you say *ee*, somewhat similar to the *ew* in *dew*.

ps that Use **Être** in the Past Tense   The Conditional (*I Would …*)

The Recent Past (*I Just …)*   Irregular Conditional

So to avoid confusion, make sure to pronounce dessus as [duh-sew] and dessous as [duh-soo]. Listen to the audio for Phrase Builder 2 a few times to hear those two words correctly pronounced by native speakers, and then repeat them out loud. This will help your mouth get used to making the sounds.

Phrase Practice 2

Choose the correct word from the word bank below to complete each sentence.

dessus	dehors
dessous	entre
nulle part	partout

1. L'école est _____ (*between*) le musée et l'hôtel de ville.

   (*The school is between the museum and city hall.*)

2. La lampe est _____ (*on top*). (*The lamp is on top.*)

3. Le journal est _____ (*underneath*). (*The newspaper is underneath.*)

4. Est-ce qu'il fait froid _____ (*outside*) ? (*Is it cold outside?*)

5. Il y a des gens _____ (*everywhere*). (*There are people everywhere.*)

6. On ne va _____ (*anywhere*). (*We're not going anywhere.*)

   ANSWER KEY:
   1. entre; 2. dessus; 3. dessous; 4. dehors; 5. partout; 6. nulle part [notice that you use ne with nulle part, in the same way as ne... jamais or ne... rien]

Giving Commands:
The Imperative

Adverbs

✎ Word Recall

Now let's review the location words and phrases that you first saw in Unit 2. Match the French words on the left to the correct English translations on the right.

1. derrière	a. *next to*
2. à côté de	b. *under*
3. en face de	c. *on*
4. sous	d. *behind*
5. sur	e. *across from*

ANSWER KEY:
1. d; 2. a; 3. e; 4. b; 5. c

Grammar Builder 2
ADVERBS

▶ 18D Lesson 18 Grammar Builder 2 (CD 6, Track 16)

An adverb is a word that describes a verb or an adjective. For example, in the phrase *I drive slowly*, the adverb *slowly* describes the verb *drive*.

Adverbs in French are usually formed by taking adjectives and adding -ment. This is very similar to English, where you add -ly to an adjective like *slow* to turn it into the adverb *slowly*.

As you know, French adjectives have different forms depending on gender and number, so how do you know which form to use? Well, that depends on how the adjective is spelled:

1. If the adjective ends in a **vowel** in the masculine singular, add -ment to the masculine singular form of the adjective to create the adverb.

ADJECTIVE IN THE MASCULINE SINGULAR	ADVERB
facile (*easy*)	facilement (*easily*)
poli (*polite*)	poliment (*politely*)
probable (*probable*)	probablement (*probably*)
vrai (*true, real*)	vraiment (*truly, really*)

2. If the adjective ends in a **consonant** in the masculine singular, add -ment to the feminine singular form of the adjective to create the adverb.

ADJECTIVE IN THE MASCULINE SINGULAR	ADVERB
lent (*slow*) (feminine singular = lente)	lentement (*slowly*)
certain (*certain*) (feminine singular = certaine)	certainement (*certainly*)
général (*general*) (feminine singular = générale)	généralement (*generally*)
seul (*alone*) (feminine singular = seule)	seulement (*only*)
actif (*active*) (feminine singular = active)	activement (*actively*)
heureux (*happy, fortunate*) (feminine singular = heureuse)	heureusement (*happily, fortunately*)

ADJECTIVE IN THE MASCULINE SINGULAR	ADVERB
malheureux *(unhappy, unfortunate)* (feminine singular = malheureuse)	malheureusement *(unhappily, unfortunately)*
léger *(light)* (feminine singular = légère)	légèrement *(lightly)*
naturel *(natural)* (feminine singular = naturelle)	naturellement *(naturally)*
doux *(sweet)* (feminine singular = douce)	doucement *(sweetly)**

* **Doux** can also mean *gentle* and *soft*, so **doucement** can mean *gently* or *softly* in addition to *sweetly*.

There are also adverbs that are irregular and don't end in **-ment**. **Bien** (*well*), for example, is the adverb form of the adjective **bon** (*good*). **Mal** (*badly*) is the adverb form of **mauvais** (*bad*). Unfortunately, when it comes to irregular adverbs, you just have to memorize them.

Now let's look at adverbs in context.

In the present tense, French adverbs are usually placed after the verb they're describing.

Elle boit lentement son café.
She drinks her coffee slowly. (lit., She drinks slowly her coffee.)

If the verb is negative, then the adverb follows the negative:
Elle ne boit pas lentement son café. (*She doesn't drink her coffee slowly.*)

Note that you can also place the adverb all the way at the end of the sentence:
Elle boit son café lentement. (or **Elle ne boit pas son café lentement.**)

In the past tense, most adverbs follow the past participle.

Elle a bu lentement son café. (or **Elle a bu son café lentement.**)
She slowly drank her coffee.

But certain common adverbs like **bien** (*well*) and **mal** (*badly*) come before the past participle, rather than after it.

Marc a bien travaillé.
Marc worked well.

Other adverbs that come before the past participle include **toujours** (*always, still*), **beaucoup** (*many, a lot, much*), **déjà** (*already*), **vite** (*quickly*), and **encore** (*again*).

Ils n'ont pas beaucoup voyagé.
They haven't traveled much. (They haven't traveled a lot.)

✏ Work Out 2
Fill in the blanks with the French translation of the adverb in parentheses.

1. **Elles dansent** _____ (*well*). (*They dance well.*)

2. **La voiture va** _____ (*quickly*) **dans la rue.** (*The car goes quickly in the street.*)

3. **Parlez** _____ (*slowly*), **s'il vous plaît.** (*Speak slowly, please.*)

4. **J'ai appris** _____ (*easily*) **la chanson.** (*I easily learned the song.*)

ANSWER KEY:
1. **bien**; 2. **vite**; 3. **lentement**; 4. **facilement**

✎ Drive It Home

A. Complete the following sentences with **y**. Don't forget to read each sentence out loud once you're done.

1. **Elle** _____ **travaille.** (*She works there.*)

2. **Nous** _____ **jouons.** (*We play there.*)

3. **Vas-**_____ **!** (*Go ahead!*)

4. **Est-ce qu'ils** _____ **sont ?** (*Are they there?*)

5. **Tu n'**_____ **habites pas.** (*You don't live there.*)

B. Rewrite the following adjectives as adverbs.

1. **actif** (*active*) _____

2. **doux** (*sweet, gentle, soft*) _____

3. **heureux** (*happy, fortunate*) _____

4. **certain** (*certain*) _____

5. **seul** (*alone*) _____

6. **naturel** (*natural*) _____

ANSWER KEY:
A. all y
B. 1. activement; 2. doucement; 3. heureusement; 4. certainement; 5. seulement; 6. naturellement

How Did You Do?

Let's see how you did! By now, you should be able to:

☐ Talk more about location
(Still unsure? Jump back to page 294)

☐ Say *I'm going there*
(Still unsure? Jump back to page 298)

☐ Say whether something is *everywhere* or *nowhere*
(Still unsure? Jump back to page 301)

☐ Talk about doing something *slowly*, *happily*, or *easily*
(Still unsure? Jump back to page 304)

Lesson 19: Sentences

By the end of this lesson, you will be able to:

☐ Ask for directions

☐ Tell someone where you *went* or if you *fell*

☐ Get around a train station

☐ Say what you *just* did

Sentence Builder 1

▶ 19A Lesson 19 Sentence Builder 1 (CD 6, Track 17)

Can you help me, please?	**Pouvez-vous m'aider, s'il vous plaît ?**
I am lost.	**Je suis perdu/perdue.**
Do you have a map of the city?	**Avez-vous un plan de la ville ?**
Where is the Louvre (Museum)?	**Où se trouve le musée du Louvre ?**
Where is the subway station?	**Où se trouve la station de métro ?**
Where is the nearest (closest) subway station?	**Où est la station de métro la plus proche ?**
Where is the bus stop?	**Où se trouve l'arrêt d'autobus ?** **(Où se trouve l'arrêt de bus) ?**

| Giving Commands: The Imperative | Adverbs |

Where is the police station?	Où se trouve le poste de police ?
Where is the post office?	Où est le bureau de poste ? (Où est la poste ?)
Do I cross the bridge?	Je traverse le pont ?
It's how many kilometers from here? (lit., It's at how many kilometers from here?)	C'est à combien de kilomètres d'ici ?
Is it far from here?	C'est loin d'ici ?
Is there a lot of traffic?	Il y a beaucoup de circulation ?
You must go straight ahead.	Il faut aller tout droit.

Take It Further

Note that in France and other European countries, distance is measured in kilometers and meters, not in miles and feet. A meter is a bit longer than a yard—about 1.09 yards actually. A kilometer is shorter than a mile—about 0.62 miles.

Now let's take a look at some of the new words you saw in Sentence Builder 1, along with a few related words and phrases:

traffic	la circulation
police station	le poste de police
post office	le bureau de poste, la poste
map, plan	le plan
map, menu, card	la carte
map of the city	le plan de la ville
map of the subway	le plan du métro
the nearest, the closest	le/la plus proche

Le bureau de poste and **la poste** are essentially interchangeable, but **le bureau de poste** sounds a little more formal.

Let's also take a closer look at the sentence:

Il faut aller tout droit.
You must go straight ahead.

As you know, **il faut** means *it's necessary to, you have to, you need to,* or *you must.* It is usually followed by an infinitive or a noun.

Il faut tourner à gauche.
You need to turn left.

Il faut boire de l'eau.
It's necessary to drink water.

Il faut de la chance !
You need luck!/You have to (have) luck!

Note that **il faut** is the present tense conjugation of the irregular verb **falloir** (*to be necessary*). **Falloir** actually **only** has an **il** form; there are no **je**, **tu**, etc. forms.

✎ Sentence Practice 1

Using **Où se trouve... ?** (*Where is ... ?*), ask where the following places are in French.

1. *the post office* _____

2. *the bus stop* _____

3. *the subway station* _____

4. *the museum* _____

5. *the police station* _____

✎ Word Recall

Rewrite the sentences below in the past tense. Remember that **traverse** comes from the verb **traverser** (*to cross*).

1. **Vous avez un plan de la ville.** (*You have a map of the city.*) _____

   _____

2. **Je suis perdu.** (*I'm lost.*) _____

3. **Il traverse le pont.** (*He's crossing the bridge.*)

   _____

4. **Je veux trouver le pont.** (*I want to find the bridge.*)

   _____

5. **Elles prennent le train.** (*They're taking the train.*)

   _____

Grammar Builder 1
VERBS THAT USE ÊTRE IN THE PAST TENSE

▶ 19B Lesson 19 Grammar Builder 1 (CD 6, Track 18)

You've already learned about verbs that use **avoir** to form the past tense: **j'ai dansé** (*I danced*), **nous avons fini** (*we finished*), **tu as bu** (*you drank*), etc. In fact, most verbs use **avoir** to form the past tense.

However, there is a select group of verbs that uses **être** (*to be*) to form the past tense, instead of **avoir**. In other words, these verbs form the past tense in the following way:

present tense of **être** + the past participle of the verb

The past participles of verbs that use **être** are formed in the same way as the past participles of verbs that use **avoir** (see Lesson 13 in Unit 4 to review), with one key exception:

The past participles of verbs that use **être** *must agree in gender and number* with the subject of the sentence.

What does that mean?

Well, for example, let's take a look at the verb **aller** (*to go*). **Aller** uses **être** in the past tense. Remember that to form the past participle of an -**er** verb, cut off the -**er** and add **é**. So the past participle of **aller** is **allé**. Here is the full conjugation of **aller** in the past tense:

ALLER *(TO GO)* - PAST			
je suis allé(e)	*I went*	nous sommes allé(e)s	*we went*
tu es allé(e)	*you went*	vous êtes allé(e)(s)	*you went*
il est allé	*he went*	ils sont allés	*they went*
elle est allée	*she went*	elles sont allées	*they went*

Notice that you say **il est allé** (*he went*) but **elle est allée** (*she went*). Since the past participle of a verb that uses **être** must agree in gender and number with the subject, an **e** must be added to **allé** in **elle est allée** because **elle** is feminine.

In other words, an **e** is added to the past participle to create the feminine form. Since **je, tu, nous,** and **vous** can refer to men or women, they can have either a masculine (no added **e**) or a feminine (an added **e**) form. For example, *I went* would be **je suis allé** if *I* am a man, and **je suis allée** if *I* am a woman. **Il** and **ils** can only be masculine (mixed company is always masculine in gender), so they only have a masculine form, and **elle** and **elles** can only be feminine, so they only have a feminine form.

Speaking of **elles**, you say **elles sont allées** because you're talking about more than one woman. You add an **e** for the feminine form, but also an **s** for the plural form. **Nous, ils,** and **elles** always refer to groups, so their past participles always end in **s**.

Since **vous** can refer to either a group of people or the formal *you* singular, it has both a plural and non-plural form. For example, if you're talking to your female boss, you'd say **vous êtes allée**, but if you were talking to a group of female friends, you'd say **vous êtes allées**. Here is another example using the verb **arriver** (*to arrive*):

...bs that Use **Être** in the Past Tense   The Conditional (*I Would* ...)

The Recent Past (*I Just* ...)   Irregular Conditional

Quand êtes-vous arrivée, Marie ?
When did you arrive, Marie?

Quand êtes-vous arrivés, messieurs ?
When did you arrive, gentlemen?

Of course, the question now is: how do you know when to use **être** instead of **avoir**?

Verbs that use **être** express a ***change of place or state of being***. For example, here are some common verbs that use **être**. Notice that many of these verbs are opposites of each other.

COMMON VERBS THAT USE ÊTRE IN THE PAST TENSE			
aller	*to go*	**venir**	*to come*
monter	*to go up*	**descendre**	*to go down (to come down)*
arriver	*to arrive*	**partir**	*to leave*
sortir	*to go out (to leave)*	**entrer**	*to enter*
naître	*to be born*	**mourir**	*to die*
rester	*to stay*	**retourner**	*to return*
revenir	*to come back (to return)*	**rentrer**	*to come home (to go home)*
devenir	*to become*	**tomber**	*to fall*

Hopefully, those examples helped give you a sense of which verbs use **être**. If not, sometimes the best method is to start by just memorizing them. The verbs above are some of the most common verbs that use **être** and are a very good place to start.

(Remember that, funnily enough, **être** itself uses **avoir** to form the past tense: **j'ai été** - *I was*.)

Here are the past participles (in the masculine singular form) of the verbs listed above. Some of them are irregular:

VERB	PAST PARTICIPLE	VERB	PAST PARTICIPLE
aller	allé	venir	venu
monter	monté	descendre	descendu
arriver	arrivé	partir	parti
sortir	sorti	entrer	entré
naître	né	mourir	mort
rester	resté	retourner	retourné
revenir	revenu	rentrer	rentré
devenir	devenu	tomber	tombé

Je suis allé/allée au cinéma.
I went to the movies. (m./f.)

Ils sont arrivés à l'hôtel.
They arrived at the hotel.

Le petit garçon est tombé.
The little boy fell.

Inversion questions and the negative are formed in the same way as verbs that use avoir. For instance, you could ask: Êtes-vous allé en France ? (*Did you go to France?*) And he could respond: Je ne suis pas allé en France. (*I didn't go to France.*)

✎ Work Out 1

Fill in the blanks with the past tense of the verbs in parentheses.

1. Christine, vous _____ (rester) une heure au musée.

   (*Christine, you stayed [for] an hour at the museum.*)

2. Ils _____ (aller) en Suisse. (*They went to Switzerland.*)

3. Hélène et Christine _____ (arriver) au théâtre.

   (*Hélène and Christine arrived at the theater.*)

4. Elle _____ (attendre) dans le magasin.

   (*She waited in the store.*)

5. Est-ce qu'il _____ (partir) ? (*Did he leave?*)

6. Nous _____ (prendre) le train. (*We took the train.*)

7. Les garçons ne _____ pas _____

   (tomber). (*The boys didn't fall.*)

   ANSWER KEY:
   1. êtes restée; 2. sont allés; 3. sont arrivées; 4. a attendu; 5. est parti; 6. avons pris; 7. sont, tombés

Sentence Builder 2

You usually need l'argent (*m.*) (*money, cash*) in order to get around town. Let's look at some phrases that will help you in those situations, and other polite expressions for getting around une gare (*a train station*).

▶ 19C Lesson 19 Sentence Builder 2 (CD 6, Track 19)

I would like to buy ...	Je voudrais acheter...
How much does that cost, please?	Combien ça coûte, s'il vous plaît ?

That's how much, please?	C'est combien, s'il vous plaît ?
I'd like to change dollars to euros.	Je voudrais changer des dollars en euros.
Do you have change?	Avez-vous de la monnaie ?
What do you want?	Que voulez-vous ?
Where can I get (take) the train for Paris? (Where can I get the train to Paris?)	Où puis-je prendre le train pour Paris ?
You must go to the ticket window.	Il faut aller au guichet.
I would like a round-trip ticket.	Je voudrais un billet aller-retour.
Here is my passport.	Voici mon passeport.
On which track is the train?	Sur quelle voie est le train ?
On what (which) platform should we wait?	Sur quel quai doit-on attendre ?
Where do I have to get off? (lit., Where should I go down?)	Où dois-je descendre ?
What is the departure time?	Quelle est l'heure du départ ?

Take It Further

You learned a lot of useful words and phrases in those sentences. Let's break them down, and add a few more:

that costs	ça coûte
to cost	coûter
to change, to exchange	changer
change, coins, currency	la monnaie

ticket window, counter, window, box office	**le guichet**
clerk (at the window/counter), teller	**le guichetier**
ticket, banknote, bill (currency)	**le billet**
check	**le chèque**
traveler's check	**le chèque de voyage**
round-trip	**aller-retour** (*m.*)
one-way	**aller simple** (*m.*)
track, lane	**la voie**
platform, quay, bank (of a river)	**le quai**
departure time	**l'heure** (*f.*) **du départ**
arrival time	**l'heure** (*f.*) **de l'arrivée**
passport	**le passeport**

You also saw the word **que** used to form a question. Sometimes **que** is used instead of **qu'est-ce que** as the question word *what*. If you do use **que** instead of **qu'est-ce que**, however, you need to use inversion:

Que voulez-vous ?
What do you want?

Qu'est-ce que vous voulez ?
What do you want?

Que sais-je ?
What do I know?

Qu'est-ce que je sais ?
What do I know?

✎ Sentence Practice 2

Match the French questions on the left to the correct English translations on the right.

1. Combien ça coûte ?	a. *Where should I get off?/ Where do I have to get off?*
2. Avez-vous de la monnaie ?	b. *How much does that cost?*
3. Où dois-je descendre ?	c. *What is the departure time?*
4. Quelle est l'heure du départ ?	d. *What do you want?*
5. Que voulez-vous ?	e. *Do you have change?*

ANSWER KEY:
1. b; 2. e; 3. a; 4. c; 5. d

✎ Word Recall

Rewrite the following sentences in the near future (*going to ...*).

1. **Je vais au guichet.** (*I'm going to the ticket window.*)

   _____

2. **Elle change des dollars en euros.** (*She's changing some dollars to euros.*)

   _____

3. **Vous prenez le train pour Paris.** (*You're taking the train to Paris.*)

   _____

4. **Ils attendent sur le quai.** (*They're waiting on the platform.*)

   _____

Grammar Builder 2
THE RECENT PAST (*I JUST ...*)

▶ 19D Lesson 19 Grammar Builder 2 (CD 6, Track 20)

Let's review the irregular verb **venir** (*to come*). Here are all of its forms:

VENIR *(TO COME)* - PRESENT			
je viens	*I come*	nous venons	*we come*
tu viens	*you come*	vous venez	*you come*
il vient	*he comes*	ils viennent	*they come*
elle vient	*she comes*	elles viennent	*they come*

D'où viens-tu ?/D'où venez-vous ?
Where do you come from? (lit., From where do you come?)

Je viens des États-Unis.
I come from the United States.

Tu viens avec nous ?
Are you coming with us? (You're coming with us?)

Il vient à dix heures dix.
He's coming at 10:10.

Remember that **venir** uses être in the past tense and that its past participle is **venu: Tu es venu(e) avec nous.** (*You came with us.*)

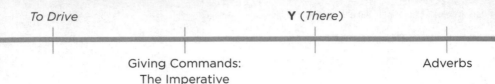
The verb venir can also be used to talk about the recent past (*I've just seen, I just left,* etc.). Simply use:

present tense of venir + de (d') + infinitive

For example, if you wanted to put the verb voir (*to see*) in the recent past, you would say: je viens de voir (*I just saw, I've just seen*).

Je viens de voir ce film.
I've just seen this movie. (I just saw this movie.)

Here is another example of a verb in the recent past:

Elle vient de sortir.
She's just left. (She just left.)

And that's all you need to know to form the recent past!

✎ Work Out 2

Fill in the blanks by placing the verb in parentheses in the recent past.

1. Nous _____ (arriver) à Washington.

   (*We've just arrived in Washington.*)

2. Robert _____ (acheter) un billet. (*Robert just bought a ticket.*)

3. Elles _____ (prendre) le train. (*They've just taken the train.*)

4. Je _____ (changer) des dollars en euros.

   (*I just changed some dollars to euros.*)

5. Le train _____ (partir). *(The train just left.)*

ANSWER KEY:
1. venons d'arriver; 2. vient d'acheter; 3. viennent de prendre; 4. viens de changer; 5. vient de partir

✎ Drive It Home

A. Rewrite each sentence in the past tense.

1. Je descends du train. *(I [m.] get off the train.)*

_____

2. Vous descendez du train. *(You [f. pl.] get off the train.)*

_____

3. Elle descend du train. *(She gets off the train.)*

_____

4. Ils descendent du train. *(They get off the train.)*

_____

5. Tu descends du train. *(You [f.] get off the train.)*

_____

6. Elles descendent du train. *(They get off the train.)*

_____

7. Nous descendons du train. *(We [m.] get off the train.)*

_____

8. Il descend du train. *(He gets off the train.)*

_____

B. Complete each sentence with the recent past.

1. **La prof** _____ (arriver). *(The teacher just arrived.)*

2. **L'avion** _____ (arriver). *(The plane just arrived.)*

3. **Marc et Paul** _____ (arriver). *(Marc and Paul just arrived.)*

4. **Sophie et Marie** _____ (arriver).

   (Sophie and Marie just arrived.)

5. **Je** _____ (arriver). *(I just arrived.)*

6. **Pierre et moi, nous** _____ (arriver).

   (Pierre and me, we just arrived.)

7. **Vous** _____ (arriver). *(You just arrived.)*

8. **Tu** _____ (arriver). *(You just arrived.)*

ANSWER KEY:

A. 1. Je suis descendu du train. 2. Vous êtes descendues du train. 3. Elle est descendue du train. 4. Ils sont descendus du train. 5. Tu es descendue du train. 6. Elles sont descendues du train. 7. Nous sommes descendus du train. 8. Il est descendu du train.

B. 1. vient d'arriver; 2. vient d'arriver; 3. viennent d'arriver; 4. viennent d'arriver; 5. viens d'arriver; 6. venons d'arriver; 7. venez d'arriver; 8. viens d'arriver

 Tip

It can be difficult to remember which common verbs use **être**. There are some acronyms that can help. One popular example is "Dr. and Mrs. Vandertramp."

D	devenir *(to become)*
R	revenir *(to come back, to return)*
M	monter *(to go up)*
R	rester *(to stay)*
S	sortir *(to go out, to leave)*

V	**venir** (*to come*)
A	**aller** (*to go*)
N	**naître** (*to be born*)
D	**descendre** (*to go down*)
E	**entrer** (*to enter*)
R	**rentrer** (*to come home, to go home*)
T	**tomber** (*to fall*)
R	**retourner** (*to return*)
A	**arriver** (*to arrive*)
M	**mourir** (*to die*)
P	**partir** (*to leave*)

How Did You Do?

Let's see how you did! By now, you should be able to:

☐ Ask for directions
(Still unsure? Jump back to page 309)

☐ Tell someone where you *went* or if you *fell*
(Still unsure? Jump back to page 313)

☐ Get around a train station
(Still unsure? Jump back to page 317)

☐ Say what you *just* did
(Still unsure? Jump back to page 321)

Lesson 20: Conversations

By the end of this lesson, you will be able to:

☐ Say what you *would* finish

☐ Say where you *would go* and who you *would be*

Conversation 1

This is the final lesson of *Intermediate French*, which means that you're almost done with the course! Congratulations!

In this dialogue, Jacques is in Paris for the first time and wants to go to the musée d'Orsay (*Orsay Museum*). He asks for directions.

▶ 20A Lesson 20 Conversation 1 (CD 6, Track 21)

Jacques :	Excusez-moi, monsieur. Pouvez-vous m'aider ?
Gendarme :	Ah, vous êtes perdu, n'est-ce pas ?
Jacques :	Je cherche le chemin pour aller au musée d'Orsay, s'il vous plaît.
Gendarme :	Eh bien, monsieur, vous n'êtes pas sur le bon chemin.
Jacques :	Il faut prendre quel chemin ?
Gendarme :	Il faut aller le long des quais, et puis vous prenez la première rue et vous tournez à gauche.
Jacques :	Est-ce que c'est loin d'ici, monsieur ?
Gendarme :	Non, pas du tout. C'est juste à un kilomètre d'ici.
Jacques :	Donc, je vais marcher le long des quais.
Gendarme :	C'est ça, et quand vous tournez à gauche, il faut continuer tout droit. Le musée d'Orsay sera juste devant vous.
Jacques :	Merci bien, monsieur !
Gendarme :	Je vous en prie. Passez une bonne journée !

Jacques:	Excuse me, sir. Can you help me?
Gendarme:	Ah, you're lost, right?
Jacques:	I'm looking for the way to go to the Orsay Museum, please.
Gendarme:	Well, sir, you are not on the correct path (lit., good path).
Jacques:	Which path do I need to take?
Gendarme:	You need to go along the quays, and then you take the first street and you turn left.
Jacques:	Is that far from here, sir?
Gendarme:	No, not at all. It's just one kilometer from here.
Jacques:	So, I'm going to walk along the quays.
Gendarme:	That's it, and when you turn left, you need to continue straight ahead. The Orsay Museum will be just in front of you.
Jacques:	Thank you very much, sir!
Gendarme:	You're welcome. Have a great day! (lit., Spend a good day!)

Take It Further

Note that les gendarmes are French guards who are sort of a cross between the National Guard in the U.S. and the state police. They're part of the military, and protect areas such as airports and coasts, but they also serve basic police functions in small towns, rural areas, or places along the border. A policier/policière is simply a *police officer*, mainly found in cities and large towns.

In the dialogue, you also saw a very useful word for asking directions:

path, way	le chemin

Je viens de demander le chemin.
I just asked for directions. (lit., I just asked the way.)

Quel chemin pour aller à Montmartre ?
Which way to go to Montmartre?

And you saw the following new vocabulary as well:

along, alongside	le long de
not at all	pas du tout
just, only	juste

✎ Conversation Practice 1

Fill in the blanks with the correct words for *straight ahead*, *left*, or *right* in French.

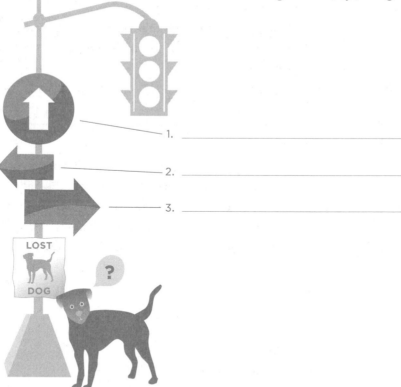

1. _____

2. _____

3. _____

ANSWER KEY:
1. **tout droit**; 2. **gauche**; 3. **droite**

Intermediate French

s that Use **Être** in the Past Tense   The Conditional (*I Would ...*)

The Recent Past (*I Just ...)*   Irregular Conditional

 ## Word Recall

Rewrite the following sentences in the future tense.

1. **Jacques est perdu.** (*Jacques is lost.*) _____

2. **Jacques n'est pas sur le bon chemin.** (*Jacques is not on the correct path.*)

   _____

3. **Jacques va le long des quais.** (*Jacques goes along the quays.*)

   _____

4. **Jacques prend la première rue.** (*Jacques takes the first street.*)

   _____

ANSWER KEY:
1. Jacques sera perdu. 2. Jacques ne sera pas sur le bon chemin. 3. Jacques ira le long des quais.
4. Jacques prendra la première rue.

Grammar Builder 1
THE CONDITIONAL (*I WOULD ...*)

 20B Lesson 20 Grammar Builder 1 (CD 6, Track 22)

Okay, so you already know how to form the past, the recent past, the present, the near future, and the future. Now let's talk about the conditional.

You've actually already learned the conditional of the verb **vouloir** (*to want, to wish*): **je voudrais** (*I would like*), **tu voudrais** (*you would like*), etc.

As you can see, the conditional corresponds to the English *would*: *would like, would dance, would finish, would sell,* etc. It expresses a possibility, a wish, or a necessity when the outcome might not occur. It is also used in polite expressions, as you know from **je voudrais.**

The conditional is very similar to the future in the way it is formed. In fact, the only difference between the future and the conditional is the verb endings. Here is how you form the conditional:

1. For -er and -ir verbs, add the following endings onto the infinitive form of the verb.

2. For -re verbs, drop the final e from the infinitive form and then add the following endings.

Here are the conditional endings:

PRONOUN	ENDING	PRONOUN	ENDING
je	-ais	nous	-ions
tu	-ais	vous	-iez
il	-ait	ils	-aient
elle	-ait	elles	-aient

Let's take a look at examples of each verb group in the conditional:

DANSER (TO DANCE) - CONDITIONAL	FINIR (TO FINISH) - CONDITIONAL	VENDRE (TO SELL) - CONDITIONAL
je danserais (I would dance)	je finirais (I would finish)	je vendrais (I would sell)
tu danserais	tu finirais	tu vendrais
il danserait	il finirait	il vendrait
elle danserait	elle finirait	elle vendrait
nous danserions	nous finirions	nous vendrions
vous danseriez	vous finiriez	vous vendriez
ils danseraient	ils finiraient	ils vendraient
elles danseraient	elles finiraient	elles vendraient

(Note that vouloir is irregular in the conditional; we'll look at verbs that are irregular in the conditional in Grammar Builder 2.)

Here are some examples of the conditional in sentences. Note that gagner means *to win, to earn,* or *to make (money).*

Nous vendrions la maison pour gagner beaucoup d'argent.
We would sell the house to get (lit., make) a lot of money.

Avec patience, tu apprendrais l'anglais.
With patience, you would learn English.

✎ Work Out 1

Translate the following sentences into English.

1. Tu finirais le film. _____

2. Elle vendrait la voiture. _____

3. Vous parleriez français. _____

4. Ils dîneraient dans un restaurant français. _____

_____

ANSWER KEY:
1. *You would finish the movie/film.* 2. *She would sell the car.* 3. *You would speak French.* 4. *They would dine/have dinner in a French restaurant.*

Conversation 2

Danielle, who is from the United States, would like to go shopping with her friend Martin. However, she first needs to exchange her dollars for euros. She asks Martin what to do.

20C Lesson 20 Conversation 2 (CD 6, Track 23)

Danielle :	D'abord, il faut changer mes dollars en euros. Qu'est-ce qu'il faut faire ?
Martin :	Pour changer de l'argent, il faut aller à la banque. Tu veux changer des chèques de voyage ?
Danielle :	Oui. J'ai des chèques et aussi de l'argent.
Martin :	C'est facile. Il faut aller à la banque du quartier. Va au guichet. Montre ton passeport au guichetier.
Danielle :	Tu peux venir avec moi ?
Martin :	Bien sûr. On y va tout de suite.

Danielle:	First, it is necessary to change my dollars into euros. What do I need to do? (lit., What is it necessary to do?)
Martin:	To change money, you need to go to the bank. Do you want to change traveler's checks?
Danielle:	Yes. I have checks and also cash.
Martin:	That's easy. You need to go to the neighborhood bank. Go to the counter. Show your passport to the teller.
Danielle:	Can you come with me?
Martin:	Of course. Let's go (there) right away.

Take It Further

Le quartier means *neighborhood, quarter,* or *area.* A famous example of this word is le Quartier Latin, or *Latin Quarter,* in Paris. La Sorbonne, a well-known college campus belonging to the University of Paris, is in the Quartier Latin.

Also, d'abord is a good word to know in conversation. It means *first.*

D'abord, nous sommes allés au cinéma. Ensuite...
First, we went to the movies. Next ...

✎ Conversation Practice 2

D'abord, re-read Conversation 2. **Ensuite,** complete the following sentences based on the dialogue.

1. **Danielle veut changer ses** _____ .

   (*Danielle wants to change her dollars into euros.*)

2. **Pour changer de l'** _____, **Danielle doit aller à la** _____ .

   (*To change money, Danielle must go to the bank.*)

3. **Danielle a des** _____ . (*Danielle has checks.*)

4. **Danielle doit montrer son** _____ **au** _____ .

   (*Danielle must show her passport to the teller.*)

ANSWER KEY:
1. dollars en euros; 2. argent, banque; 3. chèques; 4. passeport, guichetier

✎ Word Recall

Remember quantity expressions? Let's review. Choose a phrase from the word bank below to best complete each sentence.

une carafe de/d'	une tranche de/d'
une livre de/d'	une douzaine de/d'

1. **Vous voudriez** _____ **œufs.** (*You would like a dozen eggs.*)

2. **Je voudrais** _____ **pain.** (*I would like a slice of bread.*)

3. **Nous voudrions** _____ **eau.** (*We would like a pitcher of water.*)

4. **Elle voudrait** _____ **bœuf.** (*She would like a pound of beef.*)

ANSWER KEY:
1. une douzaine d'; 2. une tranche de; 3. une carafe d'; 4. une livre de

Grammar Builder 2
IRREGULAR CONDITIONAL

20D Lesson 20 Grammar Builder 2 (CD 6, Track 24)

Verbs that are irregular in the future tense are also irregular in the conditional, and they have the same irregular "stem" in both tenses. So once again, the only difference between the future and the conditional is the verb endings.

Let's review the stems. Just add the conditional endings onto the following stems to form the conditional:

VERB	CONDITIONAL STEM	
vouloir	voudr-	would like
aller	ir-	would go
avoir	aur-	would have
être	ser-	would be
faire	fer-	would do, would make
pouvoir	pourr-	could
devoir	devr-	should

Of course, you haven't seen pouvoir or vouloir in the future tense, but now that you know their conditional stems, you also know their future stems.

Notice that devoir means *should* in both the present tense and the conditional. What's the difference? The conditional of devoir is simply a more polite, less demanding way of saying it.

Tu devrais voir ce film.
You should see this movie.

Pourriez-vous nous aider ?

Could you help us?

Nous voudrions parler français.

We would like to speak French.

Voudriez-vous aller au cinéma ?

Would you like to go to the movie theater?

Ⅱ

✎ Work Out 2

Translate the following sentences into English.

1. Vous devriez aller. _____

2. Qu'est-ce que tu ferais ? _____

3. Il aurait beaucoup d'amis. _____

4. Elle serait heureuse. _____

5. J'irais à la gare. _____

ANSWER KEY:
1. *You should go.* 2. *What would you do?/What would you make?* 3. *He would have a lot of friends.* 4. *She would be happy.* 5. *I would go to the train station.*

✎ Drive It Home

A. Complete the following sentences by putting répondre in the conditional.

1. Je _____ au téléphone. (*I would answer the phone.*)

2. Tu _____ au téléphone. (*You would answer the phone.*)

3. Nous _____ au téléphone. *(We would answer the phone.)*

4. Ils _____ au téléphone. *(They would answer the phone.)*

5. Elle _____ au téléphone. *(She would answer the phone.)*

6. Vous _____ au téléphone. *(You would answer the phone.)*

7. Il _____ au téléphone. *(He would answer the phone.)*

8. Elles _____ au téléphone. *(They would answer the phone.)*

B. Now complete the following sentences by putting être in the conditional.

1. Ils _____ tristes. *(They would be sad.)*

2. Vous _____ triste. *(You would be sad.)*

3. Elle _____ triste. *(She would be sad.)*

4. Tu _____ triste. *(You would be sad.)*

5. Nous _____ tristes. *(We would be sad.)*

6. Elles _____ tristes. *(They would be sad.)*

7. Il _____ triste. *(He would be sad.)*

8. Je _____ triste. *(I would be sad.)*

ANSWER KEY:
A. 1. répondrais; 2. répondrais; 3. répondrions; 4. répondraient; 5. répondrait; 6. répondriez; 7. répondrait; 8. répondraient
B. 1. seraient; 2. seriez; 3. serait; 4. serais; 5. serions; 6. seraient; 7. serait; 8. serais

🌐 Culture Note

When you're trying to get around a foreign city, one of the first things (if not *the* first thing) you need to do is get the country's currency at **la banque** (*bank*) or **le guichet automatique/le distributeur de billets** (*ATM*). You might also find **un bureau de change** (*a currency exchange office*) at the airport, train station, or sometimes in town.

Note that the currency in France is the **euro**. There are eight **pièces** (*coins*) in the currency. There are coins worth 1, 2, 5, 10, 20, and 50 **cents** (*cents*), and there are also one- and two-euro coins. One hundred **cents** equals one **euro**. **Les billets** (*banknotes, bills*) come in denominations of 5, 10, 20, 50, 100, 200, and 500 **euros**.

How Did You Do?

Let's see how you did! By now, you should be able to:

☐ Say what you *would* finish
(Still unsure? Jump back to page 329)

☐ Say where you *would go* and who you *would be*
(Still unsure? Jump back to page 334)

Unit 5 Essentials

Don't forget to go to *www.livinglanguage.com/languagelab* to access your free online tools for this lesson: audiovisual flashcards and interactive games and quizzes.

Vocabulary Essentials

BUILDINGS

building		theater	
apartment building, office building		train station	
museum		airport	
store		library	
small shop		bookstore	
city hall, town hall, municipal building		supermarket	
school		bakery	
high school		pastry shop	
church		candy store	
cathedral		butcher shop	
synagogue		delicatessen (store that sells prepared meats)	
mosque		grocery store	

Intermediate French

bank		hardware store	
movie theater		beauty parlor, beauty salon	

[Pg. 281] (If you're stuck, visit this page to review!)

TRANSPORTATION

transportation		truck	
car		boat, ship	
bicycle		train	
bike		subway	
motorcycle		airplane	

[Pg. 286]

LOCATION

around		at the end of	
at someone's house or place		on the left	
upstairs, up above		on the right	
downstairs, down below		through, across	
this way		in the middle of	
that way			

[Pg. 295]

MORE ON LOCATION

here		underneath	
there		outside	
over there		everywhere	
between		nowhere, anywhere	
behind		far	
in front of, before		near, close	
on top			

[Pg. 301]

ASKING DIRECTIONS

Can you help me, please?	
I am lost.	
Do you have a map of the city?	
Where is the subway station?	
Where is the nearest/closest subway station?	
Where is the bus stop?	
Where is the police station?	
Is it far from here?	

[Pg. 309]

MONEY

money, cash	
I would like to buy ...	
How much does that cost, please?	
That's how much, please?	
I'd like to change dollars to euros.	
Do you have change?	

[Pg. 317]

AT THE TRAIN STATION

Where can I get the train for Paris?	
You must go to the ticket window.	
I would like a round-trip ticket.	
Here is my passport.	
On which track is the train?	
On what/which platform should we wait?	
Where do I have to get off?/ Where should I get off?	
What is the departure time?	

[Pg. 318]

ADVERBS

easily		sweetly, softly, gently	
probably		well	
truly, really		badly	
slowly		always, still	
only		many, a lot of, much	
fortunately, happily		already	
unfortunately, unhappily		quickly	
naturally		again	

[Pg. 305]

Grammar Essentials

THE IMPERATIVE

1. To form the imperative, just use the **tu**, **nous**, or **vous** form of the verb in the present tense, but without the pronoun.

2. For the **tu** form of **-er** verbs, you also need to drop the final **s**.

3. To form the negative imperative (to command someone *not* to do something), place **ne** before the verb and **pas** after it.

ALLER *(TO GO)* - IMPERATIVE	
Go! (infml.)	Va !
Let's go!	Allons !
Go! (pl./fml.)	Allez !

AVOIR *(TO HAVE)* - **IMPERATIVE**	
Have! (infml.)	Aie !
Let's have!	Ayons !
Have! (pl./fml.)	Ayez !

ÊTRE *(TO BE)* - **IMPERATIVE**	
Be! (infml.)	Sois !
Let's be!	Soyons !
Be! (pl./fml.)	Soyez !

FINIR *(TO FINISH)* - **IMPERATIVE**	
Finish! (infml.)	Finis !
Let's finish!	Finissons !
Finish! (pl./fml.)	Finissez !

Y

1. **Y** is used to replace a location word or phrase, such as à + noun.

2. **Y** is placed before the verb in sentences. However, in the imperative, **y** is placed after the verb.

3. In negative sentences, **y** is placed between **ne** (**n'**) and the verb.

4. **Y** can have the following meanings: *there, to it, in it, on it, at it, to them, in them, on them.*

FORMING ADVERBS

1. If the adjective ends in a *vowel* in the masculine singular, add **-ment** to the masculine singular form of the adjective to create the adverb.

2. If the adjective ends in a *consonant* in the masculine singular, add **-ment** to the feminine singular form of the adjective to create the adverb.

USING ADVERBS

1. In the present tense, the adverb is usually placed after the verb it's describing.

2. If the verb is negative, then the adverb follows the negative.

3. In the past tense, most adverbs follow the past participle. However, some adverbs come before the past participle. These include: bien (*well*) and mal (*badly*), toujours (*always, still*), beaucoup (*many, a lot, much*), déjà (*already*), vite (*quickly*), and encore (*again*).

FORMING THE PAST TENSE WITH ÊTRE

Some verbs use être instead of avoir to form the past tense.

1. To form the past tense of verbs that use être, use the present tense of être + the past participle of the verb.

2. The past participles of verbs that use être *must agree in gender and number* with the subject of the sentence.

VERBS THAT USE ÊTRE IN THE PAST TENSE

Verbs that use être in the past tense express a *change of place or state of being*.

	VERB	PAST PARTICIPLE
to go	aller	allé
to go up	monter	monté
to arrive	arriver	arrivé
to go out, to leave	sortir	sorti
to be born	naître	né
to stay	rester	resté
to come back, to return	revenir	revenu
to become	devenir	devenu
to come	venir	venu
to go down, to come down	descendre	descendu
to leave	partir	parti

Intermediate French

	VERB	PAST PARTICIPLE
to enter	entrer	entré
to die	mourir	mort
to return	retourner	retourné
to come home, to go home	rentrer	rentré
to fall	tomber	tombé

ALLER *(TO GO)* - **PAST**			
I went	je suis allé(e)	*we went*	nous sommes allé(e)s
you went (infml.)	tu es allé(e)	*you went (pl./fml.)*	vous êtes allé(e)(s)
he went	il est allé	*they went (m.)*	ils sont allés
she went	elle est allée	*they went (f.)*	elles sont allées

THE RECENT PAST

To form the recent past, use the present tense of present tense of venir + de (d') + infinitive.

SORTIR *(TO GO OUT, TO LEAVE)* - **RECENT PAST**			
I just left	je viens de sortir	*we just left*	nous venons de sortir
you just left (infml.)	tu viens de sortir	*you just left (pl./fml.)*	vous venez de sortir
he just left	il vient de sortir	*they just left (m.)*	ils viennent de sortir
she just left	elle vient de sortir	*they just left (f.)*	elles viennent de sortir

THE CONDITIONAL

To form the conditional:

1. For -er and -ir verbs, add the following endings onto the infinitive form of the verb.

2. For -re verbs, drop the final e from the infinitive form and then add the following endings.

PRONOUN	ENDING	PRONOUN	ENDING
je	-ais	nous	-ions
tu	-ais	vous	-iez
il	-ait	ils	-aient
elle	-ait	elles	-aient

VENDRE *(TO SELL)* - CONDITIONAL			
I would sell	je vendrais	*we would sell*	nous vendrions
you would sell (infml.)	tu vendrais	*you would sell (pl./fml.)*	vous vendriez
he would sell	il vendrait	*they would sell (m.)*	ils vendraient
she would sell	elle vendrait	*they would sell (f.)*	elles vendraient

IRREGULAR VERBS IN THE CONDITIONAL

VERB	CONDITIONAL STEM	
vouloir	voudr-	*would like*
aller	ir-	*would go*
avoir	aur-	*would have*
être	ser-	*would be*
faire	fer-	*would do, would make*
pouvoir	pourr-	*could*
devoir	devr-	*should*

Intermediate French

ALLER (*TO GO*) - **CONDITIONAL**			
I would go	j'irais	*we would go*	nous irions
you would go (infml.)	tu irais	*you would go (pl./fml.)*	vous iriez
he would go	il irait	*they would go (m.)*	ils iraient
she would go	elle irait	*they would go (f.)*	elles iraient

OTHER VERBS

CONDUIRE (*TO DRIVE*) - **PRESENT**			
I drive	je conduis	*we drive*	nous conduisons
you drive (infml.)	tu conduis	*you drive (pl./fml.)*	vous conduisez
he drives	il conduit	*they drive (m.)*	ils conduisent
she drives	elle conduit	*they drive (f.)*	elles conduisent

VENIR (*TO COME*) - **PRESENT**			
I come	je viens	*we come*	nous venons
you come (infml.)	tu viens	*you come (pl./fml.)*	vous venez
he comes	il vient	*they come (m.)*	ils viennent
she comes	elle vient	*they come (f.)*	elles viennent

Unit 5 Quiz

Ready for your final quiz of *Intermediate French*?

It's crucial that you have all of this mastered before you move on to *Advanced French*. Score yourself at the end of the quiz and see if you need to go back for further review, or if you're ready to move on to the next level.

A. Match the words on the left to their *opposites* on the right.

1. *devant*	a. **là**
2. *partout*	b. **dessous**
3. *dessus*	c. **derrière**
4. *ici*	d. **nulle part**
5. *près*	e. **loin**

B. Choose the most logical word to complete the sentence.

1. À la gare, il y a des _____.
   a. trains   c. camions
   b. voitures   d. avions

2. À l'aéroport, il y a des _____.
   a. trains   c. camions
   b. voitures   d. avions

3. À la charcuterie, il y a du _____.
   a. pain   c. lait
   b. porc   d. vin

4. À la boulangerie, il y a du _____.
   a. pain   c. lait
   b. porc   d. vin

5. Au lycée, il y a des _____.
   a. étudiants   c. bateaux
   b. métros   d. paquebots

C. Rewrite the following adjectives as adverbs.

1. vrai (true, real) _____
2. heureux (happy, fortunate) _____
3. doux (sweet, gentle, soft) _____
4. bon (good) _____
5. mauvais (bad) _____

D. Match the English phrases on the left to the correct French translations on the right.

1. *I just went*	a. **je vais aller**
2. *I will go*	b. **j'irai**
3. *I would go*	c. **je viens d'aller**
4. *I am going to go*	d. **je suis allé(e)**
5. *I went*	e. **j'irais**

ANSWER KEY:

A. 1. c (in front of, behind); 2. d (everywhere, nowhere); 3. b (on top, underneath); 4. a (here, there); 5. e (near, far)

B. 1. a. trains (At the train station, there are trains.) 2. d. avions (At the airport, there are planes.) 3. b. porc (At the delicatessen, there is pork.) 4. a. pain (At the bakery, there is bread.) 5. a. étudiants (At the high school, there are students.)

C. 1. vraiment; 2. heureusement; 3. doucement; 4. bien; 5. mal

D. 1. c; 2. b; 3. e; 4. a; 5. d

How Did You Do?

Give yourself a point for every correct answer, then use the following key to determine whether or not you're ready to move on:

0-7 points: It's probably best to go back and study the lessons again to make sure you understood everything completely. Take your time; it's not a race! Make sure you spend time reviewing the vocabulary and reading through each grammar note carefully.

8-16 points: If the questions you missed were in Section A or B, you may want to review the vocabulary again; if you missed answers mostly in Section C or D, check the Unit 5 Essentials to make sure you have your conjugations and other grammar basics down.

17-20 points: You did it! Bravo ! You've come to the end of *Living Language Intermediate French*! Feel free to move on to *Advanced French*. Of course, you can always come back to review whenever you need to.

 Points

Pronunciation Guide

Consonants

Note that the letter h can act as either a vowel or a consonant. See the end of the Pronunciation Guide for more information.

FRENCH	APPROXIMATE SOUND	PHONETIC SYMBOL	EXAMPLES
b, d, f, k, m, n, p, t, v, z	same as in English	same as in English	
ç	s	[s]	français [frah(n)-seh] (French)
c before a, o, u	k	[k]	cave [kahv] (cellar)
c before e, i, y	s	[s]	cinéma [see-nay-mah] (movie theater)
ch	sh	[sh]	chaud [shoh] (hot)
g before a, o, u	g in game	[g]	gâteau [gah-toh] (cake)
g before e, i, y	s in measure	[zh]	âge [ahzh] (age)
gn	ni in onion	[ny]	agneau [ah-nyoh] (lamb)
j	s in measure	[zh]	jeu [zhuh] (game)
l	l	[l]	lent [lah(n)] (slow)
l when it's at the end of the word and follows i	y in yes	[y]	fauteuil [foh-tuhy] (armchair)
ll	ll in ill	[l]	elle [ehl] (she)
ll between i and e	y in yes	[y]	fille [feey] (girl, daughter)
qu, final q	k	[k]	qui [kee] (who), cinq [sa(n)k] (five)

FRENCH	APPROXIMATE SOUND	PHONETIC SYMBOL	EXAMPLES
r	pronounced in the back of the mouth, like a light gargling sound	[r]	**Paris** [pah-ree] (*Paris*)
s between vowels	*z* in *zebra*	[z]	**maison** [meh-zoh(n)] (*house*)
s at the beginning of a word or before/after a consonant	*s*	[s]	**salle** [sahl] (*hall, room*), **course** [koors] (*errand*)
ss	*s*	[s]	**tasse** [tahs] (*cup*)
th	*t*	[t]	**thé** [tay] (*tea*)
w	*v*	[v]	**wagon-lit** [vah-goh(n)-lee] (*sleeping car*)
x usually before a vowel	*x* in *exact*	[gz]	**exact** [ehgz-ahkt] (*exact*)
x before a consonant or final e	*x* in *exterior*	[ks]	**extérieur** [ehks-tay-ree-uhr] (*outside*)

Keep in mind that most final consonants are silent in French, as with the -s in **Paris** [pah-ree] (*Paris*). However, there are five letters that are often (but not always) pronounced when final: **c**, **f**, **l**, **q**, and **r**.

French speakers also pronounce some final consonants when the next word begins with a vowel or silent **h** (see the end of the Pronunciation Guide for more information on the "silent **h**"). This is known as **liaison** [lyeh-zoh(n)] (*link*).

For example, the -s in **nous** [noo] (*we*) normally isn't pronounced. However, if it's followed by a word that begins with a vowel, such as **allons** [ah-loh(n)], then you do pronounce it: **nous allons** [noo zah-loh(n)] (*we go*). Notice that, when you use **liaison**, the s is pronounced *z* and it is "linked" to the following word: [zah-loh(n)].

Here's another example of **liaison**: **un grand arbre** [uh(n) grah(n) tahr-bruh] (*a big tree*). Normally, the -d in **grand** [grah(n)] is not pronounced, but, when you use **liaison**, it is pronounced *t* and linked to the following word.

Vowels

FRENCH	APPROXIMATE SOUND	PHONETIC SYMBOL	EXAMPLES
a, à, â	*a* in *father*	[ah]	**laver** [lah-vay] (*to wash*), **à** [ah] (*in, to, at*)
é, er, ez (end of a word), et	*ay* in *lay*	[ay]	**été** [ay-tay] (*summer*), **aller** [ah-lay] (*to go*), **ballet** [bah-lay] (*ballet*)
è, ê, ei, ai, aî	*e* in *bed*, with relaxed lips	[eh]	**père** [pehr] (*father*), **forêt** [foh-reh] (*forest*), **faire** [fehr] (*to do*)
e without an accent (and not combined with another vowel or r, z, t)	*a* in *above*, or *e* in *bed* with relaxed lips, or silent	[uh] or [eh] or n/a	**le** [luh] (*the*), **belle** [behl] (*beautiful*), **danse** [dah(n)s] (*dance*)
eu, œu followed by a consonant sound	*u* in *fur* with lips very rounded and loose	[uh]	**cœur** [kuhr] (*heart*)

FRENCH	APPROXIMATE SOUND	PHONETIC SYMBOL	EXAMPLES
eu, œu not followed by any sound	*u* in *fur* with lips very rounded and tight	[uh]	feu [fuh] (*fire*)
eille, ey	*ey* in *hey*	[ehy]	bouteille [boo-tehy] (*bottle*)
euille, œil	*a* in *above* + *y* in *yesterday*	[uhy]	œil [uhy] (*eye*)
i	*ee* in *beet*	[ee]	ici [ee-see] (*here*)
i plus vowel	*ee* in *beet* + *y* in *yesterday*	[y]	violon [vyoh-loh(n)] (*violin*)
o, au, eau, ô	*o* in *both*	[oh]	mot [moh] (*word*), eau [oh] (*water*), hôtel [oh-tehl] (*hotel*)
oi	*wa* in *watt*	[wah]	moi [mwah] (*me*)
ou	*oo* in *boot*	[oo]	vous [voo] (*you*)
ou before a vowel	*w* in *week*	[w]	ouest [wehst] (*west*), oui [wee] (*yes*)
oy	*wa* in *watt* + *y* in *yesterday*	[wahy]	foyer [fwahy-ay] (*home*)
u	keep your lips rounded as you pronounce *ee* in *beet*	[ew]	tu [tew] (*you*)
ui	*wee* in *week*	[wee]	lui [lwee] (*he, him, her*)

Nasal Vowels

FRENCH	APPROXIMATE SOUND	PHONETIC SYMBOL	EXAMPLES
an/en or am/em	*a* in *balm*, pronounced through both the mouth and the nose	[ah(n)] or [ah(m)]	France [frah(n)s] *(France)*, entrer [ah(n)-tray] *(to enter)*, emmener [ah(m)-muh-nay] *(to take along)*
in/yn/ain/ein or im/ym/aim/eim	*a* in *mad*, pronounced through both the mouth and the nose	[a(n)] or [a(m)]	vin [va(n)] *(wine)*, vain [va(n)] *(vain)*, sympa [sa(m)-pah] *(cool, nice, good)*, faim [fa(m)] *(hunger)*
ien	*ee* in *beet* + *y* in *yesterday* + nasal *a* in *mad*	[ya(n)]	rien [rya(n)] *(nothing)*
oin	*w* + nasal *a* in *mad*	[wa(n)]	loin [lwa(n)] *(far)*
on or om	*o* in *song*, pronounced through both the mouth and the nose	[oh(n)] or [oh(m)]	bon [boh(n)] *(good)*, tomber [toh(m)-bay] *(to fall)*
ion	*ee* in *beet* + *y* in *yesterday* + nasal *o* in *song*	[yoh(n)]	station [stah-syoh(n)] *(station)*
un or um	*u* in *lung*, pronounced through both the mouth and the nose	[uh(n)] or [uh(m)]	un [uh(n)] *(one, a/an)*, parfum [pahr-fuh(m)] *(perfume)*

The Letter H

In French, the letter h is not pronounced. For example, huit (*eight*) would be pronounced [weet].

However, there are actually two different types of h in French: the silent or mute h and the aspirated h. While you wouldn't pronounce either one, they behave differently.

The silent h acts like a vowel. For example, words like le, la, se, de, and so on become "contracted" (l', s', d', etc.) before a silent h:

l'homme (le + homme)	the man
s'habiller (se + habiller)	to get dressed

Also, you usually use liaison with a silent h. For instance, les hommes would be pronounced [lay zohm].

However, the aspirated h acts like a consonant. Words like le, la, se, de, etc. do ***not*** become l', s', d', and so on before an aspirated h:

le homard	the lobster
se hâter	to rush

Also, you do not use liaison with an aspirated h: les homards would be pronounced [lay oh-mahr].

Most "h"s are silent, not aspirated. Still, there are many words that begin with an aspirated h. Unfortunately, there isn't an easy way to tell which are which. Just start by learning the common ones, and then continue memorizing others that you come across.

Apart from **homme** and **habiller**, here are some other examples of common words that begin with a silent **h**: **habiter** (*to live*), **heure** (*hour*), **heureux/heureuse** (*happy*), **hier** (*yesterday*), **hôpital** (*hospital*), **horaire** (*schedule*), and **huile** (*oil*). Apart from **homard** and **hâter**, here are some other examples of common words that begin with an aspirated **h**: **huit** (*eight*), **héros** (*hero*), **haine** (*hatred*), **hasard** (*chance*), **hâte** (*haste*), **haut** (*high*), **honte** (*shame*), and **hors** (*outside*).

Grammar Summary

Here is a brief snapshot of French grammar from *Essential* and *Intermediate French*. Keep in mind that there are exceptions to many grammar rules.

1. NUMBERS

CARDINAL		ORDINAL	
un/une	one	premier/première	first
deux	two	deuxième, second/seconde	second
trois	three	troisième	third
quatre	four	quatrième	fourth
cinq	five	cinquième	fifth
six	six	sixième	sixth
sept	seven	septième	seventh
huit	eight	huitième	eighth
neuf	nine	neuvième	ninth
dix	ten	dixième	tenth

2. ARTICLES

	DEFINITE		INDEFINITE	
	Singular	Plural	Singular	Plural
Masculine	le	les	un	des
Feminine	la	les	une	des

Note that l' is used instead of le and la before words beginning with a vowel or silent h.

3. CONTRACTIONS

de + le = du (*some/of the, masculine*)

de + les = des (*some/of the, plural*)

à + le = au (*to/at/in the, masculine*)

à + les = aux (*to/at/in the, plural*)

There is no contraction with la or l'. In a negative sentence, de la, de l', du, and des change to de/d'.

4. PLURALS

Most nouns add -s to form the plural. If a noun ends in -s, -x, or -z in the singular, there is no change in the plural.

Nouns ending in -eau or -eu, and some nouns ending in -ou, add -x instead of -s to form the plural. Many nouns ending in -al and -ail change to -aux in the plural.

5. ADJECTIVES

Adjectives agree with the nouns they modify in gender and number; that is, they are masculine if the noun is masculine, plural if the noun is plural, etc.

a. The feminine of an adjective is normally formed by adding -e to the masculine singular.

b. If the masculine singular already ends in -e, the adjective has the same form in the feminine.

c. Some adjectives double the final consonant of the masculine singular form and then add -e to form the feminine.

d. If the masculine singular ends in -x, change the ending to -se to form the feminine.

e. If the masculine singular ends in -**f**, change the ending to -**ve** to form the feminine.

f. If the masculine singular ends in -**er**, change the ending to -**ère** to form the feminine.

g. If the masculine singular ends in -**et**, change the ending to -**ète** or -**ette** to form the feminine.

h. The plural of adjectives is usually formed by adding -**s** to the masculine or feminine singular form. But if the adjective ends in -**s** or -**x** in the masculine singular, the masculine plural stays the same.

i. Most masculine adjectives ending in -**al** in the masculine singular, change the ending to **aux** in the masculine plural.

Adjectives usually come after the noun. However, adjectives of beauty, age, goodness, and size (B-A-G-S adjectives) usually come before the noun.

6. POSSESSIVE ADJECTIVES

Possessive adjectives agree in gender and number with the possession.

BEFORE SINGULAR NOUNS		BEFORE PLURAL NOUNS	
Masculine	Feminine	Masculine and Feminine	
mon	ma	mes	*my*
ton	ta	tes	*your (infml.)*
son	sa	ses	*his, her, its*
notre	notre	nos	*our*
votre	votre	vos	*your (pl./fml.)*
leur	leur	leurs	*their*

Before feminine singular nouns beginning with a vowel or silent h, use **mon, ton,** and **son.**

7. PRONOUNS

	SUBJECT	STRESSED	REFLEXIVE
1st singular	je/j'	moi	me/m'
2nd singular	tu	toi	te/t'
3rd masculine singular	il	lui	se/s'
3rd feminine singular	elle	elle	se/s'
1st plural	nous	nous	nous
2nd plural	vous	vous	vous
3rd masculine plural	ils	eux	se/s'
3rd feminine plural	elles	elles	se/s'

On is an indefinite subject pronoun that means *we, one,* or *people/you/they in general.*

Stressed pronouns are generally used after prepositions (**avec moi,** etc.) or for emphasis (**moi, j'ai vingt ans**).

8. QUESTION WORDS

où	*where*	de quel/quelle/ quels/quelles + noun	*what/of what + noun*
qu'est-ce que	*what*	combien (de)	*how much, how many*
quel/quelle, quels/quelles	*which, what*	à quelle heure	*at what time*
qui	*who*	pourquoi	*why*
comment	*how*	quand	*when*

9. DEMONSTRATIVE ADJECTIVES

Masculine Singular	ce	*this, that*
Masculine Singular (before a vowel or silent h)	cet	*this, that*
Feminine Singular	cette	*this, that*
Masculine Plural	ces	*these, those*
Feminine Plural	ces	*these, those*

When it is necessary to distinguish between *this* and *that*, -ci and -là are added to the noun: **Donnez-moi ce livre-ci.** (*Give me this book.*)

10. NEGATION

A sentence is made negative by placing **ne** before the verb and **pas** after it. When placed before a vowel or silent h, **ne** becomes **n'**.

To form the negative of the past tense, place **ne** (**n'**) and **pas** around the present tense form of **avoir** or **être**. To form a negative statement with a reflexive verb, place **ne** after the subject pronoun but before the reflexive pronoun, and then place **pas** immediately after the verb.

11. ADVERBS

Adverbs are generally placed after the verb. In the past tense, they're placed after the past participle. However, adverbs of quality (**bien, mal**), quantity (**beaucoup**), and frequency (**toujours**), along with some other adverbs, usually come before the past participle.

Most adverbs are formed from their corresponding adjectives. If the adjective ends in a vowel in the masculine singular, add **-ment** to the masculine singular form. If the adjective ends in a consonant in the masculine singular, add **-ment** to the feminine singular form.

12. REGULAR VERBS

There are three types of regular French verbs:

TYPE	EXAMPLE
verbs ending in -er	parler *(to speak)*
verbs ending in -re	vendre *(to sell)*
verbs ending in -ir	finir *(to finish)*

Here are the full conjugations of each example in the present tense, imperative, past tense, future tense, and conditional:

parler
to speak, to talk

je	nous
tu	vous
il/elle/on	ils/elles

Present

		Imperative	
parle	parlons		Parlons !
parles	parlez	Parle !	Parlez !
parle	parlent		

Past

		Future	
ai parlé	avons parlé	parlerai	parlerons
as parlé	avez parlé	parleras	parlerez
a parlé	ont parlé	parlera	parleront

Conditional

parlerais	parlerions		
parlerais	parleriez		
parlerait	parleraient		

vendre
to sell

je	nous
tu	vous
il/elle/on	ils/elles

Present		Imperative	
vends	vendons		Vendons !
vends	vendez	Vends !	Vendez !
vend	vendent		

Past		Future	
ai vendu	avons vendu	vendrai	vendrons
as vendu	avez vendu	vendras	vendrez
a vendu	ont vendu	vendra	vendront

Conditional			
vendrais	vendrions		
vendrais	vendriez		
vendrait	vendraient		

Intermediate French

finir
to finish

je	nous
tu	vous
il/elle/on	ils/elles

Present		Imperative	
finis	finissons		Finissons !
finis	finissez	Finis !	Finissez !
finit	finissent		

Past		Future	
ai fini	avons fini	finirai	finirons
as fini	avez fini	finiras	finirez
a fini	ont fini	finira	finiront

Conditional			
finirais	finirions		
finirais	finiriez		
finirait	finiraient		

Common Irregular Verbs

être
to be

je	nous
tu	vous
il/elle/on	ils/elles

Present		Imperative	
suis	sommes		Soyons !
es	êtes	Sois !	Soyez !
est	sont		

Past		Future	
ai été	avons été	serai	serons
as été	avez été	seras	serez
a été	ont été	sera	seront

Conditional			
serais	serions		
serais	seriez		
serait	seraient		

avoir
to have

je	nous
tu	vous
il/elle/on	ils/elles

Present

ai	avons
as	avez
a	ont

Imperative

	Ayons !
Aie !	Ayez !

Past

ai eu	avons eu
as eu	avez eu
a eu	ont eu

Future

aurai	aurons
auras	aurez
aura	auront

Conditional

aurais	aurions
aurais	auriez
aurait	auraient

aller
to go

je	nous
tu	vous
il/elle/on	ils/elles

Present		Imperative	
vais	allons		Allons !
vas	allez	Va !	Allez !
va	vont		

Past		Future	
suis allé(e)	sommes allé(e)s	irai	irons
es allé(e)	êtes allé(e)(s)	iras	irez
est allé(e)	sont allé(e)s	ira	iront

Conditional			
irais	irions		
irais	iriez		
irait	iraient		

faire
to do, to make

je		nous	
tu		vous	
il/elle/ on		ils/elles	

Present		Imperative	
fais	faisons		Faisons !
fais	faites	Fais !	Faites !
fait	font		

Past		Future	
ai fait	avons fait	ferai	ferons
as fait	avez fait	feras	ferez
a fait	ont fait	fera	feront

Conditional			
ferais	ferions		
ferais	feriez		
ferait	feraient		

Glossary

Note that the following abbreviations will be used in this glossary:
(m.) = masculine, (f.) = feminine, (sg.) = singular, (pl.) = plural,
(fml.) = formal/polite, (infml.) = informal/familiar. If a word has two
grammatical genders, (m./f.) or (f./m.) is used.

French-English

A

à *in, at, to*
  à la / à l' / au / aux (f./m. or f. before a vowel or mute h/m./pl.) *in/at/to the*
  à côté de *next to*
  à côté *at the side, on the side, to the side*
  à plein temps *full-time*
  à temps partiel *part-time*
  à quelle heure? *at what time?*
  à gauche *on the left, to the left, at the left*
  à droite *on the right, to the right, at the right*
  à travers *through, across*
  à l'heure *on time*
  à la maison *at the house, at home*
  à pied *on foot, by foot*
  À votre santé ! *To your health!*
  À la prochaine ! *See you later!*
  À plus tard ! *See you later!*
  À plus ! *See you later!* (infml.)
  À tout à l'heure ! *See you later!*
  À bientôt ! *See you soon!*
  À table ! *Dinner's ready!/The food is ready!* *(lit., To the table!)*
Absolument ! *Absolutely!*
accident (m.) *accident*
accompagner *to accompany*
  plat (m.) d'accompagnement *side dish*
accord (m.) *agreement*
  D'accord. *Okay./All right.*
acheter *to buy*
acteur / actrice (m./f.) *actor/actress*
actif / active (m./f.) *active*
action (f.) *action*
  film (m.) d'action *action film*
activement *actively*

addition (f.) *check, bill*
  L'addition, s'il vous plaît. *The check, please./ The bill, please.*
admirer *to admire*
adolescent / adolescente (m./f.) *adolescent, teenager*
adorer *to love, to adore*
adulte (m./f.) *adult, grown-up*
aéroport (m.) *airport*
affaires (f. pl.) *business, belongings*
âge (m.) *age*
âgé / âgée (m./f.) *elderly*
  personne (f.) âgée *elderly person*
agir *to act (to behave)*
agneau (m.) *lamb*
  carré (m.) d'agneau rôti *roast rack of lamb*
agréable *pleasant, enjoyable*
Ah bon ... *Oh, really ... /Oh, okay ...*
aider *to help*
  Pouvez-vous m'aider, s'il vous plaît ? *Can you help me, please?*
aigre *sour*
ailleurs *elsewhere*
aimable *kind (nice)*
aimer *to like, to love*
  J'aime (bien)... *I (really) like ...*
  J'aime ça. *I like that./I love that.*
  Je n'aime pas... *I do not like ...*
aîné / aînée (m./f.) *oldest child*
alcool (m.) *alcohol*
Algérie (f.) *Algeria*
algérien / algérienne (m./f.) *Algerian*
Allemagne (f.) *Germany*
allemand / allemande (m./f.) *German*
aller *to go*
  aller visiter *to go sightseeing*
  Allons-y. *Let's go.*
  On y va. *Let's go.* (infml.)

Comment allez-vous ?
  How are you? (pl./fml.)
Comment vas-tu ? *How are you?* (infml.)
Je vais très bien. *I'm very well.*
Va ! *Go!* (infml.)
Allez ! *Go!* (pl./fml.)
aller simple *one-way*
aller-retour *round-trip*
  Je voudrais un billet aller-retour. *I would like a round-trip ticket.*
Allô. *Hello. (only on the phone)*
allonger *to lay down, to lie down*
Alors... *Well ... /So ... /Then ...*
  Alors là... *So then ...*
alpinisme (m.) *climbing*
américain / américaine (m./f.) *American*
ami / amie (m./f.) *friend*
  petit ami / petite amie (m./f.) *boyfriend/ girlfriend*
amical / amicale (m./f.) *friendly*
amusant / amusante (m./f.) *amusing, funny*
amuser *to entertain*
  s'amuser *to have a good time, to enjoy oneself, to have fun*
  Je m'amuse. *I'm having a good time./I'm having fun.*
an (m.) *year*
  jour (m.) **de l'An** *New Year's Day*
  Nouvel An (m.) *New Year*
  avoir... ans *to be ... years old*
ancien / ancienne (m./f.) *old, former, ancient*
anglais (m.) *English language*
  en anglais *in English*
anglais / anglaise (m./f.) *English*
Angleterre (f.) *England*
animal (m.) *animal*
année (f.) *year*
  mois (m. pl.) **de l'année** *months of the year*
  Bonne Année ! *Happy New Year!*
  année (f.) **dernière** *last year*
anniversaire (m.) *birthday, anniversary*
  Joyeux / Bon anniversaire !
    Happy birthday!/Happy anniversary!
annoncer *to announce*
août *August*
apéritif (m.) *drink served before the meal*

appareil (m.) *device, telephone*
  Qui est à l'appareil ? *Who is it?/Who's calling? (on the phone)*
  appareil (m.) **photo** *camera*
appartement (m.) *apartment*
appeler *to call*
  s'appeler *to be called (to call oneself)*
appétit (m.) *appetite*
  Bon appétit ! *Enjoy your meal! (lit., Good appetite!)*
apporter *to bring*
apprendre *to learn*
  J'apprends le français. *I'm learning French.*
après *after, afterwards*
après-demain *the day after tomorrow*
après-midi (m./f.) *afternoon*
arbre (m.) *tree*
Arc (m.) **de Triomphe** *Arc de Triomphe (Arch of Triumph)*
architecte (m./f.) *architect*
argent (m.) *money, cash*
armoire (f.) *wardrobe, cabinet*
  armoire à pharmacie *medicine cabinet*
arrêt (m.) *stop*
arrêt de bus / d'autobus *bus stop*
arriver *to arrive, to get somewhere, to reach*
  arriver à (+ verb) *to be able to (do something), to manage to (do something)*
  arriver à (+ destination) *to arrive (somewhere), to get to (a destination)*
  heure (f.) **de l'arrivée** *arrival time*
art (m.) *art*
artiste (m./f.) *artist*
assez *quite, enough*
assiette (f.) *plate*
assis / assise (m./f.) *sitting (down), seated*
assistant / assistante (m./f.) *assistant*
attendre *to wait (for), to expect*
au *to/at/in the* (m.)
  Au revoir. *Good-bye.*
  au bout de *at the end of*
  au pied de *at the foot of*
  au bord de *at the edge of (at the border of)*
  au milieu de *in the middle of*
auberge (f.) *inn*
  auberge de jeunesse *youth hostel*
aujourd'hui *today*

auparavant *before*
  deux mois auparavant *two months before*
aussi *also, too*
Australie (f.) *Australia*
australien / australienne (m./f.) *Australian*
auto(mobile) (f.) *car, automobile*
autobus (m.) *bus*
  arrêt (m.) d'autobus *bus stop*
autocar (m.) *bus*
automne (m.) *fall, autumn*
  en automne *in (the) fall, in autumn*
autour de *around*
autre *other*
  un / une autre (m./f.) *another*
  de l'autre côté de *on the other side of*
autrefois *formerly, in the past*
aux *to/at/in the* (pl.)
  aux États-Unis *to/at/in the United States*
avancer *to advance*
avant *before*
  deux mois avant *two months before*
  d'avant *before last*
  semaine (f.) d'avant *the week before last*
avant-hier *the day before yesterday*
avec *with*
  Avec plaisir. *With pleasure.*
  sortir avec *to go out with, to date*
avenue (f.) *avenue*
avion (m.) *airplane*
avocat / avocate (m./f.) *lawyer*
avoir *to have*
  avoir besoin de *to need*
  avoir chaud *to be hot/warm*
  avoir envie de *to feel like*
  avoir froid *to be cold*
  avoir faim *to be hungry*
  avoir hâte *to look forward to (can't wait)*
  avoir honte *to be ashamed*
  avoir lieu *to take place, to be held*
  avoir peur *to be afraid*
  avoir raison *to be right*
  avoir soif *to be thirsty*
  avoir sommeil *to be sleepy*
  avoir tort *to be wrong*
  avoir... ans *to be ... years old*
avril *April*

B

bague (f.) *ring*
baguette (f.) *baguette (French bread), chopstick*
baignoire (f.) *bathtub*
balai (m.) *broom*
balle (f.) *ball (small – tennis, etc.)*
ballet (m.) *ballet*
ballon (m.) *ball (large – basketball, etc.)*
banane (f.) *banana*
bandage (m.) *bandage*
banlieue (f.) *suburbs*
  de banlieue *suburban*
banque (f.) *bank*
banquier / banquière (m./f.) *banker*
bar (m.) *bar/counter*
bas / basse (m./f.) *low*
  en bas *downstairs, down below*
baseball (m.) *baseball*
basket (m./f.) *sneaker, tennis shoe*
basket(-ball) (m.) *basketball*
bateau (m.) *boat, ship*
bâtiment (m.) *building*
bâtir *to build*
beau / bel / belle (m./m. before a vowel or
  silent h/f.) *beautiful, handsome, nice*
  Il fait beau. *It's beautiful (outside).*
Beaubourg *Beaubourg (area in Paris and another name for the Pompidou Center)*
beaucoup *many, a lot, much*
  beaucoup de *a lot of, many*
beau-fils (m.) *stepson, son-in-law*
beau-père (m.) *father-in-law, stepfather*
beauté (f.) *beauty*
  institut (m.) de beauté *beauty parlor, beauty
    salon*
bébé (m.) *baby*
beige *beige, tan (color)*
belge *Belgian*
Belgique (f.) *Belgium*
belle-fille (f.) *stepdaughter, daughter-in-law*
belle-mère (f.) *mother-in-law, stepmother*
Ben... *Oh well ... / Well ...* (infml.)
besoin (m.) *need*
  avoir besoin de *to need (lit., to have need of)*
beurre (m.) *butter*
  livre (f.) de beurre *pound of butter*

radis (m. pl.) au beurre *rosette-cut radishes served with butter on top (lit., radishes in butter)*
bibliothèque (f.) *library, bookshelf*
bicyclette (f.) *bicycle*
bidet (m.) *bidet*
bien *well, good, fine, really, very*
  Ça va bien. *It's going well.*
  très bien *very good, very well*
  Bien sûr. *Of course.*
  Eh bien... *Oh well ... /Well ...*
  J'aime bien... *I really like ...*
  Je veux bien... *I really want ... /I do want ...*
  Je voudrais bien... *I would really like ...*
  J'ai bien... *I do have ...*
  Merci bien. *Thank you very much.*
  Bien entendu. *I do understand./Completely understood./Of course.*
  ou bien *or even, or else, either, or*
  et bien plus *and even more, and much more*
  bien au contraire *quite the opposite, quite the contrary*
bientôt *soon*
  À bientôt ! *See you soon!*
Bienvenue. *Welcome.*
bière (f.) *beer*
bijou (m.) *jewel*
  bijoux (m. pl.) *jewelry*
billard (m.) *pool, billiards*
billet (m.) *ticket, banknote, bill (currency)*
  distributeur (m.) de billets *ATM*
biologie (f.) *biology*
bisque (f.) *bisque (creamy soup)*
  bisque de homard *lobster bisque*
bizarre *strange, bizarre*
  C'est bizarre. *It's strange.*
blanc / blanche (m./f.) *white*
  vin (m.) blanc *white wine*
blancs (m. pl.) (d'œufs) *egg whites*
blessé / blessée (m./f.) *wounded*
blesser *to hurt*
  se blesser *to hurt oneself*
bleu / bleue (m./f.) *blue*
  truite (f.) au bleu *trout cooked in wine and vinegar*
blond / blonde (m./f.) *blonde*
blouse (f.) *blouse*

bœuf (m.) *beef*
  rôti (m.) de bœuf *roast beef*
boire *to drink*
bois (m.) *wood*
  en bois *wooden*
boisson (f.) *drink*
  boisson gazeuse *soft drink*
boîte (f.) *club, nightclub, box*
  boîte de nuit *nightclub*
  sortir en boîte *to go out to clubs, to go out clubbing*
  boîte de conserve *can*
  boîte (en carton) *carton*
  boîte de jus d'orange *carton of orange juice*
bon / bonne (m./f.) *good*
  très bon / bonne (m./f.) *very good*
  Bon appétit. *Bon appetit.*
  Bonne chance. *Good luck.*
  Bon anniversaire ! *Happy birthday!/Happy anniversary!*
  Bonne Année ! *Happy New Year!*
  Bonne nuit ! *Good night!*
  Bonnes fêtes ! *Happy Holidays!*
  Ah bon... *Oh really ... /Oh okay ...*
bonbons (m. pl.) *candy*
Bonjour. *Hello./Good day.*
Bonsoir. *Good evening.*
bord (m.) *border, edge*
  au bord de *at the edge of, at the border of*
bouche (f.) *mouth*
boucherie (f.) *butcher shop*
boucle (f.) d'oreille *earring*
boulangerie (f.) *bakery*
boulevard (m.) *boulevard*
boulot (m.) *job*
bout (m.) *end*
  au bout de *at the end of*
bouteille (f.) *bottle*
  bouteille de champagne *bottle of champagne*
boutique (f.) *boutique*
bracelet (m.) *bracelet*
bras (m.) *arm*
brave *good, courageous, brave*
Bravo. *Well done.*
Brésil (m.) *Brazil*
brésilien / brésilienne (m./f.) *Brazilian*
brioche (f.) *sweet bun*
brique (f.) *carton/brick*

brochure (f.) *brochure*
brosser *to brush*
  se brosser *to brush oneself (hair, teeth, etc.)*
brouillard (m.) *fog*
brouiller *to scramble*
  œufs (m. pl.) **brouillés** *scrambled eggs*
brun / brune (m./f.) *brown*
brut / brute (m./f.) *dry (alcohol)*
bulletin (m.) **scolaire** *report card*
bureau (m.) *office, desk*
  bureau de poste *post office*
  bureau de change *currency exchange office*
bus (m.) *bus*
  arrêt (m.) **de bus** *bus stop*

C

c'est *this is, that is, it is*
  C'est nuageux. *It's cloudy.*
  C'est tout ? *Is that all?*
  Qu'est-ce que c'est ? *What is this/that?*
  C'est délicieux ! *It's delicious!*
  C'est ennuyeux. *It's boring.*
  C'est bizarre. *It's strange.*
  C'est étrange. *It's strange.*
  C'est parfait. *It's perfect.*
  C'est mauvais. *That's bad.*
ça / c' *this, that, it*
  (Comment) ça va ? *How's it going?/How are you?*
  Ça va. *I'm fine./It's going fine.*
  Ça va bien. *It's going well.*
  Ça va mal. *It's not going well./It's going badly.*
  Ça fait... *That makes ... /That is ...*
  Ça coûte... *That costs ...*
  J'aime ça. *I like that./I love that.*
câble (m.) *cable*
cadet / cadette (m./f.) *youngest child*
café (m.) *café, coffee shop, coffee*
  café-crème (m.) *coffee with cream*
cafetière (f.) *coffeemaker*
cahier (m.) *notebook*
caleçon (m.) *underpants*
calme *quiet, calm*
camion (m.) *truck*
camper *to go camping*
Canada (m.) *Canada*
canadien / canadienne (m./f.) *Canadian*

canapé (m.) *sofa, couch*
canard (m.) *duck*
  canard à l'orange *duck à l'orange, duck with orange sauce*
carafe (f.) *pitcher*
  carafe d'eau *pitcher of water*
  carafe de vin *pitcher of wine*
caramel (m.) *caramel*
  crème (f.) **caramel** *creamy dessert made with caramel*
carotte (f.) *carrot*
carré (m.) *square, rack (of meat)*
  carré d'agneau (rôti) *(roast) rack of lamb*
carte (f.) *menu, card, map*
  carte des vins *wine list*
  carte de la ville *map of the city*
  carte du métro *map of the subway*
  cartes (pl.) **à jouer** *playing cards*
  La carte, s'il vous plaît. *The menu, please.*
carton (m.) *carton*
cassis (m.) *black currant*
cathédrale (f.) *cathedral*
cave (f.) *cellar*
CD-ROM (m.) *CD-ROM*
ce / cet / cette (m./m. before a vowel or silent h/f.) *this, that*
  ce soir *tonight, this evening*
ceinture (f.) *belt*
célèbre *famous*
célébrer *to celebrate*
céleri (m.) *celery*
célibataire *single*
cent *hundred*
cent (m.) *cent*
centre (m.) *center*
  centre d'informations *information center*
  centre commercial *mall*
cerise (f.) *cherry*
certain / certaine (m./f.) *certain*
certainement *certainly*
cerveau (m.) *brain*
ces *these, those*
cette / ce / cet (f./m./m. before a vowel or silent h) *this, that*
chacun / chacune (m./f.) *each, each one*
chaîne (f.) **hi-fi** *sound system*
chaise (f.) *chair*
chambre (f.) **(à coucher)** *bedroom*

champ (m.) *field*

champagne (m.) *champagne*
  bouteille (f.) de champagne *bottle of champagne*

champignon (m.) *mushroom*

champion / championne (m./f.) *champion*

chance (f.) *luck*
  Pas de chance ! *No luck!*
  Bonne chance ! *Good luck!*

changer *to change, to exchange*
  changer de chaîne *to change channels*
  bureau (m.) de change *currency exchange office*

chanson (f.) *song*

chanter *to sing*

chanteur / chanteuse (m./f.) *singer*

chapeau (m.) *hat*

chaque *each, every*

charcuterie (f.) *delicatessen (store that sells prepared meats)*

charmant / charmante (m./f.) *charming*

charpentier (m.) *carpenter*

château (m.) *castle*

chaud / chaude (m./f.) *hot, warm*
  Il fait chaud. *It's hot./It's warm.*
  avoir chaud *to be hot/warm*
  chocolat (m.) chaud *hot chocolate*

chauffeur (m.) de taxi *taxi driver*

chaussette (f.) *sock*

chaussure (f.) *shoe*
  chaussure (f.) de basket / tennis *sneaker, tennis shoe*

chef (m.) *boss*

chemin (m.) *path, way*

chemise (f.) *shirt*

chemisier (m.) *blouse*

chèque (m.) *check*
  chèque de voyage *traveler's check*

cher / chère (m./f.) *dear, expensive*

chercher *to look for*

chéri / chérie (m./f.) *honey, dear, darling*

cheveux (m. pl.) *hair*
  cheveu (m.) *hair (single strand)*
  avoir les cheveux bruns / blonds / roux / noirs *to have brown/blond/red/black hair*

cheville (f.) *ankle*

chez *at someone's house/place*
  chez moi *at my house, at home*

chien (m.) *dog*

chimie (f.) *chemistry*

Chine (f.) *China*

chinois (m.) *Chinese language*

chinois / chinoise (m./f.) *Chinese*

chocolat (m.) *chocolate*
  gâteau (m.) au chocolat *chocolate cake*
  mousse (f.) au chocolat *chocolate mousse*
  glace (f.) au chocolat *chocolate ice cream*
  chocolat (m.) chaud *hot chocolate*

choisir *to choose*

chômage (m.) *unemployment*
  au chômage *unemployed*

chose (f.) *thing*
  Pas grand-chose. *Not a lot.*

ci *this, here*

cidre (m.) *cider*

ciel (m.) *sky*

cil (m.) *eyelash*

cinéma (m.) *movie theater, the movies*

cinq *five*

cinquante *fifty*

cinquième *fifth*

circuit (m.) en bus *bus tour*

circulation (f.) *traffic*

cirque (m.) *circus*

citron (m.) *lemon*
  citron vert *lime*

citrouille (f.) *pumpkin*
  tarte (f.) à la citrouille *pumpkin pie*

clam (m.) *clam*

classe (f.) *class, grade*

clavier (m.) *keyboard*

client / cliente (m./f.) *client*

club (m.) *club (organization)*

cochon (m.) *pig*

cœur (m.) *heart*

coin (m.) *neighborhood, corner*

coïncidence (f.) *coincidence*
  Quelle coïncidence ! *What a coincidence!*

collection (f.) *collection*

collège (m.) *secondary school, junior high school, middle school*

collègue / collègue (m./f.) *colleague*

collier (m.) *necklace*

colline (f.) *hill*

combien *how many, how much*
C'est combien, s'il vous plaît ? *That's how much, please?/It's how much, please?*
comédie (f.) *comedy*
comédie romantique *romantic comedy*
comédie musicale *musical*
commander *to order*
comme *like, as, how*
Comme ci, comme ça. *So-so.*
commencer *to begin, to start*
comment *how*
Comment ? *Pardon?/What did you say?/How?*
(Comment) ça va ? *How's it going?/How are you?*
Comment allez-vous ? *How are you?* (pl./fml.)
Comment vas-tu ? *How are you?* (infml.)
Comment vous appelez-vous ? *What's your name?* (pl./fml.)
Comment t'appelles-tu ? *What's your name?* (infml.)
commercial / commerciale (m./f.) *commercial*
centre (m.) commercial *mall*
compliqué / compliquée (m./f.) *complicated*
comprendre *to understand*
Je ne comprends pas. *I don't understand.*
comptoir (m.) *counter*
concert (m.) *concert*
concombre (m.) *cucumber*
conduire *to drive*
confiserie (f.) *candy store*
pâtisserie-confiserie (f.) *pastry and candy store*
confiture (f.) *jelly, jam, marmalade*
confortable *comfortable*
connaissance (f.) *acquaintance*
Enchanté / Enchantée (de faire votre connaissance). *Pleased to meet you./Nice to meet you.*
Je suis ravi / ravie de faire votre connaissance. *I'm delighted to make your acquaintance.*
connaître *to know, to be familiar with*
consommé (m.) *consommé (clear soup made from stock)*
consommé aux vermicelles *noodle soup (vermicelli pasta consommé)*
construire *to construct*

consulter *to consult*
consulter l'annuaire *to consult a phone book*
contraire (m.) *opposite, contrary*
bien au contraire *quite the opposite, quite the contrary*
cool *cool (great)*
copain / copine (m./f.) *boyfriend/girlfriend*
coq (m.) *rooster*
coq au vin *chicken/rooster cooked in wine*
coque (f.) *shell*
œuf (m.) à la coque *soft-boiled egg*
coquilles (f. pl.) Saint-Jacques *scallops*
costume (m.) *suit*
côte (f.) *chop, rib, coast*
côte de porc *pork chop*
côté (m.) *side*
à côté *at the side, on the side, to the side*
à côté de *next to*
de l'autre côté de *on the other side of*
coton (m.) *cotton*
cou (m.) *neck*
coucher *to lay down, to put someone to bed*
se coucher *to go to bed, to lie down (to lay oneself down)*
chambre (f.) (à coucher) *bedroom*
coude (m.) *elbow*
couloir (m.) *hall*
courriel (m.) *e-mail*
courrier (m.) électronique *e-mail*
cours (m.) *course, class*
course (f.) *errand, run, race*
course à pied *running*
faire des / les courses *to shop*
court / courte (m./f.) *short*
cousin / cousine (m./f.) *cousin*
couteau (m.) *knife*
coûter *to cost*
Combien ça coûte, s'il vous plaît ? *How much does that cost, please?*
couvert (m.) *table setting*
crémant (m.) *type of French sparkling wine*
crème (f.) *cream, creamy dessert*
crème à raser *shaving cream*
crème caramel *creamy dessert made with caramel*
crème chantilly *whipped cream (that is flavored and sweetened)*

crêpe (f.) *crêpe (tissue-thin pancake)*
  Crêpe Suzette *Crêpe Suzette (crêpe with sugar, orange, and liqueur)*
crevettes (f. pl.) *shrimp*
croire *believe (to)*
croissant (m.) *croissant*
croque-madame (m.) *grilled ham and cheese sandwich with an egg on top*
croque-monsieur (m.) *grilled ham and cheese sandwich*
cru / crue (m./f.) *raw*
crudités (f. pl.) *crudités (French appetizer of raw, mixed vegetables)*
cruel / cruelle (m./f.) *cruel*
cuiller / cuillère (f.) *spoon*
cuir (m.) *leather*
cuisine (f.) *kitchen, cooking*
  faire la cuisine *to cook, to do the cooking*
cuisiner *to cook*
cuisinier / cuisinière (m./f.) *cook*
cuisinière (f.) *stove, cook*

D

dame (f.) *lady*
dans *in, into*
  dans un mois *next month, in one month*
  dans une semaine *next week, in one week*
  dans deux semaines *the week after next, in two weeks*
danse (f.) *dancing, dance*
danser *to dance*
date (f.) *date*
de / d' *of, for, from*
  de la / de l' / du / des (f./m. or f. before a vowel or silent h/m./pl.) *of the, some*
  d'ici *from here*
  D'accord. *Okay./All right.*
  D'abord... *First ...*
  De rien. *You're welcome./It's nothing.*
  de l'autre côté de *on the other side of*
  de ma part *on my behalf, from me, on my part*
  de la part de *on behalf of, from (someone)*
  C'est de la part de qui ? *Who's calling? (on the phone)*
  de quel / quelle ? (m./f.) *what?/of what?*
debout *standing (up)*
décembre *December*

décider *to decide*
  se décider *to make up one's mind, to be decided, to be resolved (to do something)*
décrocher *to pick up (the phone)*
défendre *to defend, to forbid*
degré (m.) *degree*
dehors *outside*
déjà *already*
déjeuner *to have lunch*
déjeuner (m.) *lunch*
  petit déjeuner (m.) *breakfast (lit., little lunch)*
délicieux / délicieuse (m./f.) *delicious*
demain *tomorrow*
  après-demain *the day after tomorrow*
demander *to ask, to ask for*
  se demander *to wonder, to ask oneself*
déménager *to move out*
demi / demie (m./f.) *half*
  ... et demie *half past ...*
demi-heure (f.) *half hour*
dent (f.) *tooth*
dentiste (m.) *dentist*
déodorant (m.) *deodorant*
départ (m.) *departure*
  heure (f.) du départ *departure time*
dépêcher *to dispatch*
  se dépêcher *to hurry*
dernier / dernière (m./f.) *last, final, latest*
  lundi dernier *last Monday*
  mois (m.) dernier *last month*
  été (m.) dernier *last summer*
  nuit (f.) dernière *last night*
  année (f.) dernière *last year*
derrière *behind*
des *some (pl.), of the (pl.), plural of un / une*
descendre *to go down, to come down, to descend*
  Où dois-je descendre ? *Where do I have to get off?/Where should I get off?*
description (f.) *description*
désert (m.) *desert*
désirer *to want, to wish*
désobéir *to disobey*
désolé / désolée (m./f.) *sorry*
  Je suis désolé / désolée. *I am sorry.*
dessert (m.) *dessert*
dessous *underneath*
dessus *on top*
détester *to hate, to detest*

deux *two*
deuxième *second*
devant *in front (of), ahead, before*
devenir *to become*
devoir *to have to, must, should, to owe*
devoirs (m. pl.) *homework*
dieu (m.) *god*
  Mon dieu ! *My god!*
différent / différente (m./f.) *different*
difficile *difficult*
dimanche *Sunday*
dîner *to dine, to have dinner*
dîner (m.) *dinner*
diplôme (m.) *diploma*
  diplôme universitaire *college degree*
dire *to say, to tell*
  Dis donc ! *Man!/You don't say!/Say! (lit., Say so!)*
directeur / directrice (m./f.) *director, manager*
direction (f.) *direction, way*
discothèque (f.) *(night)club*
distributeur (m.) **de billets** *ATM*
divorce (m.) *divorce*
divorcer *to get a divorce*
dix *ten*
dix-huit *eighteen*
dixième *tenth*
dix-neuf *nineteen*
dix-sept *seventeen*
docteur (m.) *doctor*
document (m.) *document*
documentaire (m.) *documentary*
doigt (m.) *finger*
  doigt de pied *toe*
donc *so, then, therefore*
  Dis donc ! *Man!/You don't say!/Say! (lit., Say so!)*
donner *to give, to show*
  donner un coup de fil *to make a phone call (lit., to give/pass a hit of the wire)* (infml.)
doublé / doublée (m./f.) *dubbed*
doucement *sweetly, gently, softly*
douche (f.) *shower*
  gel (m.) **douche** *shower gel*
doux / douce *sweet, gentle, soft*
douzaine (f.) *dozen*
  douzaine d'œufs *dozen eggs*
douze *twelve*

drame (m.) *drama*
  drame d'époque *period drama*
drapeau (m.) *flag*
droit *straight*
  tout droit *straight ahead*
  Il faut aller tout droit. *You must go straight ahead.*
droite (f.) *right (opposite of left)*
  à droite *on the right, to the right, at the right*
drôle *funny*
du / de l' / de la / des (m./m. or f. before a vowel or silent h/f./pl.) *some, of the*
dur / dure (m./f.) *hard*
  œuf (m.) **dur** *hard-boiled egg (lit., hard egg)*

E

eau (f.) *water*
  eau de cologne *cologne*
  eau de Javel *bleach*
  eau minérale *mineral water*
  carafe (f.) **d'eau** *pitcher of water*
écharpe (f.) *scarf (winter)*
éclair (m.) *lightning, éclair (type of cream-filled pastry)*
école (f.) *school*
écossais / écossaise (m./f.) *Scottish*
Écosse (f.) *Scotland*
écouter *to listen (to)*
écran (m.) *monitor, screen*
écrire *to write*
écrivain (m.) (sometimes: **écrivaine,** f.) *writer*
effrayant / effrayante (m./f.) *scary*
égal / égale (m./f.) *equal*
église (f.) *church*
électricien (m.) *electrician*
élégant / élégante (m./f.) *elegant*
éléphant (m.) *elephant*
elle *she, it* (f.), *her*
elles *they* (f.), *it* (f. pl.), *them* (f.)
email (m.) *e-mail*
émission (f.) *television program*
emmener *to take along*
emploi (m.) *employment, job*
  emploi régulier *steady job*
  sans emploi *unemployed*
employé / employée (m./f.) *employee*

en *in, into, to, some, of it, of them*
  en effet *really, indeed*
  en avance *early*
  en face de *across from, facing*
  en général *in general, generally, usually*
  en haut *upstairs, up above*
  en bas *downstairs, down below*
  en retard *late*
Enchanté. / Enchantée. (m./f.) *Pleased to meet you./Nice to meet you.*
encore *again, still, more*
  ne... pas encore *not yet*
enfant (m./f.) *child*
enfin *finally*
ennuyer *to annoy, to bore (someone)*
  s'ennuyer *to get bored, to be bored*
  C'est ennuyeux. *It's boring.*
énorme *enormous*
enseignant / enseignante (m./f.) *teacher*
enseigner *to teach*
ensemble *together*
ensuite *then, next*
entendre *to understand, to hear*
  Entendu. *All right./Understood.*
entraîneur (m.) *coach*
entre *between*
entrée (f.) *appetizer, entrance*
entrer *to enter, to come in*
  Entre ! / Entrez ! *Come in! (infml./pl., fml.)*
envie (f.) *desire*
  avoir envie de *to feel like (lit., to have desire for)*
envoyer *to send, to throw*
  envoyer en pièce jointe *to attach a file*
  envoyer un fichier *to send a file*
  envoyer un mail / mél / email / courriel / courrier électronique *to send an e-mail*
épaule (f.) *shoulder*
épicerie (f.) *grocery store*
épinards (m. pl.) *spinach*
éponger *to mop, to soak up*
épouser (quelqu'un) *to marry (someone)*
équipe (f.) *team*
équitation (f.) *horseback riding*
  faire de l'équitation *to go horseback riding*
escaliers (m. pl.) *stairs*
escargots (m. pl.) *snails, escargots*
Espagne (f.) *Spain*

espagnol (m.) *Spanish language*
espagnol / espagnole (m./f.) *Spanish*
essentiel / essentielle (m./f.) *essential*
est (m.) *east*
est-ce ? *is it?*
estomac (m.) *stomach, abdomen*
et *and*
étage (m.) *floor (as in, second floor, third floor, etc.)*
  premier étage *first floor (one floor above the ground floor)*
étagère (f.) *shelf, bookshelf*
étang (m.) *pond*
États-Unis (m. pl.) *United States*
été (m.) *summer*
  en été *in (the) summer*
  été dernier *last summer*
étoile (f.) *star*
étrange *strange*
  C'est étrange. *It's strange.*
être *to be*
  peut-être *maybe, possibly*
  être fiancé / fiancée (à) (m./f.) *to be engaged (to)*
être (m.) humain *human being*
étudiant / étudiante (m./f.) *student*
étudier *to study*
euro (m.) *euro*
européen / européenne (m./f.) *European*
  Union (f.) européenne *European Union*
eux *them (m.)*
évier (m.) *sink*
  évier de la cuisine *kitchen sink*
exact / exacte (m./f.) *exact, correct*
examen (m.) *test*
  rater un examen *to fail a test*
  réussir à un examen *to pass a test*
excellent / excellente (m./f.) *excellent*
excuser *to excuse*
  Excusez-moi. *Excuse me.*
expression (f.) *expression*
extérieur (m.) *outside, exterior*
extra *great*

F

face (f.) *face, side*
  en face de *across from, facing*
facile *easy*

facilement *easily*
faible *weak*
faim (f.) *hunger*
  avoir faim *to be hungry*
faire *to do, to make*
  faire la cuisine *to do the cooking, to cook*
  faire la lessive *to do the laundry*
  faire la vaisselle *to do the dishes*
  faire le ménage *to do the house cleaning, to clean the house*
  faire les/des courses *to do the shopping, to go shopping, to shop*
  faire un tour *to take/do a tour*
  faire de la marche *to go hiking*
  faire du sport *to play a sport, to play sports*
  faire match nul *to tie (in a game/match)*
  faire la queue *to wait in line*
  faire suivre *to forward*
  faire de la natation *to go swimming*
  faire du ski *to ski*
  faire des achats *to run errands*
  faire une promenade *to take a walk*
  faire une réservation *to make a reservation*
  faire des réservations *to make reservations*
  Ça fait... *That makes .../That is ...*
  Il fait beau. *It's beautiful (outside).*
  Il fait chaud. *It's hot./It's warm.*
  Il fait froid. *It's cold.*
  Il fait soleil. *It's sunny.*
falloir *to be necessary*
  il faut *it's necessary to, you have/need to, you must*
famille (f.) *family*
fauteuil (m.) *armchair*
faux / fausse (m./f.) *false, wrong*
Félicitations. *Congratulations.*
femme (f.) *woman, wife*
  femme d'affaires *businesswoman*
fenêtre (f.) *window*
fer (m.) à repasser *iron*
fermer *to close*
  fermer un fichier *to close a file*
fermier / fermière (m./f.) *farmer*
fête (f.) *party, festival, holiday*
  fête nationale *national holiday*
  Bonnes / Joyeuses fêtes ! *Happy Holidays!*
feu (m.) *fire*
février *February*

fiancé / fiancée (m./f.) *fiancé/fiancée*
  être fiancé / fiancée (à) *to be engaged (to)*
fichier (m.) *file*
fier / fière (m./f.) *proud*
fille (f.) *girl, daughter*
  fille unique *only child (f.)*
film (m.) *movie, film*
  film d'action *action film*
  film policier *crime drama/film, detective drama/film*
  film à suspense *thriller*
  film d'épouvante *horror movie*
  film d'animation *animated movie*
fils (m.) *son*
  fils unique *only child (m.)*
finir *to finish*
firme (f.) *company, firm*
fleur (f.) *flower*
fois (f.) *time*
  une fois *once, one time*
foot(ball) (m.) *soccer*
football (m.) américain *(American) football*
footballeur / footballeuse (m./f.) *soccer player*
forêt (f.) *forest*
Formidable. *Fantastic.*
fort / forte (m./f.) *strong*
foulard (m.) *scarf (fashion)*
foule (f.) *crowd*
four (m.) *oven*
fourchette (f.) *fork*
foyer (m.) *home*
fraise (f.) *strawberry*
  glace (f.) à la fraise *strawberry ice cream*
  tarte (f.) aux fraises *strawberry pie*
français (m.) *French language*
  en français *in French*
français / française (m./f.) *French*
France (f.) *France*
frère (m.) *brother*
frites (f. pl.) *french fries*
  poulet (m.) frites *chicken and fries*
  steak (m.) frites *steak and fries*
  moules (f. pl.) frites *mussels and fries*
froid / froide (m./f.) *cold*
  Il fait froid. *It's cold.*
  avoir froid *to be cold*
fromage (m.) *cheese*
  sandwich (m.) au fromage *cheese sandwich*

sandwich (m.) **jambon-fromage** *ham and cheese sandwich*
tranche (f.) **/part de fromage** *slice of cheese*
front (m.) *forehead*
fruit (m.) *fruit*
  salade (f.) **de fruits** *fruit salad*

G

gagner *to win, to earn*
galerie (f.) *gallery*
gant (m.) *glove*
garage (m.) *garage*
garçon (m.) *boy*
gare (f.) *train station*
gastronomie (f.) *gastronomy*
gâteau (m.) *cake*
  gâteau au chocolat *chocolate cake*
gauche (f.) *left*
  à gauche *on the left, to the left, at the left*
gel (m.) **douche** *shower gel*
général / générale (m./f.) *general*
généralement *generally*
généreux / généreuse (m./f.) *generous*
genou (m.) *knee*
gens (m. pl.) *people*
gentil / gentille (m./f.) *nice, kind*
gérant / gérante (m./f.) *manager*
glace (f.) *ice cream*
  glace à la vanille *vanilla ice cream*
  glace à la fraise *strawberry ice cream*
  glace au chocolat *chocolate ice cream*
gourmand (m.) *lover of food, gourmand*
gourmet (m.) *gourmet, lover of fine food*
goût (m.) *taste*
grammaire (f.) *grammar*
gramme (m.) *gram*
grand / grande (m./f.) *big, large, tall*
  grand magasin (m.) *department store*
  grandes vacances (f. pl.) *summer vacation*
  Pas grand-chose. *Not a lot.*
grandir *to grow*
grand-mère (f.) *grandmother*
grand-parent (m.) *grandparent*
grand-père (m.) *grandfather*
gratiné / gratinée (m./f.) *topped with browned cheese (and possibly also breadcrumbs)*
grec / grecque (m./f.) *Greek*

Grèce (f.) *Greece*
grêle (f.) *hail*
  Il grêle. *It's hailing.*
gros / grosse (m./f.) *fat*
grossir *to gain weight*
groupe (m.) **de musique** *band*
guichet (m.) *ticket window, counter, window, box office*
  guichet automatique *ATM*
guichetier (m.) *clerk (at the window/counter), teller*
guide (m.) *guide*
gymnastique (f.) *gym (physical education), gymnastics*

H

habiller *to dress*
  s'habiller *to dress oneself, to get dressed*
habiter *to live*
haine (f.) *hatred*
haltérophilie (f.) *weight lifting*
Hanoukka / Hanoucca (f.) *Hanukkah*
haricot (m.) *bean*
  haricot vert *green bean*
hasard (m.) *chance*
hâte (f.) *haste*
  avoir hâte *to look forward to (can't wait)*
hâter *to hasten*
  se hâter *to rush*
haut / haute (m./f.) *high*
  en haut *upstairs, up above*
hériter *to inherit*
héros / héroïne (m./f.) *hero/heroine*
heure (f.) *hour*
  Quelle heure est-il ? *What time is it?*
  heure du départ / heure de départ *departure time*
  heure de l'arrivée / heure d'arrivée *arrival time*
  à l'heure *on time*
  à quelle heure ? *at what time?*
  À tout à l'heure ! *See you later!*
heureusement *happily, fortunately*
heureux / heureuse (m./f.) *happy*
hier *yesterday*
  avant-hier *the day before yesterday*
  hier soir *last night*

histoire (f.) *story, history*
hiver (m.) *winter*
  en hiver *in (the) winter*
hockey (m.) *hockey*
homard (m.) *lobster*
  bisque (f.) de homard *lobster bisque*
homme (m.) *man*
  homme d'affaires *businessman*
honte (f.) *shame*
  avoir honte *to be ashamed*
hôpital (m.) *hospital*
horaire (m.) *schedule*
horrible *horrible*
hors *outside*
hors-d'œuvre (m.) *appetizer*
hôtel (m.) *hotel*
  hôtel de ville *municipal building, city hall*
huile (f.) *oil*
huit *eight*
huitième *eighth*
huître (f.) *oyster*
humain / humaine (m./f.) *human, humane*
  être (m.) humain *human being*

I

ici *here*
  d'ici *from here*
  par ici *this way*
idée (f.) *idea*
  Quelle bonne idée ! *What a good idea!*
il *he, it* (m.)
  Il fait beau. *It's beautiful (outside).*
  Il fait chaud. *It's hot./It's warm.*
  Il fait froid. *It's cold.*
  Il grêle. *It's hailing.*
  Il neige. *It's snowing.*
  Il pleut. *It's raining./It rains.*
  il faut *it's necessary to, you have/need to, you must*
  il y a *there is/are, ago*
  Il n'y a pas de quoi. *You're welcome.*
  Il y a du soleil / Il fait soleil. *It's sunny.*
  Il y a du vent. *It's windy.*
Île (f.) de la Cité *Île de la Cité (lit., City Island)*
ils *they* (m./mixed), *it* (m. pl.)
immeuble (m.) *apartment building, office building*

important / importante (m./f.) *important*
imprimante (f.) *printer*
Inde (f.) *India*
indien / indienne (m./f.) *Indian*
individu (m.) *individual*
ingénieur (m.) *engineer*
inquiet / inquiète (m./f.) *worried (anxious)*
institut (m.) de beauté *beauty parlor, beauty salon*
intelligent / intelligente (m./f.) *intelligent*
intéressant / intéressante (m./f.) *interesting*
intéresser *to interest*
  s'intéresser à / dans *to be interested in*
  Ça m'intéresse. *That interests me.*
  Ça ne m'intéresse pas. *That doesn't interest me.*
Internet (m.) *Internet*
interrompre *to interrupt*
intersection (f.) *intersection*
inviter *to invite*
Irlandais / Irlandaise (m./f.) *Irishman/Irishwoman*
irlandais / irlandaise (m./f.) *Irish*
Irlande (f.) *Ireland*
Italie (f.) *Italy*
italien / italienne (m./f.) *Italian*

J

jamais *ever, never*
  ne... jamais *never*
jambe (f.) *leg*
jambon (m.) *ham*
  sandwich (m.) au jambon *ham sandwich*
  sandwich (m.) jambon-fromage *ham and cheese sandwich*
janvier *January*
Japon (m.) *Japan*
japonais / japonaise (m./f.) *Japanese*
jardin (m.) *garden*
jaune *yellow*
je / j' *I*
  Je m'appelle... *My name is ... /I am called ...*
  Je ne comprends pas. *I don't understand.*
  Je vais très bien. *I'm very well.*
  Je veux... *I want ...*
  Je voudrais... *I would like ...*

Je te présente... / Je vous présente... *Let me introduce ...* (infml./pl., fml.)

Je vous en prie. *You're welcome.* (fml.)

Je suis ravi / ravie de faire votre connaissance. *I'm delighted to make your acquaintance.*

jean (m.) *jeans*

jeu (m.) *game*

  jeu électronique *electronic game*

  jeu vidéo *video game*

jeudi *Thursday*

jeune *young*

Joconde (f.) *Mona Lisa*

joli / jolie (m./f.) *nice, pretty*

joue (f.) *cheek*

jouer *to play, to perform, to act*

  cartes (f. pl.) **à jouer** *playing cards*

joueur / joueuse (m /f.) *player (games, sports, etc.)*

jour (m.) *day*

  jour de l'An *New Year's Day*

  jours (pl.) **de la semaine** *days of the week*

journal (m.) *newspaper*

journaliste (m./f.) *journalist*

journée (f.) *day*

joyeux / joyeuse (m./f.) *joyful, cheerful*

  Joyeuses fêtes ! *Happy Holidays!*

  Joyeux anniversaire ! *Happy birthday!/ Happy anniversary!*

  Joyeux Noël ! *Merry Christmas!*

juillet *July*

  14 (Quatorze) Juillet *Bastille Day, July 14th (France's national holiday)*

juin *June*

jupe (f.) *skirt*

jus (m.) *juice*

  boîte (f.) **de jus d'orange** *carton of orange juice*

jusqu'à *to, until, up to, up until*

juste *just, only*

K

kilo (m.) *kilo*

kilomètre *kilometer*

kir (m.) *white wine with black currant liqueur*

  kir royal *champagne with black currant liqueur*

L

là *there*

  là-bas *over there, there*

la / l' / le / les (f./m. or f. before a vowel or silent h/m./pl.) *the*

lac (m.) *lake*

laid / laide (m./f.) *ugly*

laisser *to leave, to let (someone do something), to let go*

  Je voudrais laisser un message. *I would like to leave a message.*

lait (m.) *milk*

  verre (m.) **de lait** *glass of milk*

laitue (f.) *lettuce*

lampadaire (m.) *streetlight*

lampe (f.) *lamp*

langue (f.) *language, tongue*

large *wide*

lavabo (m.) *sink*

lave-linge (m.) *washing machine*

laver *to wash*

  se laver *to wash up, to wash oneself*

lave-vaisselle (m.) *dishwasher*

le / l' / la / les (m./m. or f. before a vowel or silent h/f./pl.) *the*

leçon (f.) *lesson*

lecteur (m.) *player (CDs, DVDs, etc.), drive (computer)*

  lecteur de CD *CD player*

  lecteur de DVD *DVD player*

  lecteur de CD-ROM *CD-ROM drive*

léger / légère (m./f.) *light*

légèrement *lightly*

légume (m.) *vegetable*

lent / lente (m./f.) *slow*

lentement *slowly*

  Parlez plus lentement, s'il vous plaît. *Speak slower/more slowly, please.*

les *the* (pl.)

lessive (f.) *laundry detergent*

lettre (f.) *letter*

leur / leurs (m. or f./pl.) *their*

lever *to lift, to raise*

  se lever *to get up, to rise (to get oneself up)*

liaison (f.) *link*

librairie (f.) *bookstore*

libre *free*

lieu (m.) *place*
  avoir lieu *to take place, to be held (lit., to have place)*
liquide (m.) vaisselle *dishwashing detergent*
lire *to read*
lit (m.) *bed*
littérature (f.) *literature*
livre (f.) *pound*
  livre de beurre *pound of butter*
livre (m.) *book*
  livre scolaire *textbook*
loin *far*
  loin d'ici *far from here*
  plus loin *farther*
long / longue (m./f.) *long*
  le long de *along, alongside*
longtemps *long, (for a) long time*
loup (f.) *wolf*
Louvre (m.) *Louvre*
lui *him*
lundi *Monday*
  lundi dernier *last Monday*
lune (f.) *moon*
lunettes (f. pl.) *eyeglasses*
  lunettes de soleil *sunglasses*
lustre (m.) *chandelier*
lycée (m.) *high school*

M

M. *Mr.*
ma / mon / mes (f./m./pl.) *my*
macaron (m.) *meringue cookie*
machine (f.) à laver *washing machine*
madame *ma'am, Mrs., Ms., madam*
  mesdames *ladies*
mademoiselle *miss*
magasin (m.) *store*
  grand magasin *department store*
  magasin d'électronique *electronics store*
  magasin de chaussures *shoe store*
  magasin de vêtements *clothing store*
magazine (m.) *magazine*
magnifique *magnificent*
mai *May*
maigrir *to lose weight*
mail (m.) *e-mail*
maillot (m.) de bain *bathing suit, bathing trunks*

maillot (m.) de corps *undershirt*
main (f.) *hand*
maintenant *now*
maire (m.) *mayor*
mairie (f.) *city hall, municipal building*
mais *but*
maïs (m.) *corn*
maison *homemade*
maison (f.) *house, home*
  à la maison *at the house, at home*
mal *badly, bad, wrong*
  Ça va mal. *It's going badly./It's not going well.*
malade *sick*
malheureusement *unhappily, unfortunately*
malheureux / malheureuse (m./f.) *unhappy, unfortunate*
maman *Mom, Mommy*
manger *to eat*
  salle (f.) à manger *dining room*
  Qu'est-ce qu'il y a à manger ? *What is there to eat?*
manteau (m.) *coat*
marché (m.) *market*
marcher *to walk*
mardi *Tuesday*
mare (f.) *pond*
mari (m.) *husband*
marié / mariée (m./f.) *married*
Maroc (m.) *Morocco*
marocain / marocaine (m./f.) *Moroccan*
marron *brown*
marron (m.) *chestnut*
mars *March*
match (m.) *match, game*
mathématiques (f. pl.) *math*
maths (f. pl.) *math*
matin (m.) *morning*
matinée (f.) *morning*
mauvais / mauvaise (m./f.) *bad*
  C'est mauvais. *That's bad.*
me / m' (reflexive pronoun) *myself*
  Je m'appelle... *My name is .../I am called ...*
médecin (m.) *doctor*
médecine (f.) *medicine*
mél (m.) *email*
melon (m.) *melon, cantaloupe*
même *same, even*
mémoire (f.) *memory*

menacer *to threaten*

ménage (m.) *house cleaning*
   faire le ménage *to clean the house, to do the house cleaning*

menthe (f.) *mint*
   menthe à l'eau *water with mint syrup*

menton (m.) *chin*

menu (m.) *menu*
   Le menu, s'il vous plaît. *The menu, please.*

mer (f.) *sea*

merci *thank you*
   Merci bien. *Thank you very much.*

mercredi *Wednesday*

mère (f.) *mother*

mes / mon / ma (pl./m./f.) *my*

mesdames *ladies*

mesdemoiselles *misses*

message (m.) instantané *instant message*

messieurs *gentlemen*

métro (m.) *subway, metro*
   station (f.) de métro *subway station*
   plan (m.) du métro *map of the subway*
   carte (f.) du métro *map of the subway*

mettre *to put*
   mettre à la poste *to mail, to put in the mail*

meubles (m. pl.) *furniture (in general)*
   meuble (m.) *a piece of furniture*

mexicain / mexicaine (m./f.) *Mexican*

Mexique (m.) *Mexico*

micro-ondes (m.) *microwave (oven)*

midi (m.) *noon*
   Il est midi. *It is noon.*

miel (m.) *honey*

milieu (m.) *middle*
   au milieu de *in the middle of*

mille *thousand*

mince *thin*

minéral / minérale (m./f.) *mineral*
   eau (f.) minérale *mineral water*

minuit (m.) *midnight*
   Il est minuit. *It is midnight.*

miroir (m.) *mirror*

mixer (m.) *blender*

Mlle *Miss*

Mme *Mrs., Ms.*

modem (m.) *modem*

moi *me*

moins *less, minus, fewer*
   ... moins le quart *quarter to ...*
   moins de *less*

mois (m.) *month*
   dans un mois *next month, in one month*
   mois prochain *next month*
   mois dernier *last month*
   deux mois auparavant *two months before*
   deux mois avant *two months before*
   mois (pl.) de l'année *months of the year*

moment (m.) *moment*

mon / ma / mes (m./f./pl.) *my*

monde (m.) *world, people*
   tout le monde *everyone*

monnaie (f.) *change, coins, currency*

monsieur *sir, Mr.*
   messieurs *gentlemen*

montagne (f.) *mountain*

monter *to go up, to come up, to rise*

montre (f.) *watch*

montrer *to show*

monument (m.) *monument*

moquette (f.) *carpet*

morceau (m.) *piece, bite*

mosquée (f.) *mosque*

mot (m.) *word*

moto (f.) *motorcycle, motorcycling*

motocyclette (f.) *motorcycle*

moule (f.) *mussel*
   moules (pl.) frites *mussels and fries*

mourir *to die*

mousse (f.) *mousse*
   mousse au chocolat *chocolate mousse*

mousseux / mousseuse *sparkling*
   vin (m.) mousseux *sparkling wine*

moutarde (f.) *mustard*
   moutarde de Dijon *Dijon mustard*

mur (m.) *wall*

muscle (m.) *muscle*

musée (m.) *museum*

musicien / musicienne (m./f.) *musician*

musique (f.) *music*

mystérieux / mystérieuse (m./f.) *mysterious*

N

nager *to swim*

naître *to be born*

nappe (f.) *tablecloth*

natation (f.) *swimming*
faire de la natation *to go swimming*

nation (f.) *nation*

national / nationale (m./f.) *national*
fête (f.) nationale *national holiday*

nationalité (f.) *nationality*

naturel / naturelle (m./f.) *natural*

naturellement *naturally*

ne / n'... pas *not*
n'est-ce pas ? *isn't it?, isn't that so?, right?*
ne... jamais *never*
ne... plus *no longer, no more, any more, any-more*
ne... pas encore *not yet*
ne... rien *nothing, anything*

neige (f.) *snow*
vacances (f. pl.) d'hiver *winter vacation*

neiger *to snow*
Il neige. *It's snowing.*

neuf *nine*

neuf (m.) *new*
Rien de neuf. *Nothing new.*
Quoi de neuf ? *What's up?/What's new?*

neuvième *ninth*

neveu (m.) *nephew*

nez (m.) *nose*

nièce (f.) *niece*

Noël (m.) *Christmas*
Joyeux Noël ! *Merry Christmas!*
réveillon (m.) de Noël *Christmas Eve*
veille (f.) de Noël *Christmas Eve*

noir / noire (m./f.) *black*

nom (m.) *name*
sous quel nom ? *under what name?*

nombre (m.) *number*

non *no*

nord (m.) *north*

note (f.) *grade, note*

notre / nos (m. or f./pl.): *our*

nourrir *to feed*

nourriture (f.) *food*

nous *we, us, ourselves*

nouveau / nouvel / nouvelle (m./m. before a vowel or silent h/f.) *new*
Nouvel An (m.) *New Year*

nouveau-né (m.) *newborn*

nouvelles (f. pl.) *news (the news)*

novembre *November*

nuage (m.) *cloud*

nuageux / nuageuse (m./f.) *cloudy*
C'est nuageux. *It's cloudy.*

nuit (f.) *night*
Bonne nuit ! *Good night!*
nuit dernière *last night*

nul / nulle (m./f.) *no*
nulle part *nowhere, anywhere*

numéro (m.) de téléphone *phone number*

O

obéir *to obey*

occupé / occupée (m./f.) *busy*

océan (m.) *ocean*

octobre *October*

œil (m.) (yeux, pl.) *eye (eyes)*

œuf (m.) *egg*
œuf poché *poached egg*
œuf au plat, œuf sur le plat *fried egg (over easy egg)*
œuf à la coque *soft-boiled egg*
œuf dur *hard-boiled egg (lit., hard egg)*
œufs (pl.) brouillés *scrambled eggs*
blancs (m. pl.) d'œufs *egg whites*
douzaine (f.) d'œufs *dozen eggs*

Oh là là ! *Wow!/No way!*

oignon (m.) *onion*
soupe (f.) à l'oignon *onion soup*

omelette (f.) *omelette*
omelette aux champignons *mushroom omelette*

on *we (infml.), people in general, one (pronoun), you (general), they (general)*
On y va. *Let's go. (infml.)*

oncle (m.) *uncle*

onze *eleven*

onzième *eleventh*

opéra (m.) *opera*

orage (m.) *storm*

orange *orange (color)*

orange (f.) *orange (fruit)*
boîte (f.) de jus d'orange *carton of orange juice*
canard (m.) à l'orange *duck à l'orange, duck with orange sauce*

ordinateur (m.) *computer*

oreille (f.) *ear*
organiser *to organize*
  organiser une fête *to have a party*
original / originale (m./f.) *original*
origine (f.) *origin*
orteil (m.) *toe*
os (m.) *bone*
ou *or*
  ou bien *or even, or else, either, or*
où *where*
  Où sont les toilettes ? *Where is the restroom?*
  Où se trouve... ? / Où est... ? *Where is ... ?*
ouest (m.) *west*
oui *yes*
ouragan (m.) *hurricane*
ouvrier (m.) en bâtiment *construction worker*
ouvrir *to open*
  ouvrir un fichier *to open a file*

P

page (f.) web *webpage*
pain (m.) *bread*
palourde (f.) *clam*
panier (m.) *basket*
pansement (m.) *bandage*
pantalon (m.) *pants*
papa *Dad, Daddy*
papier (m.) *paper*
  papier hygiénique *toilet paper*
paquebot (m.) *cruise ship, ocean liner*
par *by, through*
  par ici *this way*
  par là *that way*
parapluie (m.) *umbrella*
parc (m.) *park*
parce que *because*
pardon *pardon (me), excuse me*
parent (m.) *relative, parent*
parfait / parfaite (m./f.) *perfect*
  C'est parfait. *It's perfect.*
parfois *sometimes*
parfum (m.) *flavor, fragrance, perfume*
Paris *Paris*
parisien / parisienne (m./f.) *Parisian*
parler *to speak, to talk*
  Parlez plus lentement, s'il vous plaît. *Speak slower/more slowly, please.*

Je parle un peu français. *I speak a little French.*
part (f.) *part, share, slice (cake, pie, pizza)*
  de la part de *on behalf of, from (someone)*
  de ma part *on my behalf, from me, on my part*
  nulle part *nowhere, anywhere*
partie (f.) *game, part, party*
partir *to leave, to go away*
partout *everywhere*
pas *not*
  ne... pas *not*
  pas du tout *not at all*
  Pas mal. *Not bad.*
  Pas grand-chose. *Not a lot.*
passeport (m.) *passport*
passer *to pass, to go past, to spend (time)*
  Je vous le / la passe. *I'm getting him/her for you. (lit., I'm passing him/her to you.)*
  passer un coup de fil *to make a phone call (lit., to pass a hit of the wire) (infml.)*
passionnant / passionnante (m./f.) *exciting*
pâté (m.) *pâté (spreadable purée of meat)*
  pâté de foie gras *goose liver pâté*
patient / patiente (m./f.) *patient*
  Sois patient. *Be patient. (infml.)*
  Soyez patient. *Be patient. (pl./fml.)*
patin (m.) *skate, skating*
  patin à glace *ice skate, ice-skating*
pâtisserie (f.) *pastry shop, pastry*
  pâtisserie-confiserie (f.) *pastry and candy store*
patron / patronne (m./f.) *boss*
pauvre *unfortunate, poor, impoverished*
payer *to pay*
peau (f.) *skin*
pêche (f.) *peach*
  pêche Melba *peaches with ice cream*
peindre *to paint*
pendule (f.) *grandfather clock*
penser *to think*
perdre *to lose*
  Il perd son temps. *He's wasting his time. (lit., He's losing his time.)*
perdu / perdue (m./f.) *lost*
  Je suis perdu / perdue. *I'm lost.*
père (m.) *father*

personne (f.) *person, no one, nobody*
  personne âgée *elderly person*
  ne / n' ... personne *no one, nobody*
  pour quatre personnes *for four people, for a party of four*
personnel (m.) *staff*
petit / petite (m./f.) *small, little, short*
  petit ami / petite amie (m./f.) *boyfriend/girlfriend*
  petit déjeuner (m.) *breakfast*
  prendre le petit déjeuner *to have breakfast*
  petits pois (m. pl.) *(green) peas (lit., little peas)*
peu *little, bit*
  peu de *little, few*
  un peu *a little*
  peu amical / peu amicale (m./f.) *unfriendly*
peur (f.) *fear*
  avoir peur *to be afraid (lit, to have fear)*
peut-être *maybe, possibly*
pharmacie (f.) *pharmacy, drugstore*
photo (f.) *photo*
  Pourriez-vous nous prendre en photo, s'il vous plaît ? *Can you take our picture (photo), please?*
phrase (f.) *phrase*
pièce (f.) *room, play (theater), piece, coin*
  pièce jointe *attachment*
pied (m.) *foot*
  à pied *on foot, by foot*
  au pied de *at the foot of*
placard (m.) *cupboard, closet*
place (f.) *place, seat, ticket, room*
plafond (m.) *ceiling*
plage (f.) *beach*
plaire *to please*
  s'il te plaît *please* (infml.)
  s'il vous plaît *please* (pl./fml.)
plaisir (m.) *pleasure*
  Avec plaisir. *With pleasure.*
plan (m.) *map, plan*
  plan de la ville *map of the city*
  plan du métro *map of the subway*
planche (f.) à repasser *ironing board*
plante (f.) *plant*
plastique (m.) *plastic*
  en plastique *made of plastic*

plat (m.) *dish*
  plat principal *main dish/course*
  plat d'accompagnement *side dish*
pleuvoir *to rain*
  Il pleut. *It's raining./It rains.*
plombier (m.) *plumber*
plonger *to dive*
pluie (f.) *rain*
plus *more*
  plus loin *farther*
  le / la plus proche (m./f.) *the nearest, the closest*
  À plus tard ! *See you later!*
  À plus ! *See you later!* (infml.)
  et bien plus *and even more, and much more*
  ne... plus *no longer, no more, any more, anymore*
  plus de *more*
pneu (m.) *tire*
poché / pochée (m./f.) *poached*
  œuf (m.) poché *poached egg*
poignet (m.) *wrist*
poire (f.) *pear*
pois (m. pl.) *peas*
  petits pois *(green) peas (lit., little peas)*
poisson (m.) *fish*
poitrine (f.) *chest*
poivre (m.) *pepper (condiment)*
poivron (m.) *pepper (vegetable)*
poli / polie (m./f.) *polite*
policier / femme policier (m./f.) *policeman/woman*
policier / policière (m./f.) *police, detective (adjective)*
  film (m.) policier *detective drama/film, crime drama/film*
poliment *politely*
pomme (f.) *apple*
  pomme de terre *potato*
  tarte (f.) aux pommes *apple pie*
  purée (f.) de pommes de terre *mashed potatoes*
  pommes (pl.) de terre en robe des champs *boiled potatoes in their skins, baked potatoes*
pont (m.) *bridge*
porc (m.) *pork, pig*
  côte (f.) de porc *pork chop*

portable (m.) *cell phone*
porte (f.) *door*
porter *to carry, to wear*
portugais / portugaise (m./f.) *Portuguese*
Portugal (m.) *Portugal*
possible *possible*
  Ce n'est pas possible ! *I don't believe it!/*
    Oh man!/It's not possible! (disappointment,
    anger)
poste (f.) *post office, mail*
  bureau (m.) de poste *post office*
poste (m.) *telephone extension*
poste (m.) de police *police station*
pot (m.) *drink* (infml.)
potage (m.) *soup*
poudre (f.) *powder*
poulet (m.) *chicken*
  poulet frites *chicken and fries*
poumon (m.) *lung*
pour *for, to*
pourquoi *why*
pouvoir *to be able to, can*
  Puis-je vous aider ? *Can I help you?*
pratiquer *to practice*
précédent / précédente (m./f.) *before last*
  semaine (f.) précédente *the week before last*
précis / précise (m./f.) *sharp, exact, precise*
  à midi précis *exactly at noon (at noon sharp)*
préféré / préférée (m./f.) *favorite*
préférer *to prefer*
premier / première (m./f.) *first*
  premier étage (m.) *first floor (one floor above*
    the ground floor)
prendre *to take, to have (food/drink)*
  prendre un bain *to take a bath*
  prendre une douche *to take a shower*
  prendre un verre *to have a drink*
  prendre le petit déjeuner *to have breakfast*
  prendre une chambre *to check in*
  prendre rendez-vous *to make an appointment*
  prendre une photo *to take a picture (photo)*
  Pourriez-vous nous prendre en photo,
    s'il vous plaît ? *Can you take our picture*
    (photo), please?
préparer *to prepare, to make, to cook*
près *close, near*
  tout près *very close, very near*
  près d'ici *nearby, near here, close to here*

présenter *to introduce, to show, to present*
  Je te présente... / Je vous présente... *Let me*
    introduce ... (infml./pl., fml.)
prêt / prête (m./f.) *ready*
prier *to ask, to beg, to pray*
  Je vous en prie. *You're welcome.* (fml.)
principal / principale (m./f.) *principal (main)*
  plat (m.) principal *main course*
printemps (m.) *spring*
  au printemps *in (the) spring*
probable *probable*
probablement *probably*
prochain / prochaine (m./f.) *next*
  mois (m.) prochain *next month*
  semaine (f.) prochaine *next week*
  À la prochaine ! *See you later! (Until next*
    time!)
proche *near, nearby, close*
  le / la plus proche (m./f.) *the nearest, the*
    closest
produire *to produce*
prof (m./f.) *professor, teacher* (infml.)
professeur / professeure (m./f.) *professor,*
  teacher
progrès (m.) *progress*
promenade (f.) *walk*
  faire une promenade *to take a walk*
promener *to take someone or something for a*
  walk
  se promener *to take a walk*
propre *clean, own*
prune (f.) *plum*
puis *then*
punir *to punish*
purée (f.) *purée*
  purée de pommes de terre *mashed potatoes*
pyjama (m.) *pajamas*

Q

quai (m.) *platform, quay, bank (of a river)*
quand *when*
quarante *forty*
quart (m.) *quarter*
  ... et quart *quarter after/past ...*
  ... moins le quart *quarter to ...*
quartier (m.) *neighborhood, quarter, area*
quatorze *fourteen*

quatre *four*
quatre-vingt-dix *ninety*
quatre-vingts *eighty*
quatrième *fourth*
que *what, that, which, whom*
  qu'est-ce que ? *what?*
  Qu'est-ce que c'est ? *What is this/that?*
quel / quelle (m./f.) *which, what*
  à quelle heure ? *at what time?*
  de quel / quelle ? (m./f.) *what?/of what?*
  Quel temps fait-il aujourd'hui ? *What is the weather today?*
  Quelle heure est-il ? *What time is it?*
  Quel soulagement ! *What a relief!*
  Quelle coïncidence ! *What a coincidence!*
  Quelle bonne idée ! *What a good idea!*
quelqu'un *someone*
question (f.) *question*
queue (f.) *line, tail*
  faire la queue *to wait in line*
qui *who, that*
  Qui est à l'appareil ? *Who is it?/Who's calling? (on the phone)*
  Qui est-ce ? *Who is it?*
quiche (f.) *quiche (baked dish made with eggs and cream)*
  quiche lorraine *type of quiche made with bacon*
quincaillerie (f.) *hardware store*
quinze *fifteen*
quinzième *fifteenth*
quitter *to leave, to depart, to quit*
  Ne quittez pas, s'il vous plaît. *Hold on, please. (lit., Don't leave, please.)*
quoi *what*
  Quoi de neuf ? *What's up?/What's new?*
quotidien / quotidienne (m./f.) *everyday, daily*

R

raccrocher *to hang up*
radis (m.) *radish*
  radis au beurre *rosette-cut radishes served with butter on top (lit., radishes in butter)*
raisin (m.) *grape(s)*
raison (f.) *reason*
  avoir raison *to be right (lit., to have reason)*
Ramadan (m.) *Ramadan*

ranger *to put away*
rapide *quick*
rappeler *to call back*
rarement *rarely*
rasoir (m.) *razor*
rater (un examen) *to fail (a test)*
ravi / ravie (m./f.) *delighted, charmed*
  Je suis ravi / ravie de faire votre connaissance. *I'm delighted to make your acquaintance.*
réception (f.) *reception desk*
recette (f.) *recipe*
recommander *to recommend*
récré(ation) (f.) *recess*
réfléchir *to think, to reflect*
réfrigérateur (m.) *refrigerator*
regarder *to watch, to look at*
régler sa note *to check out*
remplir *to fill (in)*
rencontrer (une personne/quelqu'un) *to meet (a person/someone)*
rendez-vous (m.) *meeting, appointment, date*
  prendre rendez-vous *to make an appointment*
rendre *to give back, to return*
rentrer *to go home, to come home, to return, to come back (in), to go in*
repas (m.) *meal*
répéter *to repeat*
  Répétez, s'il vous plaît. *Repeat (that), please.*
répondre *to answer, to respond, to reply*
  répondre au téléphone *to answer the phone*
reposer *to rest*
  se reposer *to rest (oneself), to relax*
réservation (f.) *reservation*
  faire une réservation *to make a reservation*
  faire des réservations *to make reservations*
réserver *to reserve*
restaurant (m.) *restaurant*
rester *to stay*
retard (m.) *delay*
  en retard *late*
retourner *to return*
retraite (f.) *retirement*
  à la retraite *retired*
réunion (f.) *meeting, reunion*
réussir *to succeed, to do well*
  réussir à (un examen) *to pass (a test)*

réveiller *to wake (someone)*
  se réveiller *to wake up (to wake oneself up)*
réveillon (m.) du jour de l'An *New Year's Eve*
réveillon (m.) de Noël *Christmas Eve*
revenir *to come back, to return*
réverbère (m.) *lamppost*
revue (f.) *magazine*
rez-de-chaussée (m.) *ground floor*
riche *rich*
rideau (m.) *curtain*
rien *nothing, anything*
  ne … rien *nothing, anything*
  De rien. *You're welcome./It's nothing.*
  Rien de neuf. *Nothing new.*
  Rien de particulier. *Nothing much.*
rivière (f.) *river*
riz (m.) *rice*
robe (f.) *dress*
rocher (m.) *rock*
rôle (m.) *role, part (in a play, movie, etc.)*
romantique *romantic*
rompre *to break*
rondelle (f.) *(round) slice of (cucumber, banana, sausage, etc.)*
rose *pink*
rosé *rosé*
  vin (m.) rosé *rosé wine*
rose (f.) *rose*
rôti (m.) *roast, joint (of meat)*
  rôti de bœuf *roast beef*
rôti / rôtie (m./f.) *roast(ed)*
  carré (m.) d'agneau rôti *roast rack of lamb*
rouge *red*
  vin (m.) rouge *red wine*
rougir *to blush, to redden*
rue (f.) *street*
rural / rurale (m./f.) *rural*
russe *Russian*
Russie (f.) *Russia*

S

s'amuser *to have a good time, to enjoy oneself, to have fun*
s'appeler *to be called, to call oneself*
  Comment vous appelez-vous ? *What's your name?* (pl./fml.)
  Comment t'appelles-tu ? *What's your name?* (infml.)
  Je m'appelle… *My name is …/I am called …*
s'ennuyer *to get bored, to be bored*
s'habiller *to get dressed, to dress oneself*
s'il te plaît / s'il vous plaît *please* (infml./pl., fml.) *(lit., if it pleases you)*
sa / son / ses (f./m./pl.) *his, her, its*
sable (m.) *sand*
Sacré-Cœur (m.) *Sacré Cœur (lit., Sacred Heart)*
Saint-Sylvestre (f.) *New Year's Eve*
salade (f.) *salad*
  salade de fruits *fruit salad*
  salade verte *green salad*
  salade niçoise *niçoise salad*
saladier (m.) *bowl*
salaire (m.) *salary*
sale *dirty*
salé / salée (m./f.) *savory*
salle (f.) *room, hall*
  salle à manger *dining room*
  salle de bains *bathroom, washroom*
  salle de classe *classroom*
  salle de réunion *meeting room*
salon (m.) *parlor, living room*
Salut. *Hello./Hi./Bye.*
samedi *Saturday*
sandwich (m.) *sandwich*
  sandwich au jambon *ham sandwich*
  sandwich au fromage *cheese sandwich*
  sandwich jambon-fromage *ham and cheese sandwich*
sang (m.) *blood*
sans *without*
santé (f.) *health*
  À votre santé ! *To your health!*
  en bonne santé *healthy*
sardines (f. pl.) *sardines*
  sardines sauce tomate *sardines in tomato sauce*
sarrasin (m.) *buckwheat*
sauce (f.) *sauce*
saucisse (f.) *sausage*
sauter *to sauté*
sauvegarder un document *to save a document*
savoir *to know*
  Je ne sais pas. *I don't know.*
savon (m.) *soap*

sculpture (f.) *sculpture*
se / s' (reflexive pronoun) *himself, herself, them-selves, oneself*
  s'amuser *to have a good time, to enjoy oneself, to have fun*
  s'appeler *to be called, to call oneself*
  s'ennuyer *to get bored, to be bored*
  s'habiller *to get dressed, to dress oneself*
  se blesser *to hurt oneself*
  se brosser *to brush oneself (hair, teeth, etc.)*
  se coucher *to go to bed, to lie down (to lay oneself down)*
  se décider *to make up one's mind, to be decided, to be resolved (to do something)*
  se demander *to wonder, to ask oneself*
  se dépêcher *to hurry*
  se hâter *to rush*
  se laver *to wash up, to wash oneself*
  se lever *to get up, to rise (to get oneself up)*
  se promener *to take a walk*
  se raser *to shave*
  se reposer *to rest (oneself), to relax*
  se réveiller *to wake up (to wake oneself up)*
  se souvenir *to remember*
  se tromper *to be mistaken, to make a mistake*
  se trouver *to find oneself (somewhere), to be situated*
sèche-linge (m.) *dryer*
second / seconde (m./f.) *second*
secrétaire (m./f.) *secretary*
seize *sixteen*
sel (m.) *salt*
semaine (f.) *week*
  dans une semaine *next week, in one week*
  semaine dernière *last week*
  semaine prochaine *next week*
  semaine précédente *the week before last*
  semaine d'après *the week after next*
  semaine d'avant *the week before last*
  semaine suivante *the week after next*
  jours (m. pl.) de la semaine *days of the week*
sept *seven*
septembre *September*
septième *seventh*
sérieux / sérieuse (m./f.) *serious*
serveur / serveuse (m./f.) *waiter/waitress, server*
serviette (f.) *napkin, towel, briefcase*
  serviette de bain *bath towel*

ses / son / sa (pl./m./f.) *his, her, its*
seul / seule (m./f.) *alone*
seulement *only*
shampooing (m.) *shampoo*
si *if, yes (negative)*
  s'il te plaît / s'il vous plaît *please* (infml./pl., fml.) *(lit., if it pleases you)*
simple *simple*
  aller simple *one-way*
sincère *sincere*
site (m.) web *website*
six *six*
sixième *sixth*
ski (m.) *skiing*
  faire du ski *to ski*
skier *to ski*
social / sociale (m./f.) *social*
société (f.) *company*
sœur (f.) *sister*
soie (f.) *silk*
soif (f.) *thirst*
avoir soif *to be thirsty*
soir (m.) *evening, night*
  ce soir *tonight, this evening*
  hier soir *last night*
  Bonsoir ! *Good evening!*
soirée (f.) *party, evening*
soixante *sixty*
soixante-dix *seventy*
sol (m.) *floor (of a room)*
sole (f.) *sole (fish)*
  sole meunière *sole covered in flour and sautéed in butter*
soleil (m.) *sun*
  Il fait soleil. / Il y a du soleil. *It's sunny.*
solex (m.) *moped*
sommeil (m.) *sleep*
  avoir sommeil *to be sleepy (lit., to have sleep)*
son / sa / ses (m./f./pl.) *his, her, its*
sonner *to ring*
sortie (f.) *exit*
sortir *to go out, to leave, to come out*
  sortir avec *to go out with, to date*
  sortir en boîte *to go out to clubs, to go out clubbing*
soulagement (m.) *relief*
  Quel soulagement ! *What a relief!*

soupe (f.) *soup*
  soupe à l'oignon *onion soup*
souper *to have a late dinner*
souper (m.) *late dinner*
sourcil (m.) *eyebrow*
sourire (m.) *smile*
souris (f.) *mouse*
sous *under*
  sous quel nom ? *under what name?*
sous-titre (m.) *subtitle*
sous-vêtements (m. pl.) *underwear*
souvent *often*
spécialité (f.) *specialty*
sport (m.) *sport*
  faire du sport *to play sports, to do sports*
sportif / sportive (m./f.) *athletic*
stade (m.) *stadium*
  stade de foot *soccer stadium*
station (f.) *station*
  station de métro *subway station, metro station*
statue (f.) *statue*
steak (m.) *steak*
  steak frites *steak and fries*
sucre (m.) *sugar*
sucré / sucrée (m./f.) *sweet*
sud (m.) *south*
suisse *Swiss*
Suisse (f.) *Switzerland*
suivant / suivante (m./f.) *following, after next*
  semaine (f.) suivante *the week after next*
sujet (m.) *subject*
super *super, great*
  Super ! *Great!*
supermarché (m.) *supermarket*
supprimer *to delete*
sur *on*
sûr / sûre (m./f.) *sure*
  Bien sûr ! *Of course!*
surprendre *to surprise*
surtout *mostly, above all, especially*
sympa *cool, nice, good*
  très sympa *very cool/nice/good*
sympathique *friendly, nice*
synagogue (f.) *synagogue*

T

ta / ton / tes (f./m./pl.) *your* (infml.)
table (f.) *table*
  table pour deux *table for two*
  À table ! *Dinner's ready! (lit., To the table!)*
tableau (m.) *painting*
taille (f.) *size*
talc (m.) *powder*
talentueux / talentueuse (m./f.) *talented*
tante (f.) *aunt*
tapis (m.) *rug*
tard *late*
  À plus tard ! *See you later!*
tarte (f.) *pie, tart*
  tarte aux fraises *strawberry pie*
  tarte aux pommes *apple pie*
  tarte à la citrouille *pumpkin pie*
tartine (f.) *bread with butter and jelly*
tasse (f.) *cup*
  tasse de thé *cup of tea*
taxi (m.) *taxi, cab*
te / t' (reflexive pronoun) *yourself* (infml.)
télé(vision) (f.) *television, TV*
télécopieur (m.) *fax machine*
téléphone (m.) *telephone*
  (téléphone) portable *cell phone*
  répondre au téléphone *to answer the phone*
  numéro (m.) de téléphone *phone number*
téléphoner *to phone, to call, to make a phone call*
télévision (f.) *television*
température (f.) *temperature*
temple (m.) *temple*
temps (m.) *time, weather*
  Quel temps fait-il aujourd'hui ? *What's the weather today?*
  Je n'ai pas le temps. *I don't have (the) time.*
  Il perd son temps. *He's wasting his time.*
tendon (m.) *tendon*
tenir *to hold*
tennis (m.) *tennis*
terminer *to finish, to end*
terre (f.) *land*
tes / ton / ta (pl./m./f.) *your* (infml.)
tête (f.) *head*
thé (m.) *tea*
  tasse (f.) de thé *cup of tea*
théâtre (m.) *theater*

théière (f.) *teakettle, teapot*
thriller (m.) *thriller*
Tiens ! *Say!/Hey! (surprise)*
timbre (m.) *stamp*
tiroir (m.) *drawer*
tisane (f.) *herbal tea*
toi *you* (infml.)
toilettes (f. pl.) *toilet, restroom*
  Où sont les toilettes ? *Where is the restroom?*
tomate (f.) *tomato*
  sardines (f. pl.) sauce tomate *sardines in tomato sauce*
tomber *to fall*
ton / ta / tes (m./f./pl.) *your* (infml.)
tonnerre (m.) *thunder*
tort (m.) *wrong*
  avoir tort *to be wrong (lit., to have wrong)*
tôt *early*
toujours *always, still*
tour (f.) *tower*
  Tour Eiffel *Eiffel Tower*
tour (m.) *tour, turn*
touriste (m./f.) *tourist*
tourner *to turn*
tout / toute / tous / toutes (m./f./m. pl./f. pl.) *all, every*
  tout le monde *everyone*
  tout droit *straight ahead*
  pas du tout *not at all*
  C'est tout ? *Is that all?*
  À tout à l'heure ! *See you later!*
train (m.) *train*
  train à grande vitesse (TGV) *high-speed train*
tranche (f.) *slice (bread, cheese)*
  tranche / part (f.) de fromage *slice of cheese*
transport (m.) *transportation*
travail (m.) *work*
travailler *to work*
travers (m.) *through*
  à travers *through, across*
traverser *to cross, to go across*
treize *thirteen*
trente *thirty*
très *very*
  très bien *very good, very well*
  très bon / bonne (m./f.) *very good*
triste *sad*
trois *three*

troisième *third*
tromper *to deceive*
  se tromper *to be mistaken, to make a mistake*
trop *too, too much*
  trop de *too much*
trottoir (m.) *sidewalk*
trouver *to find*
  se trouver *to find oneself (somewhere), to be situated*
  Où se trouve... ? *Where is ... ?*
truite (f.) *trout*
  truite au bleu *trout cooked in wine and vinegar*
T-shirt (m.) *t-shirt*
tu *you* (infml.)

U

un / une (m./f.) (plural of un / une is des) *a, an, one*
  un peu *a little*
Union (f.) européenne *European Union*
université (f.) *university, college*
urbain / urbaine (m./f.) *urban*
usine (f.) *factory*

V

vacances (f. pl.) *vacation*
  grandes vacances *summer vacation*
  vacances d'hiver *winter vacation*
vain / vaine (m./f.) *vain*
vanille (f.) *vanilla*
  glace (f.) à la vanille *vanilla ice cream*
Vas-y ! (infml.) *Go there!/Go on!/Go ahead!*
veau (m.) *veal*
veille (f.) de *the day before*
  veille de Noël *Christmas Eve*
vélo (m.) *bike*
vélomoteur (m.) *moped*
vendeur / vendeuse (m./f.) *salesman/woman*
vendre *to sell*
vendredi *Friday*
venir *to come*
vent (m.) *wind*
  Il y a du vent. *It's windy.*
vermicelle (m.) *vermicelli pasta*
  consommé (m.) aux vermicelles *noodle soup (vermicelli pasta consommé)*

verre (m.) *glass*
   prendre un verre *to have a drink*
   verre de lait *glass of milk*
vers *around, about*
version (f.) *version*
   version française (v.f.) *French version of a film (dubbed into French)*
   version originale (v.o.) *original version of a film (not dubbed into French)*
vert / verte (m./f.) *green*
   citron (m.) vert *lime*
   haricots (m. pl.) verts *green beans*
   salade (f.) verte *green salad*
veste (f.) *jacket*
vêtements (m. pl.) *clothes, clothing*
vétérinaire (m.) *veterinarian*
viande (f.) *meat*
vie (f.) *life*
vietnamien / vietnamienne (m./f.) *Vietnamese*
vieux / vieil / vieille (m./m. before a vowel or silent h/f.) *old, elderly, outdated*
village (m.) *village*
ville (f.) *town, city*
   plan (m.) de la ville *map of the city*
   carte (f.) de la ville *map of the city*
   hôtel (m.) de ville *city hall, town hall, municipal building*
vin (m.) *wine*
   vin rouge / blanc / rosé / mousseux *red/white/rosé/sparkling wine*
   carafe (f.) de vin *pitcher of wine*
   coq (m.) au vin *chicken/rooster cooked in wine*
vingt *twenty*
vingtième *twentieth*
violet / violette (m./f.) *violet, purple*
violon (m.) *violin*
visage (m.) *face*
visite (f.) guidée *guided tour*
visiter *to visit (a place)*
vite *quickly*
vocabulaire (m.) *vocabulary*
voici *here is/are, here it is/they are*
voie (f.) *track, lane*
voilà *there is/are, here is/are, there it is/they are, here it is/they are*
voile (f.) *sailing*
voir *to see*
voiture (f.) *car*

volaille (f.) *poultry*
votre / vos (m. or f./pl.) *your* (pl./fml.)
vouloir *to want*
   Je veux (bien)... *I (do) want ...*
   Je voudrais (bien)... *I would like ...*
   Que voulez-vous ? *What do you want?*
vous *you* (pl./fml.), *yourself* (fml.), *yourselves*
voyage (m.) *voyage, trip, travel*
   chèque (m.) de voyage *traveler's check*
voyager *to travel*
vrai / vraie (m./f.) *true, real*
vraiment *truly, really*

W

wagon (m.) *car (on a train)*
   wagon-lit (m.) *sleeping/sleeper car*
week-end (m.) *weekend*
western (m.) *western*

Y

y *there*
   il y a *there is/are, ago*
yeux (m. pl.) (œil, sg.) *eyes (eye)*
   avoir les yeux bleus / bruns / verts *to have blue/brown/green eyes*

Z

zéro *zero*
zoo (m.) *zoo*

English-French

A

a, an *un / une* (m./f.) (plural of *un / une* is *des*)
   a little *un peu*
   a lot *beaucoup*
   a lot of *beaucoup de*
abdomen *estomac* (m.)
able to (to be) *pouvoir, arriver à* (+ verb)
above all *surtout*
Absolutely! *Absolument !*
accident *accident* (m.)

accompany (to) *accompagner*
across *à travers*
  across from *en face de*
act (to) *agir, jouer*
action *action* (f.)
  action film/movie *film* (m.) *d'action*
active *actif / active* (m./f.)
actively *activement*
actor/actress *acteur / actrice* (m./f.)
admire (to) *admirer*
adolescent *adolescent / adolescente* (m./f.)
adore (to) *adorer*
adult *adulte* (m./f.)
advance (to) *avancer*
afraid (to be) *avoir peur*
after *après*
  after next *suivant/suivante, d'après*
afternoon *après-midi* (m./f.)
afterwards *après*
again *encore*
age *âge* (m.)
ago *il y a*
ahead *devant*
airplane *avion* (m.)
airport *aéroport* (m.)
alcohol *alcool* (m.)
Algeria *Algérie* (f.)
Algerian *algérien / algérienne* (m./f.)
all *tout / toute / tous / toutes* (m./f./m. pl./f. pl.)
  Is that all? *C'est tout ?*
  All right. *D'accord. / Entendu.*
alone *seul / seule* (m./f.)
along *le long de*
alongside *le long de*
already *déjà*
also *aussi*
always *toujours*
American *américain / américaine* (m./f.)
amusing *amusant / amusante* (m./f.)
and *et*
animal *animal* (m.)
animated movie *film* (m.) *d'animation*
ankle *cheville* (f.)
anniversary *anniversaire* (m.)
  Happy anniversary! *Joyeux /*
    Bon anniversaire !
announce (to) *annoncer*
annoy (to) *ennuyer*

another *un / une autre* (m./f.)
answer (to) *répondre*
  answer the phone (to) *répondre au téléphone*
anxious *inquiet / inquiète* (m./f.)
any more, anymore *ne … plus*
anything *rien, ne … rien*
anywhere *nulle part*
apartment *appartement* (m.)
  apartment building *immeuble* (m.)
appetizer *entrée* (f.), *hors-d'œuvre* (m.)
apple *pomme* (f.)
  apple pie *tarte* (f.) *aux pommes*
appointment *rendez-vous* (m.)
April *avril*
Arc de Triomphe (lit., Arch of Triumph) *Arc* (m.) *de Triomphe*
architect *architecte* (m./f.)
area *quartier* (m.)
arm *bras* (m.)
armchair *fauteuil* (m.)
around *autour de, vers*
arrive (to) *arriver*
  arrive (somewhere) (to) *arriver à* (+ destination)
  arrival time *heure* (f.) *de l'arrivée / heure d'arrivée*
art *art* (m.)
artist *artiste* (m./f.)
as *comme*
ashamed (to be) *avoir honte*
ask (for) (to) *demander*
  ask oneself (to) *se demander*
assistant *assistant / assistante* (m./f.)
at *à*
  at the *au / à la / à l' / aux* (m./f./m. or f. before a vowel or silent h/pl.)
  at someone's house/place *chez*
  at home *chez moi, à la maison*
  at what time? *à quelle heure ?*
athletic *sportif/sportive* (m./f.)
ATM *guichet* (m.) *automatique, distributeur* (m.) *de billets*
attach a file (to) *envoyer en pièce jointe*
attachment *pièce* (f.) *jointe*
August *août*
aunt *tante* (f.)
Australia *Australie* (f.)
Australian *australien / australienne* (m./f.)

automobile *automobile* (f.)
autumn *automne* (m.)
  in autumn *en automne*
avenue *avenue* (f.)

B

baby *bébé* (m.)
bad *mauvais / mauvaise* (m./f.), *mal*
badly *mal*
  It's going badly. *Ça va mal.*
bakery *boulangerie* (f.)
ball *ballon (large – basketball, etc.)* (m.), *balle (small – tennis, etc.)* (f.)
ballet *ballet* (m.)
banana *banane* (f.)
band *groupe* (m.) *de musique*
bandage *bandage* (m.), *pansement* (m.)
bank *banque* (f.), *quai (of a river)* (m.)
banker *banquier / banquière* (m./f.)
banknote *billet* (m.)
baseball *baseball* (m.)
basket *panier* (m.)
basketball *basket(-ball)* (m.)
bath towel *serviette* (f.) *de bain*
bathing suit/trunks *maillot* (m.) *de bain*
bathroom *salle* (f.) *de bains*
bathtub *baignoire* (f.)
be (to) *être*
  be able to (to) *pouvoir*
  be bored (to) *s'ennuyer*
  be born (to) *naître*
  be called (to) *s'appeler*
  be decided (to) *se décider*
  be engaged (to) (to) *être fiancé / fiancée (à)* (m./f.)
  be familiar with (to) *connaître*
  be held (to) *avoir lieu*
  be mistaken (to) *se tromper*
  be necessary (to) *falloir*
  be resolved (to do something) (to) *se décider*
  be situated (to) *se trouver*
  be afraid (to) *avoir peur*
  be ashamed (to) *avoir honte*
  be cold (to) *avoir froid*
  be hot/warm (to) *avoir chaud*
  be hungry (to) *avoir faim*
  be thirsty (to) *avoir soif*
  be sleepy (to) *avoir sommeil*

  be right (to) *avoir raison*
  be wrong (to) *avoir tort*
  be... years old (to) *avoir ... ans*
beach *plage* (f.)
bean *haricot* (m.)
  green bean *haricot vert*
beautiful beau / bel / belle (m./m. before a vowel or silent h/f.)
  It's beautiful (outside). *Il fait beau.*
beauty parlor (beauty salon) *institut* (m.) *de beauté*
because *parce que*
become (to) *devenir*
bed *lit* (m.)
bedroom *chambre* (f.) *(à coucher)*
beef *bœuf* (m.)
beer *bière* (f.)
before *devant, avant, auparavant*
  the day before *la veille de*
  before last *précédent / précédente* (m./f.), *d'avant*
beg (to) *prier*
begin (to) *commencer*
behave (to) *agir*
behind *derrière*
beige *beige*
Belgian *belge*
Belgium *Belgique* (f.)
believe (to) *croire*
  I don't believe it! *Ce n'est pas possible !*
belongings *affaires* (f. pl.)
belt *ceinture* (f.)
between *entre*
bicycle *bicyclette* (f.)
bidet *bidet* (m.)
big *grand / grande* (m./f.)
bike *vélo* (m.)
bill *billet (currency)* (m.), *addition (restaurant, café, etc.)* (f.)
  The bill, please. *L'addition, s'il vous plaît.*
billiards *billard* (m.)
biology *biologie* (f.)
birthday *anniversaire* (m.)
  Happy birthday! *Joyeux / Bon anniversaire !*
bisque (creamy soup) *bisque* (f.)
  lobster bisque *bisque de homard*
bite *morceau* (m.)
black *noir / noire* (m./f.)

black currant *cassis* (m.)
bleach *eau* (f.) *de Javel*
blender *mixer* (m.)
blonde *blond / blonde* (m./f.)
blood *sang* (m.)
blouse *chemisier* (m.), *blouse* (f.)
blue *bleu / bleue* (m./f.)
blush (to) *rougir*
boat *bateau* (m.)
bone *os* (m.)
book *livre* (m.)
bookshelf *étagère* (f.), *bibliothèque* (f.)
bookstore *librairie* (f.)
border *bord* (m.)
   at the border of *au bord de*
bore (someone) (to) *ennuyer*
   be bored (to), get bored (to) *s'ennuyer*
   It's boring. *C'est ennuyeux.*
born (to be) *naître*
boss *patron / patronne* (m./f.), *chef* (m.)
bottle *bouteille* (f.)
   bottle of champagne *bouteille de*
      champagne
boulevard *boulevard* (m.)
boutique *boutique* (f.)
bowl *saladier* (m.)
box *boîte* (f.)
box office *guichet* (m.)
boy *garçon* (m.)
boyfriend *copain* (m.), *petit ami* (m.)
bracelet *bracelet* (m.)
brain *cerveau* (m.)
brave *brave*
Brazil *Brésil* (m.)
Brazilian *brésilien / brésilienne* (m./f.)
bread *pain* (m.)
   bread with butter and jelly *tartine* (f.)
break (to) *rompre*
breakfast *petit déjeuner* (m.)
   have breakfast (to) *prendre le petit déjeuner*
bridge *pont* (m.)
briefcase *serviette* (f.)
bring (to) *apporter*
brochure *brochure* (f.)
broom *balai* (m.)
brother *frère* (m.)
brown *brun / brune* (m./f.), *marron*

brush (to) *brosser*
   brush oneself (hair, teeth, etc.) (to) *se brosser*
buckwheat *sarrasin* (m.)
build (to) *bâtir*
building *bâtiment* (m.), *immeuble* (apartment, office) (m.)
bus *bus* (m.), *autobus* (m.), *autocar* (m.)
   bus stop *arrêt* (m.) *de bus / d'autobus*
   bus tour *circuit* (m.) *en bus*
business *affaires* (f. pl.)
businessman/woman *homme / femme d'affaires* (m./f.)
busy *occupé / occupée* (m./f.)
   The line is busy. *La ligne est occupée.*
but *mais*
butcher shop *boucherie* (f.)
butter *beurre* (m.)
buy (to) *acheter*
by foot *à pied*
Bye. *Salut.*

C

cab *taxi* (m.)
cabinet *armoire* (f.)
   medicine cabinet *armoire à pharmacie*
cable *câble* (m.)
café *café* (m.)
cake *gâteau* (m.)
   chocolate cake *gâteau au chocolat*
call (to) *appeler, téléphoner, donner / passer un coup de fil* (infml.)
   call back (to) *rappeler*
   Who's calling? (on the phone) *C'est de la part de qui ? / Qui est à l'appareil ?*
called (to be) *s'appeler*
calm *calme*
camera *appareil* (m.) *photo*
can (container) *boîte* (f.) *de conserve*
can (verb) *pouvoir*
   Can I help you? *Puis-je vous aider ?*
   can't wait (to look forward to) *avoir hâte*
Canada *Canada* (m.)
Canadian *canadien / canadienne* (m./f.)
candy *bonbons* (m. pl.)
   candy store *confiserie* (f.)
   pastry and candy store *pâtisserie-confiserie* (f.)

cantaloupe *melon* (m.)

car *voiture* (f.), *automobile* (f.), *auto* (f.), *wagon (on a train)* (m.)

caramel *caramel* (m.)

card *carte* (f.)

  playing cards *cartes* (pl.) *à jouer*

card *carte* (f.)

carpenter *charpentier* (m.)

carpet *moquette* (f.)

carrot *carotte* (f.)

carry (to) *porter*

carton *boîte* (f.) *(en carton), carton* (m.), *brique* (f.)

  carton of orange juice *boîte* (f.) *de jus d'orange*

cash *argent* (m.)

castle *château* (m.)

cathedral *cathédrale* (f.)

CD player *lecteur* (m.) *de CD*

CD-ROM *CD-ROM* (m.)

  CD-ROM drive *lecteur* (m.) *de CD-ROM*

ceiling *plafond* (m.)

celebrate (to) *célébrer*

celery *céleri* (m.)

cell phone *(téléphone) portable* (m.)

cellar *cave* (f.)

cent *cent* (m.)

certain *certain / certaine* (m./f.)

certainly *certainement*

chair *chaise* (f.)

champagne *champagne* (m.)

  bottle of champagne *bouteille* (f.) *de champagne*

  champagne with black currant liqueur *kir* (m.) *royal*

champion *champion / championne* (m./f.)

chance *hasard* (m.)

chandelier *lustre* (m.)

change *monnaie* (f.)

change (to) *changer*

  change channels (to) *changer de chaîne*

charming *charmant / charmante* (m./f.)

check *chèque* (m.), *addition (restaurant, café, etc.)* (f.)

  The check, please. *L'addition, s'il vous plaît.*

check in (to) *prendre une chambre*

check out (to) *régler sa note*

cheek *joue* (f.)

cheese *fromage* (m.)

  slice of cheese *tranche* (f.) *de fromage*

  cheese sandwich *sandwich* (m.) *au fromage*

  ham and cheese sandwich *sandwich* (m.) *jambon-fromage*

  grilled ham and cheese sandwich *croque-monsieur* (m.)

  grilled ham and cheese sandwich with an egg on top *croque-madame* (m.)

chemistry *chimie* (f.)

cherry *cerise* (f.)

chest *poitrine* (f.)

chestnut *marron* (m.)

chicken *poulet* (m.)

  chicken and fries *poulet frites*

  chicken/rooster cooked in wine *coq* (m.) *au vin*

child *enfant* (m./f.)

chin *menton* (m.)

China *Chine* (f.)

Chinese *chinois / chinoise* (m./f.)

  Chinese language *chinois* (m.)

chocolate *chocolat* (m.)

  chocolate cake *gâteau* (m.) *au chocolat*

  chocolate ice cream *glace* (f.) *au chocolat*

  chocolate mousse *mousse* (f.) *au chocolat*

  hot chocolate *chocolat* (m.) *chaud*

choose (to) *choisir*

chop *côte* (f.)

  pork chop *côte de porc*

chopstick *baguette* (f.)

Christmas *Noël* (m.)

  Merry Christmas! *Joyeux Noël!*

  Christmas Eve *réveillon* (m.) *de Noël, veille* (f.) *de Noël*

church *église* (f.)

cider *cidre* (m.)

circus *cirque* (m.)

city *ville* (f.)

  city hall *mairie* (f.), *hôtel* (m.) *de ville*

clam *palourde* (f.), *clam* (m.)

class *cours* (m.), *classe* (f.)

classroom *salle* (f.) *de classe*

clean *propre*

clean the house (to) *faire le ménage*

clerk *guichetier (at the window/counter)* (m.)

client *client / cliente* (m./f.)

climbing *alpinisme* (m.)

close *près*
  very close *tout près*
  close to here *près d'ici*
  the closest *le / la plus proche* (m./f.)
close (to) *fermer*
  close a file (to) *fermer un fichier*
closet *placard* (m.)
clothing/clothes *vêtements* (m. pl.)
  clothing store *magasin* (m.) *de vêtements*
cloud *nuage* (m.)
cloudy *nuageux / nuageuse* (m./f.)
  It's cloudy. *C'est nuageux.*
club (nightclub) *boîte* (f.) *(de nuit), discothèque* (f.)
  go out to clubs (to), go out clubbing (to) *sortir en boîte*
club (organization) *club* (m.)
coach *entraîneur* (m.)
coast *côte* (f.)
coat *manteau* (m.)
coffee *café* (m.)
  coffee with cream *café-crème* (m.)
  coffee shop *café* (m.)
coffeemaker *cafetière* (f.)
coin *pièce* (f.)
  coins *pièces* (pl.), *monnaie* (f.)
coincidence *coïncidence* (f.)
  What a coincidence! *Quelle coïncidence !*
cold *froid / froide* (m./f.)
  It's cold. *Il fait froid.*
  be cold (to) *avoir froid*
colleague *collègue / collègue* (m./f.)
collection *collection* (f.)
college *université* (f.)
  college degree *diplôme* (m.) *universitaire*
cologne *eau* (f.) *de cologne*
come (to) *venir*
  come back (to) *revenir*
  come back (in) (to), come home (to) *rentrer*
  come in (to) *entrer*
  come up (to) *monter*
  come down (to) *descendre*
  come out (to) *sortir*
comedy *comédie* (f.)
  romantic comedy *comédie romantique*
comfortable *confortable*
company *société* (f.), *firme* (f.)
complicated *compliqué / compliquée* (m./f.)

computer *ordinateur* (m.)
concert *concert* (m.)
Congratulations. *Félicitations.*
consommé (clear soup made from stock) *consommé* (m.)
  vermicelli pasta consommé (noodle soup) *consommé aux vermicelles*
construct (to) *construire*
construction worker *ouvrier* (m.) *en bâtiment*
consult (to) *consulter*
  consult a phone book (to) *consulter l'annuaire*
cook *cuisinier / cuisinière* (m./f.)
cook (to) *cuisiner, préparer, faire la cuisine*
cooking *cuisine* (f.)
cool (great) *sympa, cool*
corn *maïs* (m.)
corner *coin* (m.)
correct *exact / exacte* (m./f.)
cost (to) *coûter*
  That costs ... *Ça coûte...*
cotton *coton* (m.)
couch *canapé* (m.)
counter *bar* (m.), *comptoir* (m.), *guichet* (m.)
courageous *brave*
course *cours* (m.)
cousin *cousin / cousine* (m./f.)
cream, creamy dessert *crème* (f.)
  creamy dessert made with caramel *crème caramel*
  whipped cream (that is flavored and sweetened) *crème chantilly*
  shaving cream *crème à raser*
crêpe (tissue-thin pancake) *crêpe* (f.)
  crêpe Suzette (crêpe with sugar, orange, and liqueur) *crêpe Suzette*
crime drama/film *film* (m.) *policier*
croissant *croissant* (m.)
cross (to) *traverser*
crowd *foule* (f.)
cruel *cruel*
cruise ship *paquebot* (m.)
cucumber *concombre* (m.)
cup *tasse* (f.)
  cup of tea *tasse de thé*
cupboard *placard* (m.)

currency *monnaie* (f.)
  currency exchange office *bureau* (m.) *de change*
curtain *rideau* (m.)

D

Dad/Daddy *papa*
daily *quotidien / quotidienne* (m./f.)
dance (to) *danser*
dance/dancing *danse* (f.)
darling *chéri / chérie* (m./f.)
date (to) *sortir avec*
date *date* (f.), *rendez-vous* (m.)
daughter *fille* (f.)
daughter-in-law *belle-fille* (f.)
day *jour* (m.), *journée* (f.)
  the day after tomorrow *après-demain*
  the day before yesterday *avant-hier*
dear (adjective) *cher / chère* (m./f.)
dear (term of endearment) *chéri / chérie* (m./f.)
deceive (to) *tromper*
December *décembre*
decide (to) *décider*
decided (to be) *se décider*
defend (to) *défendre*
degree *degré* (m.)
degree (college) *diplôme* (m.) *universitaire*
delete (to) *supprimer*
delicatessen *charcuterie* (f.)
delicious *délicieux / délicieuse* (m./f.)
delighted *ravi / ravie* (m./f.)
dentist *dentiste* (m.)
deodorant *déodorant* (m.)
depart (to) *quitter*
department store *grand magasin* (m.)
departure time *heure* (f.) *du départ*
descend (to) *descendre*
description *description* (f.)
desert *désert* (m.)
desire *envie* (f.)
desk *bureau* (m.)
dessert *dessert* (m.)
detective (adjective) *policier / policière* (m./f.)
  detective drama/film *film* (m.) *policier*
detest (to) *détester*
device *appareil* (m.)
die (to) *mourir*

different *différent / différente* (m./f.)
difficult *difficile*
dine (to) *dîner*
dining room *salle* (f.) *à manger*
dinner *dîner* (m.)
  have dinner (to) *dîner*
  Dinner's ready! *À table !*
  late dinner *souper* (m.)
diploma *diplôme* (m.)
direction *direction* (f.)
director *directeur / directrice* (m./f.)
dirty *sale*
dish *plat* (m.)
  side dish *plat d'accompagnement*
dishwasher *lave-vaisselle* (m.)
dishwashing detergent *liquide* (m.) *vaisselle*
disobey (to) *désobéir*
dispatch (to) *dépêcher*
dive (to) *plonger*
divorce *divorce* (m.)
  get a divorce (to) *divorcer*
do (to) *faire*
  do well (to) *réussir*
  do the cooking (to) *faire la cuisine*
  do the dishes (to) *faire la vaisselle*
  do the house cleaning (to) *faire le ménage*
  do the laundry (to) *faire la lessive*
  do the shopping (to) *faire les/des courses*
  do a tour (to) *faire un tour*
doctor *médecin* (m.), *docteur* (m.)
document *document* (m.)
documentary *documentaire* (m.)
dog *chien* (m.)
door *porte* (f.)
downstairs, down below *en bas*
dozen *douzaine* (f.)
  dozen eggs *douzaine d'œufs*
drama *drame* (m.)
  period drama *drame d'époque*
drawer *tiroir* (m.)
dress *robe* (f.)
dress (to) *habiller*
  get dressed (to), dress oneself (to) *s'habiller*
drink (to) *boire*
drive (computer) *lecteur* (m.)
  CD-ROM drive *lecteur de CD-ROM*
drive (to) *conduire*
drugstore *pharmacie* (f.)

dry (alcohol) *brut / brute* (m./f.)
dryer *sèche-linge* (m.)
dubbed *doublé / doublée* (m./f.)
duck *canard* (m.)
  duck à l'orange, duck with orange
    sauce *canard à l'orange*
DVD player *lecteur* (m.) *de DVD*

E

each *chaque, chacun / chacune* (m./f.)
ear *oreille* (f.)
early *en avance, tôt*
earn (to) *gagner*
earring *boucle* (f.) *d'oreille*
easily *facilement*
east *est* (m.)
easy *facile*
eat (to) *manger*
éclair (type of cream-filled pastry) *éclair* (m.)
edge *bord* (m.)
  at the edge of *au bord de*
egg *œuf* (m.)
  egg whites *blancs* (m. pl.) *(d'œufs)*
  fried egg (over easy egg) *œuf au plat, œuf sur*
    le plat
  hard-boiled egg *œuf dur*
  poached egg *œuf poché*
  scrambled eggs *œufs* (pl.) *brouillés*
  soft-boiled egg *œuf à la coque*
Eiffel Tower *Tour* (f.) *Eiffel*
eight *huit*
eighteen *dix-huit*
eighth *huitième*
eighty *quatre-vingts*
either *ou bien*
elbow *coude* (m.)
elderly *âgé / âgée* (m./f.)
  elderly person *personne* (f.) *âgée*
electrician *électricien* (m.)
electronic game *jeu* (m.) *électronique*
electronics store *magasin* (m.) *d'électronique*
elegant *élégant / élégante* (m./f.)
elephant *éléphant* (m.)
eleven *onze*
eleventh *onzième*
elsewhere *ailleurs*

e-mail *mail* (m.), *mél* (m.), *email* (m.), *courriel*
  (m.), *courrier* (m.) *électronique*
employee *employé / employée* (m./f.)
employment *emploi* (m.)
end (to) *terminer*
  at the end of *au bout de*
engaged (to) (to be) *être fiancé / fiancée (à)*
engineer *ingénieur* (m.)
England *Angleterre* (f.)
English *anglais / anglaise* (m./f.)
  English language *anglais* (m.)
  in English *en anglais*
enjoy oneself (to) *s'amuser*
Enjoy your meal! *Bon appétit !*
enjoyable *agréable*
enormous *énorme*
enough *assez*
enter (to) *entrer*
entertain (to) *amuser*
entrance *entrée* (f.)
equal *égal / égale* (m./f.)
errand *course* (f.)
escargots *escargots* (m. pl.)
especially *surtout*
essential *essentiel / essentielle* (m./f.)
euro *euro* (m.)
European *européen / européenne* (m./f.)
  European Union *Union* (f.) *européenne*
even *même*
  even more *bien plus*
evening *soir* (m.), *soirée* (f.)
  this evening *ce soir*
ever *jamais*
every *tout / toute / tous / toutes* (m./f./m. pl./f.
  pl.), *chaque*
everyday *quotidien / quotidienne* (m./f.)
everyone *tout le monde*
everywhere *partout*
exact *exact / exacte* (m./f.), *précis / précise* (m./f.)
excellent *excellent / excellente* (m./f.)
exchange (to) *changer*
exciting *passionnant / passionnante* (m./f.)
excuse (to) *excuser*
  Excuse me. *Pardon. / Excusez-moi.*
exit *sortie* (f.)
expect (to) *attendre*
expensive *cher / chère* (m./f.)
expression *expression* (f.)

extension (telephone) *poste* (m.)
exterior *extérieur* (m.)
eye (eyes) *œil* (m.) *(yeux,* pl.)
  blue/brown/green eyes *les yeux bleus / bruns / verts*
eyebrow *sourcil* (m.)
eyeglasses *lunettes* (f. pl.)
eyelash *cil* (m.)

F

face *visage* (m.)
facing *en face de*
factory *usine* (f.)
fail (a test) (to) *rater (un examen)*
fall (season) *automne* (m.)
  in (the) fall *en automne*
fall (to) *tomber*
false *faux / fausse* (m./f.)
familiar with (to be) *connaître*
family *famille* (f.)
famous *célèbre*
Fantastic. *Formidable.*
far *loin*
  far from here *loin d'ici*
  farther *plus loin*
farmer *fermier / fermière* (m./f.)
fat *gros / grosse* (m./f.)
father *père* (m.)
father-in-law *beau-père* (m.)
favorite *préféré / préférée* (m./f.)
fax machine *télécopieur* (m.)
fear *peur* (f.)
February *février*
feed (to) *nourrir*
feel like (to) *avoir envie de*
festival *fête* (f.), *féstival* (m.)
fewer *moins*
fiancé/fiancée *fiancé / fiancée* (m./f.)
field *champ* (m.)
fifteen *quinze*
fifteenth *quinzième*
fifth *cinquième*
fifty *cinquante*
file *fichier* (m.)
fill (in) (to) *remplir*
film *film* (m.)
  action film *film d'action*

crime/detective film, crime/detective
  drama *film policier*
original version of a film (not dubbed into
  French) *version* (f.) *originale (v.o.)*
French version of a film (dubbed into
  French) *version* (f.) *française (v.f.)*
final *dernier / dernière* (m./f.)
finally *enfin*
find (to) *trouver*
  find oneself (somewhere) (to) *se trouver*
fine *bien*
finger *doigt* (m.)
finish (to) *finir, terminer*
fire *feu* (m.)
firm (company) *firme* (f.)
First ... *D'abord ...*
first *premier / première* (number) (m./f.)
  first floor (one floor above ground
    floor) *premier étage* (m.)
fish *poisson* (m.)
five *cinq*
flag *drapeau* (m.)
flavor *parfum* (m.)
floor *étage* (as in, second floor, third floor, etc.)
  (m.), *sol* (of a room) (m.)
  ground floor *rez-de-chaussée* (m.)
flower *fleur* (f.)
fog *brouillard* (m.)
food *nourriture* (f.)
foot *pied* (m.)
  on foot, by foot *à pied*
  at the foot of *au pied de*
football (American) *football* (m.) *américain*
for *pour, de / d'*
  for a party of four, for four people *pour
    quatre personnes*
  for me *pour moi*
forehead *front* (m.)
forest *forêt* (f.)
fork *fourchette* (f.)
former *ancien / ancienne* (m./f.)
formerly *autrefois*
fortunately *heureusement*
forty *quarante*
forward (to) *faire suivre*
four *quatre*
fourteen *quatorze*
fourth *quatrième*

fragrance *parfum* (m.)
France *France* (f.)
free *libre*
French *français / française* (m./f.)
 French language *français* (m.)
 French version of a film (dubbed into
  French) *version* (f.) *française (v.f.)*
 in French *en français*
french fries *frites* (f. pl.)
Friday *vendredi*
friend *ami / amie* (m./f.)
friendly *amical / amicale* (m./f.), *sympathique*
fries *frites* (f. pl.)
 chicken and fries *poulet* (m.) *frites*
 mussels and fries *moules* (f. pl.) *frites*
 steak and fries *steak* (m.) *frites*
from *de / d'*
 from here *d'ici*
 from (someone) *de la part de*
 from me *de ma part*
front *devant*
 in front (of) *devant*
fruit *fruit* (m.)
 fruit salad *salade* (f.) *de fruits*
full-time *à plein temps*
funny *amusant / amusante* (m./f.), *drôle*
furniture *meubles* (m. pl.)
 a piece of furniture *meuble* (m.)

G

gain weight (to) *grossir*
gallery *galerie* (f.)
game *jeu* (m.), *match* (m.)
garage *garage* (m.)
garden *jardin* (m.)
gastronomy *gastronomie* (f.)
general *général / générale* (m./f.)
generally *généralement, en général*
generous *généreux / généreuse* (m./f.)
gentle *doux / douce* (m./f.)
gentlemen *messieurs*
gently *doucement*
German *allemand / allemande* (m./f.)
Germany *Allemagne* (f.)
get a divorce (to) *divorcer*
get bored (to) *s'ennuyer*
get dressed (to) *s'habiller*

get somewhere (to) *arriver*
 get to (a destination) (to) *arriver à (+ destination)*
get up (to) *se lever*
girl *fille* (f.)
girlfriend *copine* (f.), *petite amie* (f.)
give (to) *donner*
 give back (to) *rendre*
glass *verre* (m.)
 glass of milk *verre de lait*
glove *gant* (m.)
go (to) *aller*
 Let's go. *Allons-y. / On y va.* (infml.)
 Go on!/Go ahead!/Go there! *Vas-y !* (infml.) / *Allez-y !* (pl./fml)
 go across (to) *traverser*
 go away (to) *partir*
 go out (to) *partir, sortir*
 go out clubbing (to), go out to clubs (to) *sortir en boîte*
 go out with (to) (to date) *sortir avec*
 go down (to) *descendre*
 go up (to) *monter*
 go home (to), go in (to) *rentrer*
 go (past) (to) *passer*
 go shopping (to) *faire des / les courses*
 go sightseeing (to) *aller visiter*
 go to bed (to) *se coucher*
 go swimming (to) *faire de la natation*
 go hiking (to) *faire de la marche*
 go camping (to) *camper*
 go horseback riding (to) *faire de l'équitation*
god *dieu* (m.)
 My god! *Mon dieu !*
good *bon / bonne* (m./f.), *bien, sympa, brave*
 very good *très bien, très bon / bonne* (m./f.), *très sympa*
 Good luck. *Bonne chance.*
 Good day. *Bonjour.*
 Good evening. *Bonsoir.*
 Good night. *Bonne nuit.*
 Good-bye. *Au revoir.*
 I'm having a good time. *Je m'amuse.*
grade *note (score)* (f.), *classe (year)* (f.)
gram *gramme* (m.)
grammar *grammaire* (f.)
grandfather *grand-père* (m.)
 grandfather clock *pendule* (f.)

grandmother *grand-mère* (f.)
grandparent *grand-parent* (m.)
grape(s) *raisin* (m.)
great *formidable, extra, super*
  Great! *Super !*
  It's great. *C'est extra.*
Greece *Grèce* (f.)
Greek *grec / grecque* (m./f.)
green *vert / verte* (m./f.)
  green bean *haricot* (m.) *vert*
  green salad *salade* (f.) *verte*
grocery store *épicerie* (f.)
grow (to) *grandir*
grown-up *adulte* (m./f.)
guide *guide* (m.)
guided tour *visite* (f.) *guidée*
gym (physical education) *gymnastique* (f.)
gymnastics *gymnastique* (f.)

H

hail *grêle* (f.)
  It's hailing. *Il grêle.*
hair *cheveux* (m. pl.)
  hair (single strand) *cheveu* (m.)
  brown/blond/red/black hair *les cheveux bruns / blonds / roux / noirs*
half *demi / demie* (m./f.)
  half past ... *... et demie*
  half hour *demi-heure* (f.)
hall *couloir* (m.), *salle* (f.)
ham *jambon* (m.)
  ham and cheese sandwich *sandwich* (m.) *jambon-fromage*
  ham sandwich *sandwich* (m.) *au jambon*
  grilled ham and cheese sandwich *croque-monsieur* (m.)
  grilled ham and cheese sandwich with an egg on top *croque-madame* (m.)
hand *main* (f.)
handsome *beau / bel / belle (m./m. before a vowel or silent h/f.)*
hang up (to) *raccrocher*
Hanukkah *Hanoukka* (f.), *Hanoucca* (f.)
happily *heureusement*
happy *heureux / heureuse* (m./f.)
  Happy birthday!/Happy anniversary! *Joyeux / Bon anniversaire !*
  Happy Holidays! *Joyeuses / Bonnes fêtes !*
  Happy New Year! *Bonne Année !*
hard *dur / dure* (m./f.), *difficile*
  hard-boiled egg *œuf* (m.) *dur*
hardware store *quincaillerie* (f.)
haste *hâte* (f.)
hasten (to) *hâter*
hat *chapeau* (m.)
hate (to) *détester*
hatred *haine* (f.)
have (to) *avoir*
  have (food/drink) (to) *prendre*
  have a drink (to) *prendre un verre*
  have breakfast (to) *prendre le petit déjeuner*
  have lunch (to) *déjeuner*
  have dinner (to) *dîner*
  have a late dinner (to) *souper*
  have a good time (to), have fun (to) *s'amuser*
  have a party (to) *organiser une fête*
  have to (to) *devoir*
he *il*
head *tête* (f.)
health *santé* (f.)
  To your health! *À votre santé !*
  healthy *en bonne santé*
hear (to) *entendre*
heart *cœur* (m.)
held (to be) *avoir lieu*
Hello. *Bonjour. / Salut.*
  Hello. (on the phone) *Allô.*
help (to) *aider*
her *son / sa / ses* (m./f./pl.), *elle*
herbal tea *tisane* (f.)
here *ici, ci*
  from here *d'ici*
  here is/are, here it is/they are *voici, voilà*
hero/heroine *héros / héroïne* (m./f.)
herself (reflexive pronoun) *se / s'*
Hey! *Tiens !* (surprise)
Hi. *Salut.*
high *haut / haute* (m./f.)
  high-speed train *train* (m.) *à grande vitesse (TGV)*
high school *lycée* (m.)
hill *colline* (f.)
him *lui*
himself (reflexive pronoun) *se / s'*
his *son / sa / ses* (m./f./pl.)

history *histoire* (f.)
hockey *hockey* (m.)
hold (to) *tenir*
  Hold on, please. *Ne quittez pas, s'il vous plaît.*
holiday *fête* (f.)
home *maison* (f.), *foyer* (m.)
homemade *maison*
homework *devoirs* (m. pl.)
honey *miel* (m.)
honey (term of endearment) *chéri / chérie* (m./f.)
horrible *horrible*
horror movie *film* (m.) *d'épouvante*
horseback riding *équitation* (f.)
  go horseback riding (to) *faire de l'équitation*
hospital *hôpital* (m.)
hot *chaud / chaude* (m./f.)
  It's hot./It's warm. *Il fait chaud.*
  be hot/warm (to) *avoir chaud*
  hot chocolate *chocolat* (m.) *chaud*
hotel *hôtel* (m.)
hour *heure* (f.)
house *maison* (f.)
  at someone's house/place *chez*
  house cleaning *ménage* (m.)
  do the house cleaning (to), clean the house (to) *faire le ménage*
how *comment, comme*
  how many, how much *combien*
  How? *Comment ?*
  How's it going?/How are you? *(Comment) ça va ?*
  How are you? *Comment vas-tu ?* (infml.) / *Comment allez-vous ?* (pl./fml.)
human being *être* (m.) *humain*
hundred *cent*
hunger *faim* (f.)
  be hungry (to) *avoir faim*
hurricane *ouragan* (m.)
hurry (to) *se dépêcher*
hurt (to) *blesser*
  hurt oneself (to) *se blesser*
husband *mari* (m.)

I

I *je / j'*
  I am called … (My name is …) *Je m'appelle…*
  I don't understand. *Je ne comprends pas.*

  I'm fine. *Ça va.*
  I'm very well. *Je vais très bien.*
  I want … *Je veux…*
  I would like … *Je voudrais…*
  I'm getting him/her for you. *Je vous le / la passe.*
ice cream *glace* (f.)
  chocolate ice cream *glace au chocolat*
  strawberry ice cream *glace à la fraise*
  vanilla ice cream *glace à la vanille*
ice skate/skating *patin* (m.) *à glace*
idea *idée* (f.)
if *si*
Île de la Cité (City Island) *Île* (f.) *de la Cité*
important *important / importante* (m./f.)
impoverished *pauvre*
in *à, dans, en*
  in the *au / à la / à l' / aux* (m./f./m. or f. before a vowel or silent h/pl.)
  in front (of) *devant*
  in general *en général*
  in the middle of *au milieu de*
indeed *en effet*
India *Inde* (f.)
Indian *indien / indienne* (m./f.)
individual *individu* (m.)
information center *centre* (m.) *d'informations*
inherit (to) *hériter*
inn *auberge* (f.)
instant message *message* (m.) *instantané*
intelligent *intelligent / intelligente* (m./f.)
interesting *intéressant / intéressante* (m./f.)
Internet *Internet* (m.)
interrupt (to) *interrompre*
intersection *intersection* (f.)
into *dans, en*
introduce (to) *présenter*
  Let me introduce … *Je te présente…* (infml.) / *Je vous présente…* (pl./fml.)
invite (to) *inviter*
Ireland *Irlande* (f.)
Irish *irlandais / irlandaise* (m./f.)
  an Irishman/an Irishwoman *un Irlandais / une Irlandaise* (m./f.)
iron *fer* (m.) *à repasser*
ironing board *planche* (f.) *à repasser*
Is that all? *C'est tout ?*
isn't it?/isn't that so? … *n'est-ce pas ?*

it *ça / c', il / elle / ils / elles* (m./f./m. pl./f. pl.)
  It rains. *Il pleut.*
it is *c'est*
  isn't it? *n'est-ce pas ?*
  it's necessary to *il faut*
  It's going well. *Ça va bien.*
  It's not going well./It's going badly. *Ça va mal.*
  It's beautiful (outside). *Il fait beau.*
  It's hot./It's warm. *Il fait chaud.*
  It's cold. *Il fait froid.*
  It's sunny. *Il fait soleil. / Il y a du soleil.*
  It's windy. *Il y a du vent.*
  It's hailing. *Il grêle.*
  It's snowing. *Il neige.*
  It's raining. *Il pleut.*
Italian *italien / italienne* (m./f.)
Italy *Italie* (f.)
its *son / sa / ses* (m./f./pl.)
itself (reflexive pronoun) *se / s'*

J

jacket *veste* (f.)
jam *confiture* (f.)
January *janvier*
Japan *Japon* (m.)
Japanese *japonais / japonaise* (m./f.)
jeans *jean* (m.)
jelly *confiture* (f.)
jewel *bijou* (m.)
  jewelry *bijoux* (m. pl.)
job *boulot* (m.), *emploi* (m.)
joint (of meat) *rôti* (m.)
journalist *journaliste* (m./f.)
juice *jus* (m.)
  carton of orange juice *boîte* (f.) *de jus d'orange*
July *juillet*
June *juin*
junior high school *collège* (m.)
just *juste*

K

keyboard *clavier* (m.)
kilo *kilo* (m.)
kind *gentil / gentille* (m./f.), *aimable*

kitchen *cuisine* (f.)
  kitchen sink *évier* (m.) *de la cuisine*
knee *genou* (m.)
knife *couteau* (m.)
know (to) *savoir, connaître*
  I don't know. *Je ne sais pas.*

L

lady *dame* (f.)
  ladies *mesdames*
lake *lac* (m.)
lamb *agneau* (m.)
lamp *lampe* (f.)
lamppost *réverbère* (m.)
land *terre* (f.)
lane *voie* (f.)
language *langue* (f.)
large *grand / grande* (m./f.)
last *dernier / dernière* (m./f.)
  last Monday *lundi dernier*
  last month *mois* (m.) *dernier*
  last summer *été* (m.) *dernier*
  last night *hier soir, nuit* (f.) *dernière*
  last year *année* (f.) *dernière*
late *en retard, tard*
  late dinner *souper* (m.)
latest *dernier / dernière* (m./f.)
laundry detergent *lessive* (f.)
lawyer *avocat / avocate* (m./f.)
lay down (to) *coucher, allonger*
learn (to) *apprendre*
  I'm learning French. *J'apprends le français.*
leather *cuir* (m.)
leave (to) *partir, sortir, laisser*
left *gauche* (f.)
  on the left, to the left, at the left *à gauche*
leg *jambe* (f.)
lemon *citron* (m.)
less *moins*
lesson *leçon* (f.)
let (someone do something) (to) *laisser*
let go (to) *laisser*
Let me introduce … *Je te présente…* (infml.) / *Je vous présente…* (pl./fml.)
Let's go. *Allons-y. / On y va.* (infml.)
letter *lettre* (f.)
lettuce *laitue* (f.)

library *bibliothèque* (f.)
lie down (to) *se coucher, allonger*
life *vie* (f.)
lift (to) *lever*
light *léger / légère* (m./f.)
lightly *légèrement*
lightning *éclair* (m.)
like *comme*
like (to) *aimer*
  I like ... *J'aime...*
  I do not like ... *Je n'aime pas...*
lime *citron vert* (m.)
line *queue* (f.)
  wait in line (to) *faire la queue*
link *liaison* (f.)
listen (to) (to) *écouter*
literature *littérature* (f.)
little *petit / petite* (m./f.)
  a little *un peu*
live (to) *habiter*
living room *salon* (m.)
lobster *homard* (m.)
  lobster bisque *bisque* (f.) *de homard*
lonely *seul / seule* (m./f.)
long *long / longue* (m./f.), *longtemps*
look at (to) *regarder*
look for (to) *chercher*
look forward to (to) (can't wait) *avoir hâte*
lose (to) *perdre*
  lose weight (to) *maigrir*
lost *perdu / perdue* (m./f.)
  I'm lost. *Je suis perdu / perdue.*
Louvre *Louvre* (m.)
love (to) *aimer, adorer*
low *bas / basse* (m./f.)
luck *chance* (f.)
  No luck! *Pas de chance !*
  Good luck! *Bonne chance !*
lunch *déjeuner* (m.)
  have lunch (to) *déjeuner*
lung *poumon* (m.)

M

ma'am/madam *madame*
magazine *magazine* (m.), *revue* (f.)
magnificent *magnifique*
mail *poste* (f.)

mail (to) *mettre à la poste*
main *principal / principale* (m./f.)
  main course/dish *plat* (m.) *principal*
make (to) *faire, préparer*
  make a phone call (to) *téléphoner, donner (or passer) un coup de fil* (infml.)
  make a mistake (to) *se tromper*
  make a reservation (to) *faire une réservation*
  make an appointment (to) *prendre rendez-vous*
  make up one's mind (to) *se décider*
  That makes ... *Ça fait...*
mall *centre commercial* (m.)
man *homme* (m.)
  Oh man! (disappointment, anger) *Ce n'est pas possible !*
  Man! (lit., Say so!) *Dis donc !*
manage to (do something) (to) *arriver à (+ verb)*
manager *gérant / gérante* (m./f.), *directeur / directrice* (m./f.)
many *beaucoup de, beaucoup*
map *plan* (m.), *carte* (f.)
  map of the city *plan* (m.) *de la ville, carte* (f.) *de la ville*
  map of the subway *plan* (m.) *du métro, carte* (f.) *du métro*
March *mars*
market *marché* (m.)
marmalade *confiture* (f.)
married *marié / mariée* (m./f.)
marry (someone) (to) *épouser (quelqu'un)*
match (in sports) *match* (m.)
math *maths* (f. pl.), *mathématiques* (f. pl.)
May *mai*
maybe *peut-être*
mayor *maire* (m.)
me *moi*
meal *repas* (m.)
meat *viande* (f.)
medicine *médecine* (f.)
  medicine cabinet *armoire* (f.) *à pharmacie*
meet (a person/someone) (to) *rencontrer (une personne/quelqu'un), faire connaissance*
meeting *rendez-vous* (m.), *réunion* (f.)
  meeting room *salle* (f.) *de réunion*
melon *melon* (m.)
memory *mémoire* (f.)

menu *menu* (m.), *carte* (f.)
  The menu, please *Le menu / La carte, s'il vous plaît.*
meringue cookie *macaron* (m.)
metro *métro* (m.)
  metro station *station* (f.) *de métro*
Mexican *mexicain / mexicaine* (m./f.)
Mexico *Mexique* (m.)
microwave (oven) *micro-ondes* (m.)
middle *milieu* (m.)
  in the middle of *au milieu de*
  middle school *collège* (m.)
midnight *minuit* (m.)
milk *lait* (m.)
mineral water *eau* (f.) *minérale*
mint *menthe* (f.)
minus *moins*
mirror *miroir* (m.)
miss *mademoiselle (Mlle)*
  misses *mesdemoiselles*
mistaken (to be) *se tromper*
modem *modem* (m.)
Mom/Mommy *maman*
moment *moment* (m.)
Mona Lisa *Joconde* (f.)
Monday *lundi*
money *argent* (m.)
monitor *écran* (m.)
month *mois* (m.)
  next month, in one month *dans un mois*
  next month *mois prochain*
  last month *mois dernier*
  two months before *deux mois avant / auparavant*
  months of the year *mois* (pl.) *de l'année*
monument *monument* (m.)
moon *lune* (f.)
mop (to) *éponger*
moped *solex* (m.), *vélomoteur* (m.), *mobylette* (f.)
more *plus*
  even more, much more *bien plus*
more *encore*
morning *matin* (m.), *matinée* (f.)
Moroccan *marocain / marocaine* (m./f.)
Morocco *Maroc* (m.)
mosque *mosquée* (f.)
mostly *surtout*
mother *mère* (f.)

mother-in-law *belle-mère* (f.)
motorcycle *motocyclette* (f.), *moto* (f.)
mountain *montagne* (f.)
mouse *souris* (f.)
mousse *mousse* (f.)
  chocolate mousse *mousse au chocolat*
mouth *bouche* (f.)
move out (to) *déménager*
movie *film* (m.)
  movie theater, the movies *cinéma* (m.)
Mr. *M. (Monsieur)*
Mrs. *Mme (Madame)*
Ms. *Mlle (Mademoiselle) Madame*
much *beaucoup*
  much more *bien plus*
municipal building *mairie* (f.), *hôtel* (m.) *de ville*
muscle *muscle* (m.)
museum *musée* (m.)
mushroom *champignon* (m.)
music *musique* (f.)
musical *comédie* (f.) *musicale*
musician *musicien / musicienne* (m./f.)
mussel *moule* (f.)
  mussels and fries *moules* (pl.) *frites*
must *devoir*
mustard *moutarde* (f.)
  Dijon mustard *moutarde de Dijon*
my *mon / ma / mes* (m./f./pl.)
  My name is ... *Je m'appelle...*
myself (reflexive pronoun) *me / m'*
mysterious *mystérieux / mystérieuse* (m./f.)

N

name *nom* (m.)
  under what name? *sous quel nom ?*
napkin *serviette* (f.)
nation *nation* (f.)
national *national / nationale* (m./f.)
  national holiday *fête nationale* (f.)
nationality *nationalité* (f.)
natural *naturel / naturelle* (m./f.)
naturally *naturellement*
near *près*
  very near *tout près*
  nearby, near here *près d'ici*
  the nearest *le / la plus proche* (m./f.)

necessary (to be) *falloir*
  it's necessary to *il faut*
neck *cou* (m.)
necklace *collier* (m.)
need *besoin* (m.)
need (to) *avoir besoin de*
neighborhood *quartier* (m.), *coin* (m.)
nephew *neveu* (m.)
never *jamais, ne... jamais*
new *nouveau / nouvel / nouvelle* (m./m. before a
  vowel or silent h/f.)
  New Year *Nouvel An* (m.)
  New Year's Day *jour* (m.) *de l'An*
  New Year's Eve *Saint-Sylvestre* (f.), *réveillon*
  (m.) *(du jour de l'An)*
newborn *nouveau-né* (m.)
news (the news) *nouvelles* (f. pl.)
newspaper *journal* (m.)
next *prochain / prochaine* (m./f.), *ensuite*
  next to *à côté de*
  next month *dans un mois, mois prochain*
  next week *dans une semaine, semaine*
  prochaine
nice *gentil / gentille* (m./f.), *sympa, joli / jolie*
  (m./f.), *beau / bel / belle* (m./m. before a vowel or
  silent h/f.), *sympathique, aimable*
  Nice to meet you. *Enchanté. / Enchantée.*
  (m./f.)
niece *nièce* (f.)
night *nuit* (f.), *soir* (m.)
nightclub *boîte* (f.) *de nuit, discothèque* (f.)
  go out to clubs (to), go out clubbing
  (to) *sortir en boîte*
nine *neuf*
nineteen *dix-neuf*
ninety *quatre-vingt-dix*
ninth *neuvième*
no *non*
  no longer, no more *ne... plus*
  No way! *Oh là là !*
noodle soup (vermicelli pasta
  consommé) *consommé* (m.) *aux vermicelles*
noon *midi* (m.)
north *nord* (m.)
nose *nez* (m.)
not *ne / n'... pas, pas*
  not at all *pas du tout*
  not yet *ne... pas encore*

Not bad. *Pas mal.*
Not a lot. *Pas grand-chose.*
notebook *cahier* (m.)
nothing *rien, ne... rien*
  It's nothing. *De rien.*
  Nothing much. *Rien de particulier.*
  Nothing new. *Rien de neuf.*
November *novembre*
now *maintenant*
nowhere *nulle part*
number *nombre* (m.), *numéro* (m.)
  phone number *numéro de téléphone*

O

obey (to) *obéir*
ocean *océan* (m.)
  ocean liner *paquebot* (m.)
October *octobre*
of *de / d'*
  of it, of them *en*
  of the *du / de la / de l' / des* (m./f./m. or f. before
  a vowel or silent h/pl.)
  Of course. *Bien sûr. / Bien entendu.*
office *bureau* (m.)
  office building *immeuble* (m.)
often *souvent*
Oh okay ... *Ah bon...*
Oh really ... *Ah bon...*
Oh well ... *Eh bien... , Ben...* (infml.)
oil *huile* (f.)
Okay. *D'accord.*
  Oh okay ... *Ah bon...*
old *vieux / vieil / vieille* (m./m. before a vowel or
  silent h/f.), *ancien / ancienne* (m./f.)
  oldest child *aîné / aînée* (m./f.)
omelette *omelette* (f.)
  mushroom omelette *omelette aux champi-*
  gnons
on *sur*
  on top *dessus*
  on behalf of *de la part de*
  on my behalf *de ma part*
  on foot *à pied*
  on one's own *seul / seule* (m./f.)
  on the left/on the right *à gauche / à droite*
  on the other side of *de l'autre côté de*
  on time *à l'heure*

once *une fois*
one (number) *un / une* (m./f.)
one (pronoun) *on*
oneself (reflexive pronoun) *se / s'*
one-way *aller simple*
onion *oignon* (m.)
  onion soup *soupe* (f.) *à l'oignon*
only *juste, seul / seule* (m./f.), *seulement*
only child *fils / fille unique* (m./f.)
open (to) *ouvrir*
  open a file (to) *ouvrir un fichier*
opera *opéra* (m.)
or *ou*
  or even, or else *ou bien*
orange *orange, orange* (f.)
order (to) *commander*
organize (to) *organiser*
origin *origine* (f.)
original *original / originale* (m./f.)
  original version of a film (not dubbed into
    French) *version* (f.) *originale (v.o.)*
other *autre*
our *notre / nos* (m. or f./pl.)
ourselves (reflexive pronoun) *nous*
outside *hors, dehors, extérieur* (m.)
oven *four* (m.)
over there *là-bas*
owe (to) *devoir*
own *propre*
oyster *huître* (f.)

P

paint (to) *peindre*
painting *tableau* (m.)
pajamas *pyjama* (m.)
pants *pantalon* (m.)
paper *papier* (m.)
Pardon (me). *Pardon.*
parent *parent* (m.)
Paris *Paris*
Parisian *parisien / parisienne* (m./f.)
park *parc* (m.)
parlor *salon* (m.)
part (in a play, movie, etc.) *rôle* (m.)
part-time *à temps partiel*
party *soirée* (f.), *fête* (f.), *partie* (f.)

pass (to) *passer*
  pass (a test) (to) *réussir à (un examen)*
passport *passeport* (m.)
past *passé* (m.)
  in the past *autrefois*
pastry *pâtisserie* (f.)
  pastry shop *pâtisserie* (f.)
  pastry and candy store *pâtisserie-confiserie* (f.)
path *chemin* (m.)
patient *patient / patiente* (m./f.)
pay (to) *payer*
peach *pêche* (f.)
  peaches with ice cream *pêche Melba*
pear *poire* (f.)
peas (green) *petits pois* (m. pl.)
people *gens* (m. pl.)
  people in general (pronoun) *on*
pepper *poivre (condiment)* (m.), *poivron (veg-etable)* (m.)
perfect *parfait / parfaite* (m./f.)
  It's perfect. *C'est parfait.*
perform (to) *jouer*
perfume *parfum* (m.)
person *personne* (f.)
pharmacy *pharmacie* (f.)
phone *téléphone*
  cell phone *portable* (m.)
  phone number *numéro* (m.) *de téléphone*
  answer the phone (to) *répondre au téléphone*
  telephone extension *poste* (m.)
phone (to) *téléphoner*
photo *photo* (f.)
  Can you take our picture (photo),
    please? *Pourriez-vous nous prendre en
    photo, s'il vous plaît ?*
phrase *phrase* (f.)
physical education *gymnastique* (f.)
pick up (the phone) (to) *décrocher*
pie *tarte* (f.)
  apple pie *tarte aux pommes*
  pumpkin pie *tarte à la citrouille*
  strawberry pie *tarte aux fraises*
piece *pièce* (f.), *morceau* (m.)
pig *porc* (m.), *cochon* (m.)
pink *rose*
pitcher *carafe* (f.)
  pitcher of water *carafe d'eau*
  pitcher of wine *carafe de vin*

place   *place* (f.), *lieu* (m.)
  take place (to)   *avoir lieu*
plan   *plan* (m.)
plant   *plante* (f.)
plastic   *plastique* (m.)
  made of plastic   *en plastique*
plate   *assiette* (f.)
platform   *quai* (m.)
play (theater)   *pièce* (f.)
play (to)   *jouer*
  play a sport (to)   *faire du sport*
player   *joueur / joueuse* (games, sports, etc.)
  (m./f.), *lecteur* (CDs, DVDs, etc.) (m.)
  soccer player   *footballeur / footballeuse*
    (m./f.)
  CD player   *lecteur de CD*
  DVD player   *lecteur de DVD*
playing cards   *cartes* (f. pl.) *à jouer*
pleasant   *agréable*
please   *s'il te plaît* (infml.) / *s'il vous plaît*
  (pl./fml.)
  Pleased to meet you.   *Enchanté. / Enchantée.*
    (m./f.)
pleasure   *plaisir* (m.)
  With pleasure.   *Avec plaisir.*
plum   *prune* (f.)
plumber   *plombier* (m.)
poached   *poché / pochée* (m./f.)
  poached egg   *œuf* (m.) *poché*
police (adjective)   *policier / policière* (m./f.)
  police station   *poste* (m.) *de police*
policeman/woman   *policier / femme policier*
  (m./f.)
polite   *poli*
politely   *poliment*
pond   *étang* (m.), *mare* (f.)
pool   *piscine* (swimming) (f.), *billard* (billiards)
  (m.)
poor   *pauvre*
pork   *porc* (m.)
  pork chop   *côte* (f.) *de porc*
Portugal   *Portugal* (m.)
Portuguese   *portugais / portugaise* (m./f.)
possible   *possible*
  It's not possible! (disappointment,
    anger)   *Ce n'est pas possible !*
possibly   *peut-être*
post office   *poste* (f.), *bureau* (m.) *de poste*

potato   *pomme* (f.) *de terre*
  boiled potatoes in their skins, baked
    potatoes   *pommes* (pl.) *de terre en robe des
    champs*
  mashed potatoes   *purée* (f.) *de pommes de
    terre*
poultry   *volaille* (f.)
pound   *livre* (f.)
  pound of butter   *livre de beurre*
powder   *poudre* (f.), *talc* (m.)
practice (to)   *pratiquer*
precise   *précis / précise* (m./f.)
prefer (to)   *préférer*
prepare (to)   *préparer*
present (to)   *présenter*
pretty   *joli / jolie* (m./f.)
principal   *principal / principale* (m./f.)
printer   *imprimante* (f.)
probable   *probable*
probably   *probablement*
produce (to)   *produire*
professor   *professeur / professeure* (m./f.), *prof*
  (m./f.) (infml.)
progress   *progrès* (m.)
proud   *fier / fière* (m./f.)
pumpkin   *citrouille* (f.)
  pumpkin pie   *tarte* (f.) *à la citrouille*
punish (to)   *punir*
purée   *purée* (f.)
purple   *violet / violette* (m./f.)
put (to)   *mettre*
  put in the mail (to)   *mettre à la poste*
  put away (to)   *ranger*
  put someone to bed (to)   *coucher*

Q

quarter   *quart* (m.), *quartier* (m.)
  quarter after/past ...   *... et quart*
  quarter to ...   *... moins le quart*
quay   *quai* (m.)
question   *question* (f.)
quiche   *quiche* (f.)
quick   *rapide*
quickly   *vite / rapidement*
quiet   *calme*
quit (to)   *quitter*

quite *assez, bien*
  quite the opposite, quite the contrary *bien au contraire*

R

race *course* (f.)
rack (of meat) *carré* (m.)
  rack of lamb *carré d'agneau*
radish *radis* (m.)
  rosette-cut radishes served with butter on top (lit., radishes in butter) *radis* (m. pl.) *au beurre*
rain *pluie* (f.)
rain (to) *pleuvoir*
  It's raining./It rains. *Il pleut.*
raise (to) *lever*
Ramadan *Ramadan* (m.)
rarely *rarement*
raw *cru / crue* (m./f.)
  crudités (French appetizer of raw, mixed vegetables) *crudités* (f. pl.)
razor *rasoir* (m.)
reach (to) *arriver*
read (to) *lire*
ready *prêt / prête* (m./f.)
real *vrai / vraie* (m./f.)
really *vraiment, en effet, bien*
  I really like ... *J'aime bien...*
  I really want ... *Je veux bien...*
reason *raison*
recent *dernier / dernière* (m./f.)
reception desk *réception* (f.)
recess *récré(ation)* (f.)
recipe *recette* (f.)
red *rouge*
  red wine *vin* (m.) *rouge*
redden (to) *rougir*
reflect (to) *réfléchir*
refrigerator *réfrigérateur* (m.)
relative *parent* (m.)
relax (to) *se reposer*
relief *soulagement* (m.)
  What a relief! *Quel soulagement !*
remember (to) *se souvenir*
repeat (to) *répéter*
  Repeat (that), please. *Répétez, s'il vous plaît.*
reply (to) *répondre*

report card *bulletin* (m.) *scolaire*
reservation *réservation* (f.)
  to make a reservation *faire une réservation*
  to make reservations *faire des réservations*
reserve (to) *réserver*
resolved (to do something) (to be) *se décider*
respond (to) *répondre*
rest (to) *reposer*
  rest (oneself) (to) *se reposer*
restaurant *restaurant* (m.)
restroom *toilettes* (f. pl.)
  Where is the restroom? *Où sont les toilettes ?*
retired *à la retraite*
retirement *retraite* (f.)
return (to) *revenir, rentrer, rendre, retourner*
reunion *réunion* (f.)
rib (meat) *côte* (f.)
rice *riz* (m.)
rich *riche*
right (opposite of left) *droite* (f.)
  be right (to) *avoir raison*
  right? *n'est-ce pas ?*
ring *bague* (f.)
ring (to) *sonner*
rise (to) *monter, se lever*
river *rivière* (f.)
roast (of meat) *rôti* (m.)
  roast beef *rôti de bœuf*
roast(ed) *rôti / rôtie* (m./f.)
  roast rack of lamb *carré* (m.) *d'agneau rôti*
rock *rocher* (m.)
role *rôle* (m.)
romantic *romantique*
  romantic comedy *comédie* (f.) *romantique*
room *pièce* (f.), *salle* (f.), *place* (f.)
rooster *coq* (m.)
rose *rose* (f.)
rosé (wine) *vin* (m.) *rosé*
round-trip *aller-retour*
  I would like a round-trip ticket. *Je voudrais un billet aller-retour.*
rug *tapis* (m.)
run *course* (f.)
run errands (to) *faire des achats*
running *course* (f.) *à pied*
rural *rural / rurale* (m./f.)
rush (to) *se hâter*

Russia *Russie* (f.)
Russian *russe*

S

sad *triste*
sailing *voile* (f.)
salad *salade* (f.)
  fruit salad *salade de fruits*
  green salad *salade verte*
salary *salaire* (m.)
salesman/woman *vendeur / vendeuse* (m./f.)
salt *sel* (m.)
same *même*
sand *sable* (m.)
sandwich *sandwich* (m.)
  ham sandwich *sandwich au jambon*
  ham and cheese sandwich *sandwich jambon-fromage*
  grilled ham and cheese sandwich *croque-monsieur* (m.)
  grilled ham and cheese sandwich with an egg on top *croque-madame* (m.)
sardines *sardines* (f. pl.)
  sardines in tomato sauce *sardines sauce tomate*
Saturday *samedi*
sauce *sauce* (f.)
sausage *saucisse* (f.)
sauté (to) *sauter*
save a document (to) *sauvegarder un document*
savory *salé / salée* (m./f.)
say (to) *dire*
  Say! *Tiens !* (surprise)
  You don't say!/Say! (lit., Say so!) *Dis donc !*
scallops *coquilles* (f. pl.) *Saint-Jacques*
scarf *foulard* (fashion) (m.), *écharpe* (winter) (f.)
scary *effrayant / effrayante* (m./f.)
schedule *horaire* (m.)
school *école* (f.)
  high school *lycée* (m.)
  secondary school, junior high school, middle school *collège* (m.)
Scotland *Écosse* (f.)
Scottish *écossais / écossaise* (m./f.)
screen *écran* (m.)
sculpture *sculpture* (f.)
sea *mer* (f.)

seat *place* (f.)
seated *assis / assise* (m./f.)
second *deuxième, second / seconde* (m./f.)
secondary school *collège* (m.)
secretary *secrétaire* (m./f.)
see (to) *voir*
  See you later! *À tout à l'heure ! / À plus tard ! / À plus !* (infml.) */ À la prochaine !*
  See you soon! *À bientôt !*
sell (to) *vendre*
send (to) *envoyer*
  send a file (to) *envoyer un fichier*
  send an e-mail (to) *envoyer un mail / mél / email / courriel / courrier électronique*
September *septembre*
serious *sérieux / sérieuse* (m./f.)
server *serveur / serveuse* (m./f.)
seven *sept*
seventeen *dix-sept*
seventh *septième*
seventy *soixante-dix*
shame *honte* (f.)
  be ashamed (to) *avoir honte*
shampoo *shampooing* (m.)
sharp *précis / précise* (m./f.)
  at noon sharp *à midi précis*
shave (to) *se raser*
shaving cream *crème* (f.) *à raser*
she *elle*
shelf *étagère* (f.)
ship *bateau* (m.)
shirt *chemise* (f.)
shoe *chaussure* (f.)
  shoe store *magasin* (m.) *de chaussures*
shop (small) *boutique* (f.)
shop (to) *faire des / les courses*
short *petit / petite* (m./f.), *court / courte* (m./f.)
should *devoir*
shoulder *épaule* (f.)
show (to) *montrer, présenter, donner*
shower *douche* (f.)
  shower gel *gel* (m.) *douche*
shrimp *crevette* (f.)
sick *malade*
side *côté* (m.)
  at the side of (next to) *à côté de*
  at the side, on the side, to the side *à côté*

on the other side of *de l'autre côté de*
  side dish *plat* (m.) *d'accompagnement*
sidewalk *trottoir* (m.)
silk *soie* (f.)
simple *simple*
sincere *sincère*
sing (to) *chanter*
singer *chanteur / chanteuse* (m./f.)
single *célibataire*
sink *lavabo* (m.), *évier* (m.)
sir *monsieur*
sister *sœur* (f.)
sitting (down) *assis / assise* (m./f.)
situated (to be) *se trouver*
six *six*
sixteen *seize*
sixth *sixième*
sixty *soixante*
size *taille* (f.)
skate/skating *patin* (m.)
ski (to) *faire du ski, skier*
skiing *ski* (m.)
skin *peau* (f.)
skirt *jupe* (f.)
sky *ciel* (m.)
sleep *sommeil* (m.)
sleeping car/sleeper car *wagon-lit* (m.)
sleepy (to be) *avoir sommeil*
slice *tranche (bread, cheese)* (f.), *part (cake, pie, pizza)* (f.), *rondelle (round - cucumber, banana, sausage, etc.)* (f.)
  slice of cheese *tranche / part de fromage*
slow *lent / lente* (m./f.)
slowly *lentement*
small *petit / petite* (m./f.)
  small shop *boutique* (f.)
smile *sourire* (m.)
snails *escargots* (m. pl.)
sneaker *basket* (m./f.), *chaussure* (f.) *de basket / tennis*
snow *neige* (f.)
snow (to) *neiger*
  It's snowing. *Il neige.*
so *alors, donc*
soak up (to) *éponger*
soap *savon* (m.)

soccer *foot(ball)* (m.)
  soccer player *footballeur / footballeuse* (m./f.)
  soccer stadium *stade* (m.) *de foot*
social *social / sociale* (m./f.)
sock *chaussette* (f.)
sofa *canapé* (m.)
soft *doux / douce* (m./f.)
  soft drink *boisson* (f.) *gazeuse*
softly *doucement*
sole (fish) *sole* (f.)
  sole covered in flour and sautéed in butter *sole meunière*
some *du / de la / de l' / des* (m./f./m. or f. before a vowel or silent h/pl.), *en*
someone *quelqu'un*
sometimes *parfois*
son *fils* (m.)
son-in-law *beau-fils* (m.)
song *chanson* (f.)
soon *bientôt*
  See you soon! *À bientôt !*
sorry *désolé / désolée* (m./f.)
  I am sorry. *Je suis désolé / désolée.*
So-so. *Comme ci, comme ça.*
sound system *chaîne* (f.) *hi-fi*
soup *soupe* (f.), *potage* (m.)
  onion soup *soupe à l'oignon*
  consommé (clear soup made from stock) *consommé* (m.)
  vermicelli pasta consommé (noodle soup) *consommé aux vermicelles*
sour *aigre*
south *sud* (m.)
Spain *Espagne* (f.)
Spanish *espagnol / espagnole* (m./f.)
  Spanish language *espagnol* (m.)
sparkling *mousseux / mousseuse*
  sparkling wine *vin* (m.) *mousseux*
speak (to) *parler*
  Speak slower/more slowly, please. *Parlez plus lentement, s'il vous plaît.*
  I speak a little French. *Je parle un peu français.*
specialty *spécialité* (f.)
spend (time) (to) *passer*
spinach *épinards* (m. pl.)
spoon *cuillère* (f.), *cuiller* (f.)

spring *printemps* (m.)
  in (the) spring *au printemps*
square *carré* (m.)
stadium *stade* (m.)
  soccer stadium *stade de foot*
staff *personnel* (m.)
stairs *escaliers* (m. pl.)
stamp *timbre* (m.)
standing (up) *debout*
star *étoile* (f.)
start (to) *commencer*
station *station* (f.)
  subway/metro station *station* (f.) *de métro*
statue *statue* (f.)
stay (to) *rester*
steady job *emploi* (m.) *régulier*
steak *steak* (m.)
  steak and fries *steak frites*
stepdaughter *belle-fille* (f.)
stepfather *beau-père* (m.)
stepmother *belle-mère* (f.)
stepson *beau-fils* (m.)
still *toujours, encore*
stomach *estomac* (m.)
stop *arrêt* (m.)
  bus stop *arrêt de bus / d'autobus*
store *magasin* (m.)
  candy store *confiserie* (f.)
  pastry and candy store
    pâtisserie-confiserie (f.)
  grocery store *épicerie* (f.)
  hardware store *quincaillerie* (f.)
storm *orage* (m.)
story *histoire* (f.)
stove *cuisinière* (f.)
straight *droit*
  straight ahead *tout droit*
strange *étrange, bizarre*
  It's strange. *C'est bizarre. / C'est étrange.*
strawberry *fraise* (f.)
  strawberry ice cream *glace* (f.) *à la fraise*
  strawberry pie *tarte* (f.) *aux fraises*
street *rue* (f.)
streetlight *lampadaire* (m.)
strong *fort / forte* (m./f.)
student *étudiant / étudiante* (m./f.)
study (to) *étudier*
subject *sujet* (m.)

subtitle *sous-titre* (m.)
suburban *de banlieue*
suburbs *banlieue* (f.)
subway *métro* (m.)
  subway station *station* (f.) *de métro*
succeed (to) *réussir*
sugar *sucre* (m.)
suit *costume* (m.)
summer *été* (m.)
  in (the) summer *en été*
  summer vacation *grandes vacances* (f. pl.)
sun *soleil* (m.)
  It's sunny. *Il fait soleil. / Il y a du soleil.*
Sunday *dimanche*
sunglasses *lunettes* (f. pl.) *de soleil*
super *super*
supermarket *supermarché* (m.)
surprise (to) *surprendre*
sweet *sucré / sucrée* (m./f.), *doux / douce* (m./f.)
  sweet bun *brioche* (f.)
sweetly *doucement*
swim (to) *nager*
swimming *natation* (f.)
  go swimming (to) *faire de la natation*
Swiss *suisse*
Switzerland *Suisse* (f.)
synagogue *synagogue* (f.)

T

table *table* (f.)
  table for two *table pour deux*
  table setting *couvert* (m.)
tablecloth *nappe* (f.)
tail *queue* (f.)
take (to) *prendre*
  take a bath (to) *prendre un bain*
  take a shower (to) *prendre une douche*
  take a tour (to) *faire un tour*
  take a walk (to) *faire une promenade, se promener*
  take someone or something for a walk (to) *promener*
  take along (to) *emmener*
  take a picture (to) *prendre une photo*
  Can you take our picture, please? *Pourriez-vous nous prendre en photo, s'il vous plaît ?*
talented *talentueux / talentueuse* (m./f.)

talk (to) *parler*
tall *grand / grande* (m./f.)
tan (color) *beige*
tart *tarte* (f.)
taste *goût* (m.)
taxi *taxi* (m.)
  taxi driver *chauffeur* (m.) *de taxi*
tea *thé* (m.)
  herbal tea *tisane* (f.)
  cup of tea *tasse* (f.) *de thé*
  teakettle, teapot *théière* (f.)
teach (to) *enseigner*
teacher *professeur / professeure* (m./f.), *prof* (infml., m./f.), *enseignant / enseignante* (m./f.)
team *équipe* (f.)
teenager *adolescent / adolescente* (m./f.)
telephone *téléphone* (m.), *appareil* (m.)
  cell phone *portable* (m.)
  phone number *numéro* (m.) *de téléphone*
  to answer the phone *répondre au téléphone*
  to make a phone call, to phone *téléphoner*
  telephone extension *poste* (m.)
television *télé(vision)* (f.)
  television program *émission* (f.)
tell (to) *dire*
teller *guichetier* (m.)
temperature *température* (f.)
temple *temple* (m.)
ten *dix*
tendon *tendon* (m.)
tennis *tennis* (m.)
  tennis shoe *basket* (m./f.), *chaussure* (f.) *de
    basket / tennis*
tenth *dixième*
test *examen* (m.)
  fail (a test) (to) *rater (un examen)*
  pass (a test) (to) *réussir à (un examen)*
textbook *livre* (m.) *scolaire*
thank you *merci*
  Thank you very much. *Merci bien.*
that *ce / cet / cette* (m./m. before a vowel or silent
  h/f.), *ça / c', que, qui*
  that way *par là*
  That doesn't interest me.
  Ça ne m'intéresse pas.
  That interests me. *Ça m'intéresse.*
  That makes ... /That is ... *Ça fait...*
  that is *c'est*

  That's bad. *C'est mauvais.*
  Is that all? *C'est tout ?*
the *le / l' / la / les* (m./m. before a vowel or silent
  h/f./pl.)
theater *théâtre* (m.)
  movie theater *cinéma* (m.)
their *leur / leurs* (m. or f./pl.)
them *eux / elles* (m./f.)
themselves (reflexive pronoun) *se / s'*
then *alors, donc, ensuite, puis*
there *là, là-bas, y*
  over there *là-bas*
  there is/are *il y a, voilà*
  there it is/they are *voilà*
therefore *donc*
these *ces*
they *ils / elles* (m./f.)
thin *mince*
thing *chose* (f.)
think (to) *penser, réfléchir*
third *troisième*
thirst *soif* (f.)
  be thirsty (to) *avoir soif*
thirteen *treize*
thirty *trente*
this *ce / cet / cette* (m./m. before a vowel or silent
  h/f.), *ça / c', ci*
  this is *c'est*
  this way *par ici*
those *ces*
thousand *mille*
threaten (to) *menacer*
three *trois*
thriller *film* (m.) *à suspense, thriller* (m.)
through *à travers*
throw (to) *envoyer*
thunder *tonnerre* (m.)
Thursday *jeudi*
ticket *billet* (m.), *place* (f.)
  ticket window *guichet* (m.)
  I would like a round-trip ticket. *Je voudrais
    un billet aller-retour.*
tie (in a game/match) (to) *faire match nul*
time *fois* (f.), *temps* (m.)
  at what time? *à quelle heure ?*
  What time is it? *Quelle heure est-il ?*
  arrival time *heure* (f.) *de l'arrivée / heure
    d'arrivée*

departure time *heure* (f.) *du départ / heure de départ*
one time (once) *une fois*
I don't have (the) time. *Je n'ai pas le temps.*
tire *pneu* (m.)
to *à, pour, en, jusqu'à*
to the *au / à la / à l' / aux* (m./f./m. or f. before a vowel or silent h/pl.)
To your health! *À votre santé !*
to the left/to the right *à gauche / à droite*
today *aujourd'hui*
toe *doigt* (m.) *de pied, orteil* (m.)
together *ensemble*
toilet *toilettes* (f. pl.)
toilet paper *papier* (m.) *hygiénique*
tomato *tomate* (f.)
tomorrow *demain*
tongue *langue* (f.)
tonight *ce soir*
too *aussi (also), trop (much)*
tooth *dent* (f.)
tour *tour* (m.)
tourist *touriste* (m./f.)
towel *serviette* (f.)
  bath towel *serviette de bain*
tower *tour* (f.)
  Eiffel Tower *Tour Eiffel*
town *ville* (f.)
  town hall *hôtel* (m.) *de ville*
track *voie* (f.)
traffic *circulation* (f.)
train *train* (m.)
  train station *gare* (f.)
  high-speed train *train à grande vitesse (TGV)*
transportation *transport* (m.)
travel *voyage* (m.)
travel (to) *voyager*
traveler's check *chèque* (m.) *de voyage*
tree *arbre* (m.)
trip *voyage* (m.)
  round-trip *aller-retour*
trout *truite* (f.)
  trout cooked in wine and vinegar *truite au bleu*
truck *camion* (m.)
true *vrai / vraie* (m./f.)
truly *vraiment*
T-shirt *T-shirt* (m.)

Tuesday *mardi*
turn *tour* (m.)
turn (to) *tourner*
TV *télé(vision)* (f.)
twelve *douze*
twentieth *vingtième*
twenty *vingt*
two *deux*
  two dozen *deux douzaines*
  two months before *deux mois auparavant, deux mois avant*

U

ugly *laid / laide* (m./f.)
umbrella *parapluie* (m.)
uncle *oncle* (m.)
under *sous*
  under what name? *sous quel nom ?*
underneath *dessous*
underpants *caleçon* (m.)
undershirt *maillot* (m.) *de corps*
understand (to) *comprendre*
  I don't understand. *Je ne comprends pas.*
  Completely understood. *Bien entendu.*
underwear *sous-vêtements* (m. pl.)
unemployed *au chômage, sans emploi*
unemployment *chômage* (m.)
unfortunate *malheureux / malheureuse* (m./f.), *pauvre*
unfortunately *malheureusement*
unfriendly *peu amical / peu amicale* (m./f.)
unhappily *malheureusement*
unhappy *malheureux / malheureuse* (m./f.)
United States *États-Unis* (m. pl.)
university *université* (f.)
until, up until, up to *jusqu'à*
upstairs, up above *en haut*
urban *urbain / urbaine* (m./f.)
us *nous*
usually *en général*

V

vacation *vacances* (f. pl.)
  summer vacation *grandes vacances* (f. pl.)
  winter vacation *vacances* (f. pl.) *d'hiver*
vain *vain / vaine* (m./f.)

vanilla *vanille* (f.)
  vanilla ice cream *glace* (f.) *à la vanille*
veal *veau* (m.)
vegetable *légume* (m.)
vermicelli pasta *vermicelle* (m.)
  vermicelli pasta consommé (noodle
    soup) *consommé* (m.) *aux vermicelles*
version *version* (f.)
very *très, bien*
  very good *très bien, très bon / bonne* (m./f.)
  very well *très bien*
veterinarian *vétérinaire* (m.)
video game *jeu* (m.) *vidéo*
Vietnamese *vietnamien / vietnamienne* (m./f.)
village *village* (m.)
violet (purple) *violet / violette* (m./f.)
violin *violon* (m.)
visit (a place) (to) *visiter*
vocabulary *vocabulaire* (m.)
voyage *voyage* (m.)

W

wait (for) (to) *attendre*
  wait in line (to) *faire la queue*
  can't wait (to look forward to) *avoir hâte*
waiter/waitress *serveur / serveuse* (m./f.)
wake (someone) (to) *réveiller*
  wake up (to), wake oneself up (to) *se réveiller*
walk (to) *marcher*
  take a walk (to) *se promener*
  take someone or something for a walk
    (to) *promener*
wall *mur* (m.)
want (to) *vouloir, désirer*
  I want ... *Je veux...*
  I would like ... *Je voudrais...*
wardrobe *armoire* (f.)
warm *chaud / chaude* (m./f.)
  It's warm./It's hot. *Il fait chaud.*
  be warm/hot (to) *avoir chaud*
wash (to) *laver*
  wash up (to), wash oneself (to) *se laver*
washing machine *machine* (f.) *à laver, lave-linge*
  (m.)
washroom *salle* (f.) *de bains*
waste (to) *perdre*
  He's wasting his time. *Il perd son temps.*

watch *montre* (f.)
watch (to) *regarder*
water *eau* (f.)
  mineral water *eau minérale*
  pitcher of water *carafe* (f.) *d'eau*
way *direction* (f.), *chemin* (m.)
  this way *par ici*
  that way *par là*
we *nous, on* (infml.)
weak *faible*
wear (to) *porter*
weather *temps* (m.)
  What's the weather today? *Quel temps fait-il
    aujourd'hui ?*
webpage *page* (f.) *web*
website *site* (m.) *web*
Wednesday *mercredi*
week *semaine* (f.)
  in one week *dans une semaine*
  next week *semaine prochaine, dans une
    semaine*
  the week before last *semaine précédente,
    semaine d'avant*
  the week after next *semaine d'après, semaine
    suivante, dans deux semaines*
  days of the week *jours* (m. pl.) *de la semaine*
weekend *week-end* (m.)
weightlifting *haltérophilie* (f.)
Welcome. *Bienvenue.*
  You're welcome. *De rien. / Il n'y a pas de
    quoi. / Je vous en prie.* (fml.)
well *bien*
  very well *très bien*
  It's going well. *Ça va bien.*
  Well done. *Bravo.*
  Well ... *Eh bien... / Ben...* (infml.) */ Alors... /
    Alors là...*
west *ouest* (m.)
western *western* (m.)
what *qu'est-ce que, quel / quelle* (m./f.), *quoi, que*
  what?/of what? *de quel / quelle ?* (m./f.)
  at what time? *à quelle heure ?*
  What is this/that? *Qu'est-ce que c'est ?*
  What is the weather today? *Quel temps fait-
    il aujourd'hui ?*
  What time is it? *Quelle heure est-il ?*

What's your name? *Comment vous appelez-vous ?* (pl./fml.) / *Comment t'appelles-tu ?* (infml.)

What's up?/What's new? *Quoi de neuf ?*

when *quand*

where *où*

   Where is ... ? *Où se trouve... ? / Où est... ?*

   Where is the restroom? (lit., Where are the toilets?) *Où sont les toilettes ?*

which *que, quel / quelle* (m./f.)

whipped cream (that is flavored and sweetened) *crème* (f.) *chantilly*

white *blanc / blanche* (m./f.)

   white wine *vin* (m.) *blanc*

   white wine with black currant liqueur *kir* (m.)

who *qui*

   Who is it? *Qui est-ce ?*

   Who's calling? (on the phone) *C'est de la part de qui ? / Qui est à l'appareil ?*

whom *que*

why *pourquoi*

wide *large*

wife *femme* (f.)

win (to) *gagner*

wind *vent* (m.)

   It's windy. *Il y a du vent.*

window *fenêtre* (f.), *guichet* (ticket) (m.)

wine *vin* (m.)

   red/white/rosé/sparkling wine *vin rouge / blanc / rosé / mousseux*

   white wine with black currant liqueur *kir* (m.)

   type of French sparkling wine *crémant* (m.)

   wine list *carte* (f.) *des vins*

winter *hiver* (m.)

   in (the) winter *en hiver*

   winter vacation *vacances* (f. pl.) *d'hiver*

wish (to) *désirer*

with *avec*

   With pleasure. *Avec plaisir.*

without *sans*

wolf *loup* (f.)

woman *femme* (f.)

wonder (to) *se demander*

wood *bois* (m.)

wooden *en bois*

word *mot* (m.)

work *travail* (m.)

work (to) *travailler*

world *monde* (m.)

worried *inquiet / inquiète* (m./f.)

wounded *blessé / blessée* (m./f.)

Wow! *Oh là là !*

wrist *poignet* (m.)

write (to) *écrire*

writer *écrivain* (m.) (sometimes: *écrivaine*, f.)

wrong *faux / fausse* (m./f.), *mal, tort*

   be wrong (to) *avoir tort*

Y

year *année* (f.), *an* (m.)

   be ... years old (to) *avoir... ans*

yellow *jaune*

yes *oui, si* (negative)

yesterday *hier*

you *tu* (infml.), *vous* (pl./fml.), *toi* (infml.)

   you have to/need to/must *il faut*

   You're welcome. *De rien. / Je vous en prie.* (fml.)

young *jeune*

   youngest child *cadet / cadette* (m./f.)

your (infml.) *ton / ta / tes* (m./f./pl.)

your (pl./fml.) *votre / vos* (m. or f./pl.)

yourself (reflexive pronoun) *te / t'* (infml.), *vous* (fml.)

yourselves (reflexive pronoun) *vous*

youth hostel *auberge* (f.) *de jeunesse*

Z

zero *zéro*

zoo *zoo* (m.)